WHAT PEOPLE ARE SAYING

"I read the entire book in one sitting. I could not stop-what a life lived."
  ~ *Michael Scott, Commercial Photographer, USA*

"The gut-wrenching life journey of Wendy Beth reminds us of the importance of seeing the soul within each person without placing artificial labels."
  ~ *Dr. Kashturi Henry PhD, CTP, Six Sigma Black Belt Founder & CEO, Kas Henry Inc. & Ennobled for Success Institute (Belize)*

"*Living Blueprint* is the most open, raw, and honest book I have ever read!"
  ~ *Pam Howard*

"From day one of the forty-day journey . . . it's almost like God had a hand in you choosing me to be part of this journey."
  ~*Daniel - Father*

"This book is both refreshing and compelling to read!"
  ~ *Maria Jose, Santiago, (Chile)*

"Wendy Beth and the Living Blueprint can help you emerge from a life of exhaustive pain, anxiety, and fear with no foreseeable future to a life of genuine joy, freedom, and contentment."
  ~ *Gary Little, NHA*

"My favorite part of the 'Living Blueprint' journey has been discovering new tools I can use for self-care and achieving my absolute BEST."
  ~ *Beta Reader Number Two*

"Wow, what a powerful gift Wendy has given readers!"
~ *Joan Wife, Mother, Grandma, RN*

"This story will help people gain their own strength and resolve so that they too can live a life that was meant for them, uncovering their own strengths so that they too can do it freely without having their pasts destroy their present or future."
~ *Steven Zeiger*

"This book is soulfully honest with a raw look into the author's true journey to find who they are. This book is well written and is full of tools to help the reader find where you are at in life, and help you find your true happiness in your own life's journey."
~ *Priscilla Miller*

"Wendy Beth's courage to share the intimate details of her journey is a beacon of hope, showing that even in the darkest moments, healing is possible."
~ *Brita Bigler Peterson#1 International Bestselling Author www.brita-peterson.com*

" I love that this book is a product of Wendy Beth overcoming her very difficult challenges and her willingness to share proven self-help tools with us in an encouraging and loving way."
~ *Rebecca Westfall (Germany)*

"In this day and age, where the market is saturated with numerous self-help books, *The Living Blueprint* is a breath of fresh air, an inspiring, intimate conversation."
~ *Masha Maria, (Russia) artist @itsmashamaria earthisforlovers.com*

This book is worth the read. It is well written with a clearly laid-out path for the reader to follow to create a better life for themselves."

~ *Madison Frederick #1 International best-selling author* <u>*https://www.*</u> <u>*madisonfrederick.com/*</u>

" After reading this book, I feel confident that you will love and appreciate Wendy Beth the way I do."

~Jo Skeen

"*Living Blueprint* includes her raw and vulnerable story of how she trans-formed her life from unbelievable pain to incredible happiness."

~ *Spencer Cozzens (President, IA3 Consulting)*

FIVE PRINCIPLES TO CREATING AN
AUTHENTIC, JOY-FILLED LIFE

Living
Blueprint

a true story

WENDY BETH

Living Blueprint
A True Story
Five Principles to Creating an Authentic, Joy-Filled Life

Inspired Legacy Publishing is a division of (DBA) Inspired Legacy, LLC
PO Box 900816
Sandy UT 84090-0816.

Changing Names & Medical Advice
Some names and identifying details have been changed to protect the privacy of individuals.
This book is not intended as a substitute for the medical advice of physicians. The reader
should regularly consult a physician in matters relating to his/her health and particularly
with respect to any symptoms that may require diagnosis or medical attention.

ISBN 979-8-9896174-0-1 (paperback)
ISBN 979-8-9896174-1-8 (hardcover)

Printed in the United States of America.

Dedicated to:

My children, for teaching me what unconditional love is

Spencer, my soulmate and champion

C.W., J.H., S.A. . . . . . you are sunshine to my soul

The Reader, You were born for joy

DISCLAIMER

Everything in my story is true.

And, to protect the innocent and for legal purposes,
I have changed, omitted, or been vague in sharing
names, dates, places, and specific relationships.

The information herein is not intended to be a substitute
for medical advice, diagnosis, or treatment.

Mature readership is advised–this book contains
violence, abuse, incest, and rape.

ASK FOR HELP

If you or someone you know is dealing with any of the following feelings, or if any of these thoughts come up as you work through Living Blueprint, ask for help and/or call or text **988**:

- Looking for a way to end life

- Talking about feeling hopeless or having no reason to live

- Talking about feeling trapped or in unbearable pain

- Talking about being a burden to others

- Increasing the use of alcohol or drugs

- Giving away personal items for no reason

- Acting anxious or agitated or behaving recklessly

- Withdrawing or isolating

- Showing rage or talking about seeking revenge

- Displaying extreme mood swings

when we live from truth
the battle within ceases
living is joy-filled

Haiku is a Japanese art form that offers its reader a snapshot
of a single impression or idea. It utilizes seventeen syllables
and traditionally contains no punctuation.

Since childhood, I have loved haiku and often find myself creating them in
my mind, to counter non-productive thoughts, as I go through my day.

In place of chapter titles, I have written a haiku poem offering a
glimpse of a concept we are about to explore. I hope you enjoy them.

TABLE OF CONTENTS

LETTER TO MY READER

Dear Friend,

If you've ever hung by a thread, or if you're struggling to find hope now, I won't downplay your pain or pretend it isn't real. The confusion you may feel and the battle you're fighting, the one that no one else sees, making it impossible to move forward or create the life you desire, is absolutely real. The turmoil you feel can seem like it's never going to end.

But it can. And although I haven't felt your pain, I've experienced my own living hell, more than once. I know what it feels like to be confused, alone, without hope, stuck, unable to move forward, barely hanging on for dear life.

Thankfully, I also know what it feels like to be open to a nearly invisible, gossamer-like thread of hope to keep going. I've experienced the pain subsiding, the battle inside of me ceasing, and a single ray of sunlight breaking through the darkness. At that moment, options emerged that I hadn't thought of before, and I found the strength to move forward in a positive direction. So can you.

Within these pages, you'll find a combination of storytelling and teaching that I've taken exquisite amounts of time structuring lovingly just for you. After reading through more than thirty years of my own journals, I've decided to share some of my life's most raw, vulnerable moments with you. Yes, it's a risk. But I'm willing to take that risk, knowing that at the same time, you're living your own real, raw unfiltered life.

My hope is that in the forging of yours and my traumatic and triumphant stories, an immutable connection will evolve. And in that bond, you'll know and feel that you're not alone in this world, that you can be safe and at peace, moving forward in a positive direction no matter what has happened in your past.

The five principles of Living Blueprint were learned and experienced through my own sheer pain and desperation. They're not of my making. They are universal axioms, self-evident facts that are universally acknowledged, that I was open to and instinctively learned to live by. They moved me out of an internal battle that caused immense suffering–even attempting suicide at twenty years old–into the healing and awakening of my own heart, mind, and soul. Today at fifty-five years old, I can honestly say that I love myself and the person I'm becoming, am deliciously happy in my relationship, and am living my purpose every day, even when life is not perfect. Joy and peace fill my soul and my life.

Every day (and I do mean every day), I get out of bed excited to be alive, ready to serve, love, build, and help others. Living from my Blueprint renews and restores my brain, my heart, and my body. It is a compass that leads me to my highest potential and the greatest compassion and loving kindness I've ever experienced over and over again, year after year! Even and especially when I'm afraid, or when I feel less capable than the obstacle before me. Living from my Blueprint has never failed me.

And here's the good news for you: as you progress through this book, our journey together will reveal your own unique Living Blueprint, giving you the choice to move out of confusion, destructive patterns, and suffering into awakening and innovating your own peaceful, magnificent life. I invite you to leave nothing unturned as you dive deep into your own beautiful, undeniable life! The five fundamental principles of Living Blueprint, when lived consistently, create equanimity, a mental calmness in your mind and in your life, regardless of your past relationships, age, race, gender, socio-economic status, culture, or religion. Peace is available for you!

To begin, I'll have a couple of stories to share with you about times in my life when I've faced enormous challenges. Where I've failed, where I've learned, and where I've moved forward. Together we'll make sure you're safe first and then dive into your Blueprint. We'll walk together through how you can pull out the threads of your own life and apply them to a new, powerful picture of existence.

It may be difficult to read what I have to share, but I promise it's worth it. And it may seem laborious to finish working through forty activities in discovering your Living Blueprint. But guess what? That'll be worth it too.

If there are days when you want to stop, you are completely normal, but please don't. Just take one day at a time, do what you can, try to not judge yourself, and be patient with where you are right now. Hang in there on the day at hand and pick up where you left off the next day. Try hard not to miss a day. Just keep going until you have completed all forty activities, using your free will to live from them along the way. Trust the process—it's unveiling your Blueprint.

Over the past thirty-four years, I've been healing, learning, and teaching others what I'm sharing with you now, though Living Blueprint is not what I called it back then.

Today, I cherish my work as a Soul Guide. If you're not sure what that means, the Soul Guide Discourse, written in 2012, has a great definition for what I am. "The term 'Soul Guide' means coaching that transcends the rational and material mind, creating a reflective, contemplative space for truth, meaning, authenticity, and love."[1] Now I'm here to go on this journey with you.

As I work through sessions with individuals, I find that often we are putting out fires, addressing immediate or urgent issues, and managing and dealing with sudden problems and stressors, without the opportunity to address root causes. Living Blueprint-A True Story. Five Principles to Creating an Authentic, Joy-Filled Life allows anyone to gain traction towards what they most desire, leaving crisis-based living in the wake of satisfaction and contentment.

As you learn and apply the five axioms and work through the forty activities, take one day at a time. Some of them may take more than one day. I encourage you to commit to a specific time of day and length of time each day to discover and design your Blueprint. As you build it into the fabric of your daily life, remember you are the architect of your daily routine, ultimately creating your life.

Just breathing, upon waking, in order to connect to the stillness inside of you may seem simple, but I promise, those few minutes before the internal mind chatter begins that you and I both have, can do two things. First, it can reveal priceless information about who you are and the decisions you want to make throughout the day. And, secondly, it can allow you to feel peace, as you learn to let go of things you cannot change and focus on the moments that bring joy into your life.

Your words, your drawings, your thoughts, and your feelings that will be recorded here are priceless. Everything you add to this book will be relevant. All of it will matter because as you will learn, even if you don't see it at the moment, everything about you matters.

Every decision you've made and every scar you wear (especially the ones no one can see), has prepared you to live in this moment with the highest intention for self-exploration, allowing you to fully embody who you truly are and what you want to create for your life. Together, we're about to unveil a template that when utilized in your life will help you achieve what you may see as impossible: your happily ever after.

This I can promise you: one day at a time as you discover your Living Blueprint, and your commitment to your own personal evolution will change everything. And with time you will know just how vital you are to our human family.

Warmly, Wendy Beth

INTRODUCTION

In a world full of beauty, the one that you and I both inhabit, there exists a harsh reality-this planet is not an equal playing field.[1] Within the tapestry of humanity, each of our lives encounters exciting and excruciating moments as we move through the complexities of daily living. Ideally, life is a transformational process where we are safe, where we learn, and then ultimately create what we desire. However, there are times when the challenges become overwhelming, leaving us feeling unprepared to face the difficult moments that threaten to destroy our dreams. At times, we think we do not inherently possess the tools to overcome the excruciating and *live joyfully*.

Life is not easy. Unmet expectations, heavy responsibilities, ideological confusion, violence in the home or society, socio-economic hardships, sickness in the mind or the body, natural disasters, and simply decisions made by us, and around us, every day absent of love wreak havoc in our personal lives and in our societies. For many of us, it's just simply too much.

However, within each of us, there exists a distinctive Living Blueprint. This can be seen as a compass that, when utilized, can help us navigate between things we are unable to alter and everything else within our control. As individuals, we are boundless, intuitive, and indescribable beings. When we live from our unique Living Blueprint, we find relief from suffering. It has the power to intervene harmful thoughts, establish personal security, heal trauma, and reduce distractions––regardless of obstacles we may face.

A Living Blueprint woven into your everyday routine guides you towards focused actions based on your personality, your way of being, your values, and your beliefs. It shows you where you are out of integrity and supports unapologetic authenticity. It opens the path of free will towards achieving what you want and then assists you in acting in remarkable ways to reach your goals.

A Living Blueprint teaches a person to connect with their core essence, trust a Source of Inspiration, listen to their body cues, encourages them to make commitments, and enables them to take full responsibility for their decisions in order to achieve their desired results. An actualized Living Blueprint eliminates hate towards oneself and others and brings light and love into every moment.

Do you or someone you know have more bad days than good ones? Do you or someone you know want to progress but are having difficulty overcoming the obstacles in life and achieving a goal? Are you feeling mentally or physically unsteady? Does expressing your true thoughts frighten you or is being genuine something you aspire to, or perhaps both? Have you personally experienced or cared for someone going through a suicidal episode or crisis? If you answered yes to any of these questions, rest assured that you are not alone, and neither is your loved one. This book is intended for you.

We all have adversity. The World Health Organization reports that every year, over 700,000 individuals complete suicide, not realizing or remembering the exquisite dance that lies before them.[2] That's more than one person in our human family every minute ending their life. The Centers for Disease Control reports that in the United States alone 12.3 million adults seriously contemplated suicide, 3.5 million made a plan, and 1.7 million people attempted to end their lives in 2021 alone.[3] This reality we are living is heartbreaking and unnecessary.

Stigmas regarding mental illness and the taboo around suicide cause individuals and their loved ones to not seek the help and vital support they need; therefore, the suffering continues. In the wake of such tragedy, how do we, the ones actively hurting, the ones who know someone actively hurting, and those willing to move forward with our lives, how do we continue on?

As much as we may too often feel helpless, I promise you this: **these universal feelings of confusion, anxiety, and hopelessness need *not* be a life sentence. Joy is available.**

In 2019, my dear friend, a man who fiercely loved his family and friends, died by suicide. Everyone who knew him was shocked at his choice. He had the biggest heart and wanted to help others be "real, raw, and authentic." His choice to end his life propelled me forward in sharing my own story in order to help others live, ask for help, and be honest in creating an authentic, joy-filled life.

Circumstances of our lives may not be ideal, but how we choose to deal with our circumstances can be ideal when we act from the map of our unique Living Blueprint. It's what can eliminate the battle inside ourselves, take us out of the hamster wheel of reaction, and back consciously into the act of creating a safe, satisfying, peaceful life connected to love.

What qualifies me to share and teach Living Blueprint?

Thirty-three years ago, at twenty years old, while intoxicated and wanting everything to go black, I took a bottle of pills my psychiatrist had prescribed for anxiety. I'd barely survived my teenage years, which had been a cesspool of drugs, alcohol, and sexual trauma. Religious precepts were incessant thoughts reminding me how unworthy of love I was. My parents had rejected my lesbian relationship, saying I was "disgusting" and "evil." And my thoughts were a hellhole of hopelessness. Making it all stop had been my only goal. For a very dark moment, I gave up.

Gratefully, surviving suicide is a miracle I do not take for granted. The experience changed me. I hadn't known then how much that moment would impact the rest of my life—nor how healing my own trauma over thirty-plus years would inform my decisions and my destiny. My journey has given me powerful insight and healing gifts to help others today. After surviving my own self-destructive tendencies, I discovered, designed, and applied my unique Living Blueprint to create my happily ever after.

In 2020, under the guidance of a writing mentor, I began reading over thirty years of my own personal journals, then writing down my memories in chronological order. Not a light task with over fifty years bouncing around in my brain. At times, remembering was painful, but I did it! As I reviewed my timeline, I noticed a clear trajectory of my own personal evolution from surviving suicide in 1989 to living an authentic, joy-filled life in January of 2020.

Seeing the growth pattern that had worked in my life, I believed two things. First, that the universal principles I had employed could work for others dealing with similar issues like confusion, grief, PTSD, anxiety, depression, and suicidal thinking. And second, in front of my eyes was a process that had given me options in order to choose life, overcome my addictions, and heal my trauma, in addition to experiencing peace, being exquisitely happy, and living honestly, connected to the love that connects us all.

My own journey had created a cumulative process that had healed my own trauma from the inside out. The patterns and how they worked brought to mind Sir Dave Brailsford, a performance coach for British cyclists who revolutionized the sport using the theory of marginal gains. He taught that if you make a 1 percent improvement in multiple areas, the cumulative benefits are extraordinary.[4] That was it! That was exactly what I had done in my own life.

Extraordinary things had come to pass from consistently making decisions and commitments in small and simple principles across five specific areas of growth. I noticed a fluidity in the processes I'd lived. And the order I had learned and applied the axioms seemed, to me, quite significant.

Upon completion of the first draft, I sent the book to beta readers. I also sent the manuscript to a registered working nurse with recent real-time experience at a psychiatric hospital, helping individuals dealing with suicidal ideation. I wanted to make sure the book had the least amount of triggers for anyone in crisis, hoping it could potentially be used to help individuals in clinical and institutionalized settings.

For eight weeks I received valuable feedback from individuals working through the forty activities. Here are a few of their comments . . .

"I love it. I'm captivated by your story and it's a roller coaster. When you asked me to read, you didn't know that these last couple of years were the hardest in my life. You didn't know that about eighteen months ago I tried to take my own life. Thank you, with all my heart, for sharing your story. It's been healing already. Your story is unimpeachable." A. P. Beta Reader

"From day one of the Forty Day Journey, I began thinking it was a little too easy, but as I continued, I'm grateful you started slow. From pinpointing who I am and what makes me who I am; finding my true self in my integrity . . .it's been a blessing going through this whole process . . . it's almost like God had a hand in you choosing me to be part of this journey." D.P. Beta Reader

"My favorite part of the journey has been discovering new tools that I can use for self-care and achieving my absolute "BEST". The "Three Words" have been very powerful. It's only been a week since I discovered them, but in one week I am making connections from my thoughts and feelings and decisions to my three words. It's incredible. I have a new weapon to use against my demons." B.C. Beta Reader

While preparing Living Blueprint for publication, several working titles came and went. I could see that what I had before me was my own Blueprint for experiencing peace, honestly living in love, and choosing to be consciously and joyfully alive. In talking about the title with my husband, he suggested I add the word *living* since that is what the process had allowed me to do. It perfectly described what I'd experienced and now could share.

Living Blueprint-A True Story. Five Principles to Creating an Authentic, Joy-Filled Life.

What Is a Living Blueprint?

A Living Blueprint is an internal compass that embodies five key components supporting our physical, emotional, mental, and spiritual well-being while synergistically building upon each principle lived in order to create a solid foundation. The data in our own Blueprint is the truth we understand about ourselves, our values, beliefs, and personality characteristics guided by our personal guidance system and is the equation to creating our personal peace and joy-filled life.

By applying the principle of "marginal gains," the small, incremental improvements in our daily life decisions add up to an exponential improvement toward our own self-actualization. Living from a personal Blueprint 1+1+1+1+1 does not equal five, it equals *never living less than we are capable of being in each present moment*, regardless of our past.

During the Forty Activities, you will be introduced to:

- Breathing and eliminating self-harm as an option in dealing with trauma, pain, or problems.

- Creating personal safety by identifying issues and obstacles in the way of forward movement and assembling a success team for support.

- Discovering and living from who you are, focusing energy, diminishing distractions, and directing life-sustaining decisions from core attributes and personality qualities.

- Learning and designing a Personal Guidance System, including your greatest gifts and talents and connecting to your Source of Inspiration. Choosing the programs by which to consciously create a life by and deleting viruses holding you back.

- Nurturing your mind, body, heart, and soul by stimulating the parasympathetic nervous system and utilizing your own biochemistry to relieve stress, anxiety, depression, and self-destructive tendencies.

- Becoming honest and authentic, letting go of anything no longer supporting your highest and best self. Then experiencing a newfound feeling of autonomy and freedom because you are living from the truth of who you are.

- Diving into the most powerful and greatest power used to create healing effects and miracles: desiring loving kindness for others, choosing loving kindness for one's self, and opening to loving kindness from the source of love that connects us all.

- All of that, step-by-step, day by day, equals your Living Blueprint!

As we learn and then live from our own Blueprint, we automatically help others do the same. We become absolutely honest with ourselves first and then with others in our words and actions. We support others in being honest with themselves. We are not afraid of the truth. We begin to discover who we are and we realize we don't need to hide. Fear melts away. Real authentic connection to others follows.

As you consistently and diligently live from your Blueprint, the battle inside will cease, and you will learn to trust yourself. When we trust ourselves, we learn to listen and hear each other. Eventually, we learn to trust each other. We spend time pursuing our interests and achieving our personal best while celebrating others doing and enjoying the same. Our cups become full. We let go of toxic comparison and contention, first in our own hearts, and then in our relationships. We recognize that there is enough love for everyone. Kindness and compassion spill into our actions.

How to use Living Blueprint

Take one day at a time as you *work* through the forty activities and choose what is best for your life at every moment. Moving forward is more important than moving fast.

Use your free will, agency, intelligence, heart, and intuition to discover and design your Living Blueprint in the workbook pages. Perhaps something I share in *my story* resonates with you, or it piques your interest. By all means, explore your own feelings and thoughts about it, but please do not compare your Blueprint to mine or anyone else's.

Comparison is the antithesis of happiness. Let go of judgment about yourself and others. Judgment can impede progress. In fact, when we are judging others, it's very difficult, if not impossible, to see ourselves. Each of us is perfectly unique and divine in our own right. Live, choose, and experience your decisions based on your knowledge, life experience, and goals. You are the only one who can gift humanity with your presence. Don't try to be someone else. Be you, all of you! That's who we want to see and get to know.

Carve out a specific time each day to *work* on your Blueprint. Creating your Blueprint will take work, be diligent in not missing a day. Your pain, stress, and anxiety are no joke, and we live in a competitive world exploding with information. We all get overwhelmed. Focus and consistency are key to creating and utilizing your Blueprint.

Create your Living Blueprint and your DWM (daily, weekly, monthly) accountability tracker:

Step 1: Access the Templates:

- My Living Blueprint and Living Blueprint Tracker at wendybeth. org or use the provided templates My Living Blueprint and Living Blueprint in the Appendix.

Step 2: Discover and Design Your Living Blueprint:

- Fill in the provided template with detailed information about your Blueprint as you work through the forty activities. The directions will be given as you move through each of the processes. Though not all of them add a component to your Blueprint, every process is helping you discover the truth of who you are and the life you desire to create and live.

Step 3: Create (DWM) Daily, Weekly, and Monthly Accountability Tracker:

- Utilize the tracker to break down your overarching desires and plans into daily, weekly, and monthly actionable steps.

- Design your daily plan by outlining specific tasks, habits, or activities aligned with your Blueprint that create your best day.

- Develop your weekly plan by setting milestones and dividing tasks from My Living Blueprint into manageable segments for each week.

- Establish your monthly goals to assess progress, make necessary adjustments, and plan for the upcoming month.

Step 4: Accountability Strategy:

- Establish a consistent DWM accountability system to ensure you stick to your plan supporting self-regulation.

- Find an accountability partner and use tools to track and review your progress regularly. (Watch for Living Blueprint APP.)

- Schedule check-ins once per week with yourself and a success partner to evaluate how well you're following your plan and adjust when needed.

Step 5: Implement and Monitor:

Start utilizing your Blueprint as you discover it. Don't wait. Remember focused. Small, and simple steps add up to extraordinary results. Regularly review and monitor your progress against your set goals and make adjustments as necessary.

Live what you know now and let tomorrow take care of itself. Happy moments strung together turn into a joyful day. Joy–filled days strung together turn into a happy life. Embrace and enjoy each and every moment, today.

Life-changing songs that inspire us, exhilarating athletic achievements we celebrate, healthy relationships we aspire to enjoy, and beautiful architecture we marvel at are designed first in the imagination, then rendered into plans and blueprints before they are actualized in the physical world. Creating a peace-filled life connected to love takes no less intention, effort, or time.

So, let's go. It's time to discover and design your own Living Blueprint.

PROLOGUE

Gangly limbs, oversized feet, bottle cap eyeglasses, and eczema splotches covering my face made me an easy mark as the new girl in a small, rural town in Idaho.

First thing every morning, a supersized seventh grader whose arms were as big as my waist cornered me in the girl's locker room. Hovering over me, she seethed threats so close to my face I could smell her breath and feel the drops of spittle fly out of her mouth. After which a pretty eighth grader, who just happened to go to my same church, and her besties surrounded me, then taunted me to never talk to her boyfriend again.

The mean girls didn't know it, but they were just the warm-up act.

For my entire seventh-grade year, I walked to the assigned desk placed purposefully in the middle of the science classroom. My teacher, a potbellied man with a dark black, bushy mustache, and his towheaded son, along with the rest of the class, would serenade me:

"Marmaduke, Marmaduke,
She is a big and ugly puke.
She has a diaper rash on her face.
She wears her shades in the wrong place.
Marmaduke, Marmaduke."

At the end of science, I would go to English, lay my head down on the desk, stare at the red and pink geraniums in the tin cans on the window sills, and fall asleep. Every few minutes I'd lift my head, peek my eyes open, and watch Mrs. Welch write on the chalkboard. The next year, my family moved to Montana.

From the first day of class, I laid my head down on the desk. One time after falling asleep, my teacher yelled at me. Jerking upright in my chair, saliva ran down the side of my mouth. Everyone laughed. After that, I started ditching class, hiding out in the bathroom stalls.

Soon thereafter, a boy offered me a white pill. I took it. Before the semester ended, I was popping white pills, diet pills, smoking marijuana, drinking alcohol, and huffing Rush–an inhalant that made me wane consciousness every time I breathed it in. I loved it and wanted more of it.

By seventeen I'd overdosed three times and been taken to the hospital once. I was arrested for shoplifting once but could have been busted a hundred times. I'd been expelled from two high schools, fired from my job for going to work high, and caused a head-on car collision because I'd been drinking–not to mention the other two car wrecks I caused.

My home was a battlefield. Neither I nor my religious mother nor my alcoholic father had any conflict communication skills. We were always fighting. Since grade school, I often went to school with tears running down my cheeks. More than once I hid behind gym lockers so that no one would see the bruises on my arms and legs. As I grew older, fighting with my parents worsened. Running away was my answer.

My body meant nothing to me, and so, when boys and men touched me inappropriately, I froze, let whatever happened happen, then scurried away. Sexual trauma transpired because I had no boundaries, no voice, no self, and no ability to stop what was happening. Safety did not exist for me.

The summer before my eighteenth birthday my parents found me and put me in Shodair Children's Hospital Detox and Rehab Center for thirty days. I stayed sober for six months, then started using again by drinking a bottle of tequila till I was dry heaving into a friend's toilet all night. After that, I called my dad. "If I don't get out of this town, I'm going to die." Leaving was my answer.

While living with an aunt who loved me dearly, life calmed down. I went back to high school. I met a nice man, had sex once, then started spiraling again. This time I ended the relationship.

Then I met a woman.

For the first time, my heart felt something other than pain. I told her everything about me, even Marmaduke. I loved her fiercely. She loved me back. When my parents found out, my mother said, "You're disgusting. You're evil. You're nothing. Change your name; you're a disgrace to your grandparents."

For two years, I tried to convince them to accept me. To accept us as a couple. They would not. I was not allowed to see my siblings. I could see nothing left worth fighting for. At twenty years old, making everything go black was my answer. A bottle of pills nearly stopped my world, but I didn't die; I survived.

This book is how I learned to live an authentic, joy-filled life, one moment at a time.

STEP 1 WHO BLUEPRINT

CHAPTER 1 CREATING PERSONAL SAFETY

our life is a dance
between our destiny and
all our decisions

The culture you were raised in, the people in your life both past and present, and the decisions you've made have downloaded intricate programs and viruses onto the motherboard of your mind, heart, and body. However, there is another circuit and a vital energy animating within you. This part of you is WHO you are and is individually distinct, immortal, irreplaceable, and connected to love.

Discovering and living from WHO you are will not only affect your decisions, it will support you in forging a chosen path out of the programming inside your brain towards the destiny you desire. Whether the programs and viruses are creative or destructive, today you have the power to follow and/or unlearn, delete, and choose to create new ones in order to get out of bed excited to be alive, every day.

Sharing my story with you is a decision I've made for one reason: no matter how confused, alone, lost, sad, or angry you are, **there is a way for you to not live less than you are capable of being**. You can live from your essence of WHO you are. It is the truth of you, your light, and it is connected to an everlasting love that can lead you out of the darkness. You can create a meaningful life, no matter what.

My life's purpose, and with every fiber of my being, I believe that your unique Living Blueprint honors, validates, and enlivens your own magnificent soul. Within the story pages, you'll find a roadmap to creating a life that resonates with meaning, love, and fulfillment, one moment at a time. Your own powerful journey of uncovering and then utilizing your Blueprint everyday will help you create the life you were born to live and enjoy.

A midnight sky loomed overhead as my breathing formed fleeting mists of puffy clouds reminding me of my undeniable existence, which brought me neither peace nor joy. My left hand held me steady as my right hand groped to find the keyhole to my newly rented house in Bountiful, Utah. Once inside, I moved briskly toward the phone on the wall, crumpling to the floor in an anguished heap, then laid my head back. *Breathe, Wendy. Just breathe.* Staring at the popcorn ceiling, flashes from the previous summer inspired my next decision. I wanted to live.

Sadness choked me while my thoughts screamed at me all day, just like they did every day. *You're nothing. You'll never be good enough. You're disgusting. You just want attention.* My heart raced and tears stung my eyes. I didn't know how to keep going. I wanted everything to go black. A bottle of pills nearly stopped my world.

With my bourbon in hand, I walked into my bathroom and picked up the prescription of Xanax my psychiatrist had refilled for me the previous day. With shaking palms, I pushed down and unscrewed the lid. Tipping the bottle, I poured the pills into my hand and then washed them down with my drink. When Sage, my lesbian lover of almost two years, came home unexpectedly, I lost consciousness in her arms. She took me to the hospital. My head hung off the right side of the gurney. Blinking from the bright lights above, I could see people rushing all around me.

Shaking off the memory, I focused on breathing, then pulled myself up just enough to grab the phone receiver, and pushed the buttons of Orlo's number, then slid back to the ground. "Please help me," I whispered when

CHAPTER 1 CREATING PERSONAL SAFETY

she answered, knowing I needed something to change in my life. *Maybe she can help me . . .* I didn't know.

Orlo and her buckaroo husband, Waylon, had shown up at my work, out of the blue, in October, three months prior, and three months after my surviving suicide, telling me that if I ever needed anything to just call. And so with Sage gone, out of desperation, I turned to them because I believed they cared.

"Wendy Beth, it's the middle of the night! Are you okay?"

"Yes, I'm okay. I'm feeling the same way I did last summer," I admitted. "Sage moved to Seattle and I don't know who else to ask for help."

"Ya did good to call, sis. Lemme talk to Waylon. I'll get back to ya, are ya okay now?"

I took a slow, deep breath, relaxing my grip on the phone a little bit. "Yes," I nodded, even though she couldn't see me. "I'm just going to sleep."

"Okay, young lady. Get some rest. We'll talk to ya soon."

Before I'd even woken up the next morning, Orlo was on my doorstep. The snow-capped Wasatch Mountains came into view the moment I opened my back door, a golden hint of the rising sun warmed the chilly January morning. This woman lived one state over in Idaho and was the mother of six children. I couldn't believe she'd dropped everything and was standing outside my door merely eight hours after I'd called her.

Orlo Walker was a smallish woman in her forties with a firecracker personality. She wore her hair short and I noticed her dark brown hair had a lot more gray than I remembered. Her gaze penetrated mine while her eyelashes fluttered as she talked. Their aliveness almost matched her personality; they always had. She was the most unapologetic, authentic person I'd ever known. Once I got over the shock of her standing at my back door, I invited her in.

"Thank you for coming! I can't believe you're here. I didn't mean for you to drive all this way!" We walked into my bedroom and I got back in bed, still exhausted despite sleeping all night.

Orlo sat on the end of the mattress. "What's going on, sis?"

Shaking my head, I began, "Sage and I broke up. I don't know what to do. Last night I felt like I was falling again, like last summer with all those pills. I, I don't want to get that low again, Orlo."

"I know, sis. I know ya don't." Her presence helped me to feel safe. Since Sage had left, I'd been sexually assaulted twice. It felt like everywhere I went, even the gym wasn't safe. I didn't know how to stop men from hurting me.

Confusion tormented me. Inside my head, I had two lives battling to be lived. One part of me wanted Sage, creating our life together no matter what my family thought. The other part of me wanted my family. I missed my brothers and sisters. I didn't know how to live without them. There was no right answer.

I'd felt safe with Sage. But one thing was for certain: my parents were never going to accept us as a couple. The battle inside my brain was killing me.

So, that's who I called, in the depths of my despair, frustration, and hopelessness: Waylon and Orlo. They didn't understand my feelings for Sage either, but at least they were kind to me and her. They'd welcomed me into their family openly as a twelve-year-old girl less than a decade ago. Orlo had been a teacher at my church, my "Beehive" leader until we moved back to Montana when I was thirteen.

They scared the hell out of me when they talked to their own children-tough love had been their parenting style, but never with me. Whenever we could be together, they treated me like a cowgirl princess, teaching me how to move cows on horseback and sleeping in a tent at cow camp. Even when the dust caused my eczema to ooze and bleed, I didn't care. I felt safe with them. It was worth it to be with them, outside, at their ranch.

Thankfully, as an adult, my eczema, the "diaper rash on my face," over time and with a lot of intention, had healed. But even the thought of middle school made me cringe. *Weak. Vulnerable. An ugly duckling.* No one knew about the Marmaduke song except Sage. She was the only person I'd ever felt safe enough to tell. Now she was gone.

"Come back to the ranch with me," Orlo suggested, pulling me back to the present moment in my bed. "Lambin' season is comin' and you can go up the Snake River on the jet boat to Hells Canyon. You need to get outta this city and get some fresh air, sis."

I gave her a hesitant glance, opening my eyes wider. She was still the same. She said what she wanted to say and she didn't hold back. But she was right. I did need to get out of the city. Since Sage had left I hadn't been up to Park City, a mountain town outside of the Salt Lake Valley, once. I was stuck and I didn't know how to move forward.

"We need help bringin' the sheep from the Snake River back to the lambin' sheds," Orlo continued. "You could take care of the newborns whose mamas won't feed 'em. The baby animals will be healing to your soul, Wendy Beth." She'd called me Wendy Beth when I was in middle school. It endeared her to me now, just as it had then.

But I shook my head. "I can't leave, Orlo. I'm really good at what I do and the people in my company love me. I make enough money to take care of myself here. I just needed to talk. I didn't mean for you to drive all this way. Really, I'm okay."

We talked for the rest of the day. At one point Orlo just stopped mid-conversation, then stared into my eyes. "Sis, ye shall know the truth and the truth will set you free."[1]

Confused but still smiling, I replied, "I'll trust you on that, Orlo."

I have no idea what those words even mean. I'd been grappling with finding answers in my life for a long time. I needed truth: my own truth, not someone else's truth imposed upon me. Everyone had a different answer to my questions, and so far, none of their answers had helped me experience the joy I was looking for. Not even Sage, as much as she loved me and I loved her. Her truth was not mine.

The same was true for what Orlo just offered. Going to her ranch wasn't an option. I loved my job. Decorating wedding cakes was the first thing I'd ever excelled at. Sage had taught me. She was the best and I was her protégé. My cakes, especially ones with fresh flowers, were magnificent, and every time I created one, people loved them. I just couldn't leave!

Orlo stayed with me for the next five days, trying to convince me to leave my job and move to her ranch. I wouldn't budge. On the sixth day of her visit, I was surprised when she called me at work and asked me to come home early. I was pretty sure she was leaving. Actually, I was flabbergasted that she'd stayed so long.

When I arrived home from work, however, I was surprised to see two men in dark suits with colored ties in my living room. They reminded me of the men I'd seen every week at church as a child. Seeing them in *my* house felt odd. After a few minutes of small talk, they asked me a question: "Can we give you a blessing?"

"Sure," I said, not knowing what I was agreeing to, still a bit dazed from their presence. I was open to what they were offering. In fact, I was open to *anything* that would help me find answers to my questions and peace in my heart. I sat in the chair and they put their hands on my head and began speaking.

As they were saying the blessing, deep inside, I felt an unyielding impression. Crystal clear, I experienced an indelible understanding that if I did not leave with Orlo that day, I would die. I did not hear a voice. There was no emotion attached to the experience. It was simply a choice: to leave and live . . . or to stay and die. The decision was mine.

Three hours later, the impossible happened. The lease for my house was broken and a leave of absence for ninety-nine years at my work was secured for whenever I wanted to return to my employment. As I followed Orlo's truck out of town, we drove by the first place Sage and I had lived in Utah. Her most recent letter was tucked away in my glove box. Gratitude filled my heart while tears formed in my eyes as I thought of my ex-girlfriend and our last two years together. She was starting over, and so was I.

The truth was just breathing had given me enough clarity of mind to ask for help. I had no answers except the absolute knowledge that an influence apart from my own intellect had infiltrated my thoughts and conveyed a message to my heart and mind. Going with Orlo was me following that thought and choosing to find the answers I was looking for.

Money in my bank account and Orlo's job offer at the ranch would continue to take care of my needs while I stepped into the unknown and explored a new world. Listening to music on the radio, I followed Orlo's farm truck, as if it were a lighthouse in the dark, down the highway for the next three hours.

We drove to her nephew's house, in Idaho, to spend the night, arriving late. A young man in his twenties, the same age as me, with strong shoulders, a slender waist, and brown curls tucked behind his ears met us at the door with a kind smile. "Ryder, I've brought you a mail order bride!" Orlo announced with a joking grin as we stepped through his doorway.

True Principles for Creating Safety for Yourself:

- When life is too much and you don't know what to do, when it feels like the walls are collapsing around you, **just breathe**. It's enough. Even if you think there's more you must do, even if you think others expect things from you, just breathe.

- Your **personal safety is essential** to moving forward and creating the life you want. Just breathe. Inhale. Exhale. Repeat.

- You're the only one who can **utilize your agency and make the conscious, deliberate decision to live** your life. Taking self-harm off the table as an option to deal with trauma, pain, and problems can uncover options not yet seen and help you move forward and create a sustainable future.

- In my experience, self-harm and suicidality not only inhibit our ability to see all the solutions to our problems, they thwart our ability to thrive and decrease our resilience.

- **Staying focused on the present moment and practicing gratitude** can help lift you out of despair and help you see the good that you have experienced in the past.

- As you move forward, ask yourself, "Am I physically, emotionally, and mentally safe? Do I have enough food to feed myself? Do I have shelter?" **Taking care of your basic human physiological and safety needs is essential in order to create a satisfying life.**

- As humans, we are born to connect. Somewhere along the journey of life, we may learn that it's far safer to keep everything inside rather than being honest in our deepest needs and wants. And for some of us, this can be deadly! This program must be unlearned and deleted.

- **Asking for help and organizing your success team** can save your life. Your success partners don't have to agree with everything you do or how you live, but they do need to be safe, kind, and supportive of you living from WHO you are.

Throughout the forty engaging activities, you will be filling in key elements, your My Living Blueprint Template. By the time you finish all forty processes, you'll hold in your hands a convenient and comprehensive reference to your very own Living Blueprint, a powerful tool to use in order to structure and create your daily life with purpose and intention. After which, you can organize what you do every day into your DWM--daily, weekly, and monthly tracker as a way to keep your life going in the positive direction you desire.

Get ready to embark on a transformational journey that will empower you to create the life you deeply desire.

While completing activities 1-5, you will be:

- **Activity 1: Experiencing Stillness Every Morning**

- **Activity 2: Living by Choice in Gratitude**

- **Activity 3: Unlocking True Potential by Meeting Basic Needs**

- **Activity 4: Identifying Success Partners and Asking for Help**

- **Activity 5: Going to Bermuda**

ACTIVITY 1: EXPERIENCING STILLNESS EVERY MORNING

Rumi said, "Let silence take you to the core of life." In a world of constant motion, disconnection, trauma, problems, and pain, days can go by without a moment of stillness. I invite you, as soon as you wake up, even before you get out of bed to *just breathe* and learn to experience stillness. Inhale. Exhale. Repeat. For at least five minutes. The point is to be present with yourself.

What does "stillness" feel like? As you practice just breathing every morning for a few minutes, you'll learn what it feels like *for you.*

For me, stillness feels like a lake at dusk when the water is so calm I can see my reflection. As I begin to notice my breath, within just a minute I feel a gentle flow of energy in an outward expansion deep within my core separated from my thoughts.

Everything is still a bit hazy, but I'm aware of WHO I am, my body, how my heart feels, and how my brain is working. The soft sheets touching my knees in particular bring mindfulness and pleasure upon waking. Vulnerability and honesty within myself begin in these first few moments each day.

Still a bit sleepy in that space I feel free or I feel tired or sick or happy or sad . . . Often, I feel like I'm floating. Whatever I am feeling and experiencing, I connect to the deepest part of me, WHO I am. After a few minutes of gentle, mindful breathing, I place one hand on each shoulder and give myself a hug.

If I'm sad or upset or if I'm dealing with heavy things in my life, it takes longer to connect with myself. But I do it; I connect with WHO I am, *every single day* before I get out of bed. Why? Because I have learned that what I think and feel and WHO I am are two separate things. Addressing my state of consciousness every morning gives me vital information, allowing me to choose the thoughts I focus on, feel my heart energy, and get out of bed excited, connected to love and myself, every day.

Experiment with the following breathing techniques or just breathe on your own for five minutes.[2] See what feels natural for you.

Square breathing allows you to inhale and exhale in a pattern of equal counts.

1. Inhale through your nose for the count of four.

2. Hold your breath for the count of four.

3. Exhale through your mouth for the count of four.

4. Gently hold your breath for the count of four.

5. Repeat.

Belly breathing calms the mind, allowing you to drop deeper into being present.

1. Close your eyes.

2. Inhale slowly through your nose from your belly.

3. Exhale from your mouth from your belly

4. Repeat.

What did you notice? Does the mind chatter start immediately? Do you go into a state of autopilot? Would it support your process to use the structured breathing routine? Getting curious about you can change the trajectory of each and every day as you discover and design your Living Blueprint. Remember self-discovery is never selfish.

Connecting with WHO we are and being honestly curious with ourselves upon waking creates our starting point for each day. From this we choose what is appropriate to be done to create the life we want, that day. Feeling excited when we get out of bed is possible, even if we don't immediately have the answers to our questions. Taking the time to connect, listen, hear, feel, and understand what we need is vitally important to our happiness, and it starts the moment we wake up.

Discovery Activity

- **Breathe. Do this for at least five minutes.** *After today, do this every morning before you get out of bed.*

- **To experience your own stillness, try the following:**

  1. Lie awake for a moment, before getting out of bed.

  2. Be still, and just breathe in whatever way feels natural to you.

3. Let go of everything except the present moment.

4. Rest in the awareness or stillness of being, noticing what you feel inside.

Important note-If you feel you might fall asleep by staying in bed by all means, sit up, sit in the shower, sit on the couch, or sit outside. Do whatever you need to do in order to be still and experience you, while being awake first thing each morning.

- **Write about your experience of being in stillness. What do you notice?**

_____

_____

_____

_____

_____

Are you in pain? Can you pinpoint where the pain is?

_____

_____

_____

Did you notice an overload of thoughts or was your mind calm?

_____

_____

_____

Did you use one of the breathing techniques or did you prefer to breathe naturally?

_____

_____

_____

- **Store your phone in a different room.**

  As you discover your Blueprint, you're teaching yourself how to unplug from the rest of the world's pace and expectations to find WHO you are. Adam Grant on his Instagram page teaches, "Reducing your smartphone use is better for your well-being than stopping cold turkey. Digital moderation beats digital abstinence." For the duration of creating your Living Blueprint, I invite you to store and charge your phone and computer in a different room away from your bed.

ACTIVITY 2: LIVING BY CHOICE IN GRATITUDE

Deciding to embrace life fully is a conscious commitment you and I get to make every single day. From my own journey, I have learned that when we are entertaining even the slightest thoughts of self-harm and suicidality, it can be challenging to see the other choices and opportunities that can lift us out of despair.

The twenty-two-year-old poet laureate Amanda Gorman during the 2021 presidential inauguration read "There is always light if only we're brave enough to see it, if only we're brave enough to be it."[3] Choosing to live, no matter what, opens a universe of options ahead of us that can bring experiences, even miracles, into our lives leading to happiness. Many times I've not known how I would get through a specific problem or a deep emotional wound. But there is a way through. There is light in you. Go towards the light.

When we begin experiencing stillness, choosing life no matter what and living with gratitude is one of the greatest gifts we can give ourselves. As we become aware of, then more clearly see the small and large victories of daily living, they can help us move out of negative thought patterns and self-destructive behaviors. For the rest of our journey together here, I invite you to write down three things you are grateful for every day.

- Breathing deeply

- Feeding myself

- Taking a shower

- Landing a big deal

- Having a baby

- Kissing my son's head as he goes out the door

- Handing in my homework

- Winning the World Cup

As you are breathing every morning and documenting your gratitudes, I invite you to explore music as a way to experience peace and inspiration. My son shared with me the song, "Illusion," by VNV Nation at a very difficult period of my life. The message touched my heart so deeply that I reached out to Ronan Harris, the song's creator, to see if I could share his song in this book.

I received a personal note from the songwriter with the following explanation that said he'd "lost count of the number of people who felt deeply inspired to find light in the dark from this song," adding, "Absolutely, please do share it with anyone whom it will help."

Listen here: *https://open.spotify.com/track/2h90T02jHEfnEAtnq4Mz7n ?si=a4da89e785744dd7.*

- **What feelings, thoughts, or images did Ronan's song bring up for you?**

_____

Discovery Activities

- **Breathe, before you even get out of bed. Do this for at least five minutes today.**

- **List gratitudes**

  1. _____

  2. _____

  3. _____

- **Create a playlist of songs that empower you, supporting feelings of hope and living your best life.**

_____

ACTIVITY 3: UNLOCKING POTENTIAL BY MEETING YOUR BASIC NEEDS

Abraham Maslow, an American psychologist from 1931-1970 revolution-ized the idea that for humans to *self-actualize* or live at their highest poten-tial, their basic needs must be met. He said, "When people appear to be something other than good and decent, it is only because they are reacting to stress, pain, or the deprivation of basic human needs such as security, love, and self-esteem."[4] Assuring that you have the necessities to sustain life is fundamental to discovering, designing, and utilizing your Living Blueprint.

The basic physiological and safety needs we will address here include homeostasis, meaning basic sustenance for functioning in your physical body, hydration, nutrition, clothing, shelter, and financial safety necessities. Reaching out to family, friends, church services, government, and community outreach programs and pride centers in your area might feel scary, but people want to help you. **988** is a twenty-four-hour crisis hotline created by people who care. Please call this number in case of emergency and find out what help is available in your area.

Discovery Activity

- **Breathe, before you even get out of bed. Do this for at least five minutes today.**

- **List Gratitudes**

  1. _____

  2. _____

  3. _____

- **Are your basic needs met?** Look at the list below. If any of these things are not currently present in your daily life, resolve any missing pieces. CIRCLE any item that relates to your basic needs that are NOT being met:

  - My body is functioning at a level that I am able to care for my basic needs.

  - I have an adequate amount of clean drinking water.

  - I have enough food for my needs.

  - I have adequate clothing to wear.

  - My medical needs are met and I am taking any needed supplementation.

  - I have shelter and housing where I feel safe and protected.

- I am safe and free from any form of physical, emotional, or mental abuse.

- I have financial means to take care of my basic needs.

If any of the above items are CIRCLED, focused energy must be spent in fulfilling your basic needs. I've been there, and it's a tough place to be. You are the only one who can really answer the question: what do you need to do, today?

I love this quote by American actor Ben Affleck about resilience. "You have to work harder than you think you possibly can. You can't hold grudges. It's hard and it doesn't matter how you get knocked down because that's going to happen. All that matters is that you gotta get back up." Celebrate yourself for surviving.

- **Write about one of these:**

  1. My basic needs are met and I am grateful for this blessing in my life, or

  2. This is the first thing I need to do to have my basic needs met, and my plan is . . .

  _____

  _____

  _____

  _____

  _____

- **If your basic needs are NOT all met,** begin today by making the necessary phone calls and reaching out to remedy your current situation. Look on the Internet or in the local phone book and write down the phone numbers of available help for you, then call them today.

_____

_____

_____

_____

My next action steps to having my basic needs met are . . .

_____

ACTIVITY 4: IDENTIFYING SUCCESS PARTNERS AND ASKING FOR HELP

Transformational power comes from human connection. Knowing there are people available in our lives who care what happens to us, who we can call if we need something, and who we feel safe with can make all the difference at some of the lowest points in our lives. It has in mine, more than once. Are you like me, a person who gets revitalized from being alone, or do you get energized from being with other people? Even the most introverted of us need someone, sometimes. Who do you turn to in times of need?

Do you find the question, "How are you?" difficult to answer. And when you want to answer, do you really feel heard and understood? Asking for help might feel awkward and vulnerable. It can often feel laborious if not impossible to find the words to express what we're feeling. But people want to help! Helen Keller said, "Alone, we can do so little; together, we can do so much."[5] One easy communication strategy I've found in either asking for help, or knowing when someone else might need my support is to use the How Am I Scale?

"How Am I Scale"

- 10-Exuberant. Life's never been better. I want to share my gifts with the world!

- 9-Fantastic. I feel happy and excited for the day ahead. Let's go!

- 8-Awesome. Nothing is bothering me, I feel satisfied and can help others.

- 7-Good. Low energy, a bit tired, but still doing well.

- 6-Okay. Feeling down physically, mentally, or emotionally. Increasing self-care.

- 5-Unsure. Feeling stuck, paralyzed, unable to move forward.

- 4-Unhappy. Mostly distressed, self-loathing, blaming. Looking for answers.

- 3-Very Dissatisfied. Self-destructive, cutting, substance abuse. Asking for help.

- 2-Hanging on. Self-harm, intermittent thoughts. Needs not being met.

- 1-Hopelessness. Self-harm plan on forefront of mind. Not seeking help.

This scale is an easy way to know where you are today and every day from here on out. Share this scale with your success partners in this next activity. It's a good way to easily and succinctly communicate how we are. I use this scale every day to check in with myself when I first wake up in the morning, with my partner, and with many of the people I interact with in my life. It's a great way to support ourselves and the people we love. (Eventually, you can record your number each day in the space provided as you create your Living Blueprint Tracker.)

Discovery Activity

- **Breathe, before you even get out of bed. Do this for at least five minutes today.**

- **What is your number today?** _____

- **List Gratitudes**

  1. _____

  2. _____

  3. _____

- **Create your success team.**

  Write down the names and phone numbers of five people, organizations, or hotlines that you *would* call if you needed anything. This includes friends, family, clergy, community assistance, pride centers, therapists, outreach programs, and hotlines.

  ○ _____

  ○ _____

  ○ _____

  ○ _____

  ○ _____

One overly self-sufficient man, not in the habit of reaching out to others, while working on his Blueprint, struggled to come up with people he felt comfortable reaching out to. Finally, he identified five individuals he could reach out to if he ever needed help. He wrote them each a brief note and thanked them for being someone he could ask for help—even though most likely he never would.

In response, he then received heartfelt thoughts of gratitude and love from each of them.

If you believe you are alone, I invite you to reach out to a local food bank, shelter, church, or outreach program. Call a mental health advisor associated with your healthcare provider and ask for help. Keep looking until you find two people who will be your success partners.

- Write down two people's names whom you will ask for support as you create your Living Blueprint. Transfer these two (2) names to My Living Blueprint, Success Partners.

    o _____

    o _____

1. Share the "How Am I Scale" with success partners. Ask the above two individuals if it would be okay for you to reach out to them from time to time. Assure them it won't be too much; just a few conversations and a couple of activities as you work this program. Once they agree, add their contacts to your favorites on your phone.

2. Send the two people you added to your favorites a note/text of gratitude.

3. Look over the checklist of physiological and safety needs on **Activity 3.** Be prepared to discuss these needs with your success partner. Brainstorm with them how to best make sure all your basic needs are taken care of.

ACTIVITY 5: GOING TO BERMUDA

Today we will explore one of the greatest treasures I found on my healing journey-the transformative power of Going to Bermuda. Though my story reveals this gift given to me much later, its significance can no longer be contained. Going to Bermuda is one of the easiest tools I have ever used in bringing equanimity to my heart, my mind, and my day-to-day life. I use it every day, and so do my loved ones.

About seven years into my healing journey, a registered nurse named Cheryl invited me to *Go to Bermuda* three times per day. She knew I was under a great deal of stress and explained that going to Bermuda was similar to a yoga posture also known as *Viparita Karini*[6], and that it could help me into a peaceful state of mind any time of the day.

In this pose, I laid on the ground and put my feet up the wall at a seventy-degree angle, then rested there for twenty minutes. No, I'm not kidding. Three times! And I had four young children at the time.

From our conversations, Cheryl knew that my body and my mind were in a place of constant flight and fight mode and that my sympathetic nervous system was always on alert. She wanted to see me in my parasympathetic nervous system so that I could recover and allow my body to rest and heal. She told me that listening to soft meditation music could enhance my process, but she didn't want me to read or talk while my feet were up the wall. Had I had a cell phone then, I'm sure she would have told me to put away my smart phone.

The benefits were almost immediate. Within the first few days of "Going to Bermuda" three times every day, I began to experience a welcomed level of peace in my whole being. The inversion was restorative and relaxing. Cheryl taught me that the posture would regulate my blood pressure, allowing hormones and blood to better circulate throughout my body.

As you begin to "Go to Bermuda," intrusive thoughts that make you want to move out of the pose may try to dissuade your peace. I'm going to invite you to do two things.

- First, just let them float right on by, imagining automatic thoughts like clouds; they come and they go . . . you don't need to attach to or follow any thought.

- And second, let's create some affirmations that could bust some of those recurring negative thoughts that may be bothering you, not only when you're in Bermuda, but at other times as well.

Discovery Activity

- **Breathe, before you even get out of bed. Do this for at least five minutes today.**

- **What is your number today?** _____

- **List Gratitudes**

    1. _____

    2. _____

    3. _____

- **As you go through the following thoughts, write down an affirmation that helps you recreate the negative thought presented.**

    <u>Thought #1</u>-*I've tried everything. There is no hope for my happiness.*

    - You were born to experience joy. You're not an exception. You're not a lost cause. You just don't know your unique Blueprint, yet!

    - _____

      _____

    <u>Thought#2</u>-*I'm too broken. I've made too many mistakes to believe I can ever be happy.*

    - You are never too broken. You can forgive yourself, recenter, and start today learning and becoming WHO you were born to become–- your highest and best self!

    - _____

_____

Thought #3-*I'm too "different" (too old, too non-conforming, too weird, too angry, too anything) for anything to really work for me.*

- You are never "too anything." You can grow at any time in any place of your life. You have the strength and courage to make this life work for you.

- _____

_____

Thought #4-*I need money, love, perfect physical appearance, and fame to bring me happiness.*

- Your happiness comes from inside, not from the world around you or the things in it. You have the power to let go of social comparisons and find peace within yourself.

- _____

_____

- **Go to Bermuda at least 1x today.**

Music, love, prayer, a breeze, a smell . . . none of these can be seen or touched; however, these immaterial things can change and shift our perspective in a moment. Just breathing can do the same thing.

Walls or distractions in the way of thoughts, feelings, and emotions can block us from experiencing the feeling of safety. But breathing and being still can show us and then help dissolve barriers we have within ourselves.

Creating safety for yourself is a process and a gift that only you can give yourself. You are worth whatever it takes to feel secure in your body and safe in your life. Taking care of your material needs, practicing gratitude, asking for support, listening to music you love, and Going to Bermuda are all things that will create safety in your daily existence and move you forward toward a peaceful, joy-filled life.

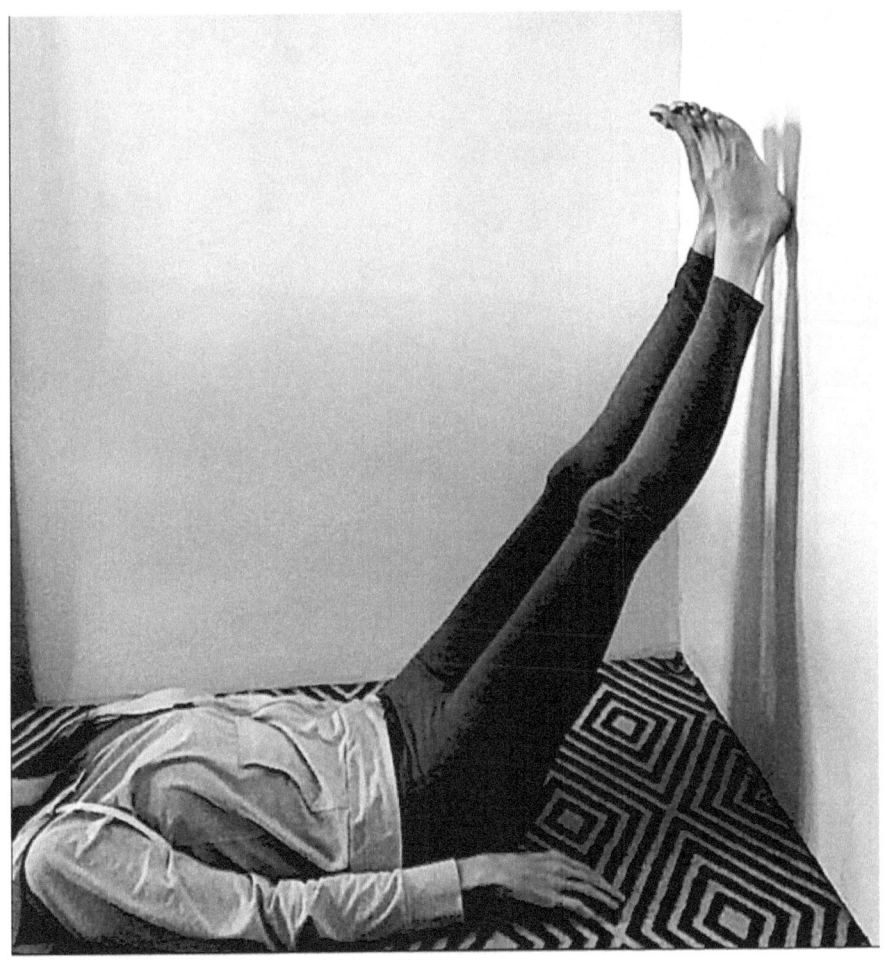

Going to Bermuda

CHAPTER 2 DISCOVERING WHO YOU ARE

lost in shadows deep
the light in who you are keeps
awaken from sleep

Unveiling the ultimate key in designing a Living Blueprint is a journey that delves into the very essence of your identity-a process where every decision you make *can* be grounded from the epicenter of WHO you are. In this place, you are free, untouched, reminiscent of the innocent child you once were. When you live from WHO you are, you catalyze every decision towards what you were born to create and you connect to the love that connects us all.

WHO you are is an unscathed, limitless, loving core essence. WHO you are transcends the roles you choose, the manner in which you make money, the labels you wear, the house you live in, or the titles you bear, though these things can be outward indicators of your true nature. WHO you are, are the qualities, attributes, and characteristics that are innate and untouched by circumstance. WHO you are is infinite.

Some of us have a clear understanding of our true self, while for others WHO we are is hidden behind barriers and walls, pain and regret, trauma and lies. When this happens, we find ourselves reeling, experiencing (and creating) chaos, pain, often in autopilot and reaction. This is how we've learned to survive.

However, by becoming aware of WHO you truly are, you practice connecting, nurturing, and bringing forth your true self, making effective decisions and consciously creating your life, instead of reacting to it and everything in your environment. You become powerful and directed. You live from your talents, your gifts, your strengths, and the truth you know.

If you've ever had a difficult time knowing what it takes to make you truly happy, think about what made you exuberant as a child. When did you lose track of time before you started worrying about to-do lists, assignments, and responsibility? For me, I loved being outside. That meant playing in the woods, tramping through the swamps, catching pollywogs, and swimming in the rivers with my brothers and sister. Those were the best parts of my childhood. As an adult, being in nature always connects me to the core essence of WHO I am. What activities readily bring you back to yourself, the truth of WHO you are?

The ranch kitchen was a treasure trove of pans clanging, children laughing, sometimes crying, along with the smell of pancakes coming off the hot griddle. My senses were eliciting a part of myself I hadn't connected with since leaving my own parents' home years before.

Two days around Orlo's farm-style table with six children felt like a whole new yet familiar world. Still, I didn't have my legs under me yet. After breakfast, everyone began doing their chores without being asked.

"Would you like to make bread with us?" asked Orlo's teenage daughters thoughtfully.

"Yes," I replied. Doing so reminded me of my mother's kitchen growing up, especially her delicious, hot, whole wheat bread.

As one of them poured the seemingly endless amount of white flour into the wet, frothy ingredients of water, yeast, and sugar, the other one kneaded the dough with her bare hands. The bowl they were using was the biggest one I'd ever seen—even bigger than my own mother's bread bowl. In my mind, I estimated that we would get at least ten loaves out of the batch. They would need all of that to feed their large family. Nothing would go to waste.

Later that morning, as Orlo drove through the fields, my mind began to slow down after the rousing morning I'd just experienced. I'd forgotten how much energy children possessed. We were checking the heifers to see if any of them needed help birthing their first calf. The sun was out and I rolled down the window to breathe in the fresh morning air. Wide open land filled in the background as the cows, with heads down in the hay, breath floated, then dissipated in the cold morning air.

Being with Orlo's family made me miss my own family even more. It had been two years since I had been "allowed" to see my brothers and sisters. Now that I wasn't with Sage, my parents had consented for me to have a relationship with them again.

Serendipitously, Orlo questioned, "Would ya like to see your family, sis?"

"Yes, I would like that," I said, trying to keep the longing out of my voice.

Upon returning to the farmhouse, I enjoyed Orlo's decorative touch of lace and cowboy paraphernalia littered on the walls and counters. The horse-hide sprawled on the bench by the front door reminded me of riding out on the range with her and Waylen when I was a young girl.

I heard Orlo call my parents and invite them to the ranch. I wondered where everyone would sleep. I was already sleeping in a bed with their two teenage girls and the four other children were in another bedroom. It wasn't a big farmhouse, but they made it work.

My parents and my eight brothers and sisters all lived in Montana. I was surprised when everyone came to Idaho to visit me. Even my brother, who didn't live at home and his wife, pregnant with their first baby, made the drive. Though I did not show it, trepidation filled my heart as tumultuous memories of my childhood and my teenage years resurfaced at the prospect of seeing my parents again. I was walking back into their lives, craving their love and approval.

Talking back and arguing came naturally to me as a child. My willful spirit did not sit well with either of my parents, especially my mom. But my dad's volatile anger when I would *talk back* terrified me. I loved him, was scared of him, and at times used him to protect me from my mother. She was always angry at me. At least when he wasn't screaming or threatening me, I felt like *he* actually liked me. When they arrived at the ranch, I let go of the memories and genuinely hugged them.

My heart exploded with happiness when I saw my brothers and sisters coming down the dirt road. There was so much unresolved pain in our relationships too, but I'd missed them more than I could bear. Alcohol and drug addiction–first our dad's and then mine–had caused havoc in our family and in our home. Now, I couldn't wait to throw my arms around them.

Orlo had planned a traditional American Thanksgiving meal the day they arrived. With Waylen and Orlo's family of eight and my family of eleven, we had a lot of people around a not-so-large table. Somehow, we all squeezed in. I looked across the serving bowls piled high with mashed potatoes and gravy at my parents and my brothers and my sisters. My thoughts drifted to the past.

As little children, after our chores were finished, we scampered out the back door of our double-wide trailer, onto our dad's freshly cut, green grass and into the woods. We passed the tool shed and passed the rabbit hutch. Our little feet scrambled past our parent's garden. Beets, radishes, leafy greens, and an assortment of other vegetables grew so that our mother could then put them up in quart jars for the winter.

One by one, we'd crawled under the wooden-framed fence too tall to climb, through jagged, wire fencing. Placing one leg through and then another, we'd stepped onto the path that led us to the thicket of willows and brush hollowed out by our small hands, looking to make our fort.

Then, all around our little woodland fortress deep in the woods, I gathered twigs, sprouts, leaves, and different colored grasses and plants. I began to create the grandest, most sublime food for my pretend children.

Gathering and making a feast for my brothers and sister made me happy. I'd been undeterred finding a few berries and adding those to my hodge-podge salad. I had a purpose, even then, in our make-believe house. I loved helping others. I knew it was important.

Coming back to the present moment, as everyone ate their dinner and chatted to the person sitting next to them, I had a moment to contemplate how I was feeling. For the first time *in my entire life* while sitting at that table, with my whole family, I felt wanted by them–all of them, even my mother.

Dad asked me a question from the other side of Orlo's table. "Wendy, why don't you come home?"

While I contemplated his invitation, my belly full, we pushed ourselves away from the table so I could respond, away from the sound of all the kids chatting. "I will, Dad. But I've committed to stay here and go up the Snake River to help with the sheep. I need to make some money. I'll come home soon." Relief and anguish rushed through me at the same time.

My family spent the night and then left the next day. When my mother hugged me good-bye, I felt loving kindness flow from her to me. After she left, I went into my shared bedroom and cried. *I want to go home.* Still, Orlo's was a soft place for me to land, for now.

Getting off the bed and wiping my nose and my face, I went outside. Tipping my head back, the brim of my borrowed cowboy hat softly touched my back. The morning sun rose up over the mountain, its rays touching the newly fallen snow, turning the wide, open landscape into a sea of diamonds. *My mother.* Feeling her love had touched the deepest part of my soul, something I'd yearned for my whole life. *Maybe she and I can have a close relationship after all. What could that look like?* I wondered.

Anxious to get to the mountains and try my hand at sheepherding, Orlo, myself, and Ryder, her nephew (the one she'd told I was his "mail order bride" as a joke) left for sheep camp. Our job was to move the band of sheep from the high hills in Hells Canyon down to White Bird, Idaho, a tiny town where the lambing sheds were located. We were in for a load of work.

Ryder was a bit taller than me with a welcoming smile. He was about my age, a quiet man, but spoke with a strong voice. He laughed uneasily around his family, though he and Waylen seemed to get along quite well. He too was a cowboy, who only wore Wranglers, western shirts, and a braided cord belt that I had a feeling he'd made himself. His eyes were a bit sad and he had the cutest pug nose. Observing people seemed to be what he liked to do the most.

Over the next two months, Ryder and I talked freely. He made me laugh. For the first time since leaving Salt Lake City, my heart didn't feel so heavy. Our conversations were long and deep and when it was time to sleep, we'd pick up where we left off the next morning. It seemed "Black Velvet" by Alannah Myles was playing on the radio every time we got in a pick-up truck. We lived on Pepsi and Baby Ruth candy bars.

Questions raging in my heart and mind quieted on the banks of the Snake River. It was easy to be with Ryder; he wasn't like the other men I'd dated. He didn't ignore my boundaries and he never forced himself on me. Holding his hand as our relationship graduated beyond friendship happened naturally. I relaxed.

The wind on my face felt like a soft answer to my mind and heart. With no city lights, the stars above seemed close enough to reach out and touch. With Ryder close by in his bed roll and me in mine, the blackness of the sky felt like a soft blanket in the unknown. For the first time in a long time, I felt like I could just breathe.

Sheep camp on the Snake was rustic living at its best. I hated the bugs, especially the spiders! Just the sight of one made me want to crush it! Food was sparse. Once we ran out of soda and candy bars, I'd turned to the sheep camp cupboards. Rice, carrots, cloves of garlic, canned tomatoes, salt, pepper, brown sugar, coffee, and a leg of mutton felt like a cornucopia of food. Orlo would be back in a week with more supplies, till then this would do.

As a child I'd watched and helped my industrious mother cook from her pantry every day. Now, it was my turn. I started with carrots and garlic, then added the rice and tomatoes. When the rice was soft, I added chunks of mutton. We ended our meal with coffee and brown sugar. It was the best food I'd ever tasted. Looking across the fire, I caught Ryder's eye and he nodded approvingly.

Slowly, our band of sheep with us trailing behind made our way out of the canyon and back to the sheds. Soon lambing pens were bursting with babies. Their bleating was a constant invitation to love. Holding the babies soothed my soul. They were soft and warm. Their little tender noises, especially the weakest ones, demanded our attention. Sometimes their mothers would abandon them and we would then feed them from a bottle. My heart fell in love with every lamb I took care of and whenever one would die, my heart ached.

Orlo's family, though I loved them, was not my family. I'd felt my mom's compassion while she was at the ranch, and the heartfelt hug she'd given me as she left made me hungry to be with her more. We'd been estranged my entire life. For the first time ever, I thought I might be able to live at home, in peace.

Lambing season finished and we headed back to Waylen's and Orlo's ranch. Ryder lived in town and we spent a bit more time together before I left for home in Montana. Then, standing next to my truck, we looked into each other's eyes.

"Thank you for everything, Ryder. I'm not sure when we'll see each other again."

"Take care of yourself." We kissed good-bye. It was early in the day, and I had a six-hour drive to my family.

After a lifetime of fighting with my parents, chaos, and running away, finally I was home. Including me, my parents had a bursting household with eight of their nine children under one roof. Before bed we all met in the living room and knelt in a circle for family prayer. As I looked around at my family, I realized how much I'd hurt them and how much time we'd missed during my drug and alcohol days. *What an absolute mess I was.* I felt so sorry. I had wasted so much time. In that circle, I felt my mother's forgiveness as I knelt there that night. Her love was like sunshine in my heart. I was happy to be home.

She listened to me chatter endlessly as I settled into my new life. For the first time, I felt heard by her and we didn't fight. She wanted to hear what I had to say. She was beautiful and open and I could see how hard she worked to take care of our family. I wanted to be like her– the mother she was to me, now.

I had taken a leap of faith, leaving Salt Lake with Orlo, following a feeling deep inside myself. So far everything was working out upon my return. I could feel my mother's love. That meant life for me. Then, a few weeks after settling at home, I realized I'd missed my period.

Telling my parents I was pregnant was easy. They seemed genuinely happy to have me home, and I could feel it. My mother had a surprised look on her face, but compassion in her eyes. She asked me what I wanted to do.

"I want to take care of my baby," was my response.

My dad seemed sad, but he told me he would help me any way possible. Their support helped me to feel safe. The past was gone. All I felt was love.

Calling Ryder wasn't hard either. He immediately drove to Montana to be with me. When he got to town, he rented a hotel room, explaining to me that we could be together in private and talk about what we wanted to do.

"I want to take care of you and the baby," he told me.

Hearing his words gave me an even stronger feeling of support and safety. *We can do this together.* Talking about marriage and what colors we would want for our wedding seemed appropriate and exciting. Teal blue was a shade we both loved.

When I returned home and told my mother that I was getting married, she gasped.

"No, Wendy. You don't have to get married. I thought you wanted to go to college."

"I did, Mom, but I'm pregnant. I want to get married."

"Dad and I already told you we'd help you. Do you and Ryder have the same goals? Do you have the slightest idea of what he wants in life?"

"He wants to marry me, Mom. He wants to take care of the baby. He wants us to be a family."

Shocked, I'd assumed she would expect me to get married since I was pregnant and unwed, a taboo in the religion she'd raised me in. Overwhelmed at what I was feeling, my brain did a complete 180-degree turn in my mind from what Ryder and I had just planned. Maybe she was right. And I couldn't lose my mom again.

Trusting her direction and needing her approval more than I needed anything else, I told Ryder that I wasn't ready to get married. I needed time. He said he'd do whatever was best for me and the baby. He did not push me.

Immediately, I gave up drinking alcohol. It didn't feel like a sacrifice. Thankfully, I'd quit smoking a couple of months before I left Salt Lake with Orlo. I wanted the cleanest body I could have in order to grow my baby.

Going to church just kind of fell into my weekly routine since everyone at home attended. Often my dad and I would skip out of Sunday School and go see my sister at work. Sitting in the passenger's seat, listening to music on the radio, reminded me of happy times in my childhood. As a child, I loved to hear my mom sing in choirs, at weddings, and in church. At home I would listen to my dad play his vinyl records of ABBA, Crystal Gayle, Kenny Rogers, and so many more artists while I snuggled down into our family beanbag behind our brown recliner. As a child, in music, I felt loved.

Finding a job I liked, since I enjoyed decorating wedding cakes and was good at it, wasn't difficult. But waking up at 4:00 a.m. five days a week with morning sickness was so hard. And my boss wasn't the nicest guy. He simply told me to put a five-gallon bucket next to my workstation, to vomit in, to keep me from going to the bathroom too many times on my shift.

I only worked at that bakery for a short time because another bakery manager walked by the cake case and exclaimed, "Hey, is this your work? Pretty nice stuff for this town! You want a job?"

I started my new job two weeks later. Working was heavenly after that.

My baby's first little movements deep inside my belly felt like butterfly wings flapping. It was the softest sensation I'd ever felt. At times I'd sit quietly just to see if I could experience my baby flutter. I was in love.

While pregnant, two significant things happened. First, we found out my mother was pregnant with her tenth child. Second, my mother asked me if I wanted to receive my patriarchal blessing–an optional practice in my church where an ordained male called a patriarch would put his hands on my head and give me a blessing[1]. After what had happened in Salt Lake City with the blessing there, I thought a patriarchal blessing sounded like a good thing.

She told me that this particular blessing would be accompanied by words of promise, counsel, and lifelong guidance intended just for me. Mom added that the words would be formally recorded, transcribed, and kept in the records of the church. I made the necessary arrangements to receive one. There was a six-week wait for the next available appointment.

By the time my blessing day arrived, I felt like I was going to pop. At eight and a half months pregnant, I was eminently excited as I drove to the patriarch's home. Walking in the front door, I sensed a tranquility like I'd never experienced before in my life. The vintage lamps with painted flowers were turned down and the home had an ethereal glow about it.

After a bit of small talk, the patriarch placed his hands on my head. A sweet peace filled my soul. He spoke many words, but the ones that lingered in my mind until I received my transcribed copy were these:

"You had a personal relationship with Heavenly Father and Jesus. If you stay active in the church, you will meet an elder, a worthy elder who can take you to one of the Lord's temples where you will be married.

"You will be a mother and you'll be able to guide your children along a path that will give them the greatest happiness. They will follow those things they know are true."

As if a lodestar was implanted in my soul, the direction of my life was solidified that night. The questions I'd been grappling with for years were answered as I listened, felt, and experienced receiving my patriarchal blessing. For the first time in my life, I knew exactly what I wanted and I believed God's guidance, even though I didn't really know who He was, would help me achieve it. I was His daughter and He would help me create a happy family.

On a cold December afternoon in Helena, Montana, Rhodes Winter was born. His black eyes stared deep into a part of me I didn't know existed. Holding him in my arms while looking into my son's eyes felt like being in the night sky away from all the city lights. He was infinite–a universe all of his own.

My baby looked just like Ryder, especially his little pug nose. He was fragile, soft, and sweet. While holding his tiny body in both of my hands, I would kiss his velvety little neck. His dark eyes followed mine. He was perfect.

Becoming a mother burst open my innate nurturing capability. Loving my baby came naturally. Never wanting to put him down, I held him for hours, looking into his eyes. Being his protector was instinctual.

"You get some rest," one nurse offered in the hospital. "He'll be just fine; we'll take care of him."

"No, thank you. I'll have him sleep with me."

"He needs a bottle. He's not getting enough milk from you," said another nurse.

"I don't want you to give him water or formula. I'll just nurse him," I said defiantly. "My milk will come in." And it did.

From the moment I became a mother, I did three things every day. First, I read the scriptures, the Bible, and The Book of Mormon to myself and my baby. Petrified that some injury would come upon my child, I prayed for help to be a good mom and to protect my child. And third, I wrote in a journal in order to keep myself steady and moving in a positive direction.

Relentlessly completing these three rituals every day became a habit. I knew why I was doing them. I was a daughter of God and a mother. These three things, along with going to church every week, made me feel like I was keeping up my part of the deal so that I could have the blessings I'd been promised in my patriarchal blessing. Once my blessing arrived in the mail, I added it to my scriptures and read them every day in order to keep myself focused on my goals.

Ryder came to visit soon after Rhodes was born. He was patient with me as I had no idea what to do about our relationship, especially now that I knew I was going to marry an elder in the temple. I gave him a Book of Mormon, hoping he might read it and explore my religion. He never said a cross word to me, ever. He trusted me as a mother and told me so often. He loved us both, mostly from Idaho, while I lived in Montana.

Since I was still living at home, my brothers and sisters adored playing with the baby all the time. When my maternity leave ended after six weeks, my heart broke to be separated from Rhodes, but my little sister took care of him part-time when I went back to work. When my sister was in school, a kind woman from my church offered to babysit Rhodes. With three young children of her own and her husband deployed in Afghanistan, she'd said she had time to help me.

Six months later, when she stopped taking care of my baby because I was relocating for college, she handed me back all of my uncashed checks. "It just doesn't feel right getting paid to love Rhodes. You take these back and use them as you start the next chapter of your life." Her loving kindness for my son and for me compounded my trust that everything would work out, even if I didn't have all the answers.

The truth was, in my role as a mother, parts of my true self emerged, and my awareness of my potential expanded. My willingness to act from faith flourished. Nurturing another human being, to be the giver in a relationship, and sacrificing my own gratification for my child grew within me. Sometimes the days were long as a single mom and I was far from perfect, but I was growing and progressing. So was my baby.

Looking for answers and figuring out what was true for me and my baby was a journey that felt purposeful. What I did mattered. Every choice was important. I loved my child and I could see so many possibilities for both of our futures. In fact, I believed the possibilities ahead of us were endless. I felt happy and my heart was wide open as were my eyes for the next chapter of our lives.

True Principles for Discovering Your WHO Blueprint:

- **Understanding WHO you are will be absolutely unique to you**. Comparison can wreak havoc on your happiness, so try not to judge yourself or others.

- **Discover your interests and do things that bring the truth of WHO you are into the forefront of your life.** Satisfying and meaningful moments strung together can create a life that feels worth living.

- A philosophy or code is consciously and unconsciously governing you. As you **identify what ideology is guiding your life,** you then have the power to adjust the thoughts, feelings, and attitudes driving your behaviors. You're better able to make choices from what you want and WHO you are instead of being at the whim of emotions or the preferences of others and your environment.

- **Remembering WHO you were as a child can be a springboard to understanding your greatest character attributes as an adult.** Take the time to reconnect with the child within you. You'll notice innocent and irreplaceable parts of yourself to treasure.

- Being in nature can teach us so much about how the world works and how we interact within its influence, if we're willing to slow down and pay attention. When was the last time you felt the wind on your face, or let the deep, dark night sky inform your life? **Being in nature and letting the sun shine upon you can open your imagination and allow your curiosity to run wild and free.**

While completing activities 6-9, you will discover:

- **Activity 6: Creating Your Circle of Interests, Enjoying Each Moment**

- **Activity 7: Writing and Identifying Beliefs Guiding Your Life**

- **Activity 8: Honoring Your Child Within**

- **Activity 9: Immersing Yourself in Nature: Walking in the Sunshine**

ACTIVITY 6: CREATING YOUR CIRCLE OF INTERESTS, ENJOYING EACH MOMENT

Discovering and then nurturing WHO you are expands your highest qualities and attributes. Noticing and living from your true self will lessen confusion, stress, and overwhelm because being true to you lessons inner dissonance. If you're confused about who you are, I don't blame you. Cultural labels, the world around you, and other people's expectations try to identify us and tell us who *they* think we should be. Globally, $299 billion was spent in 2020[2] marketing to you and me to buy or do or be something. Anything.

Protection from labels, expectations, and philosophies that don't fit WHO you are will come when you center on WHO you were born to become and what your specific purpose is. It's a journey–one that not everyone takes, which is why we can stay lost.

Being curious, self-discovery, and deep introspection take courage and time, are not selfish, and require practicing what we learn about ourselves as we become more aware. You've got this!

Discovery Activities:

Breathe before you even get out of bed. Do this for at least five minutes today.

- **What is your number today?** _____

- **List Gratitudes**

  1. _____

  2. _____

  3. _____

- **Create a Circle of Interests or what I like to call "My Happy Basket": In the circle provided, write activities you like doing, foods you like eating, places you like visiting, and hobbies you enjoy pursuing. Imagine carrying these things with you, and doing them often.** What creates a satisfied, excited, or contented feeling for you? That's different for everyone, right? Throughout many of the Forty Activities, you will be referring back to this list so make sure you have activities of varying duration.

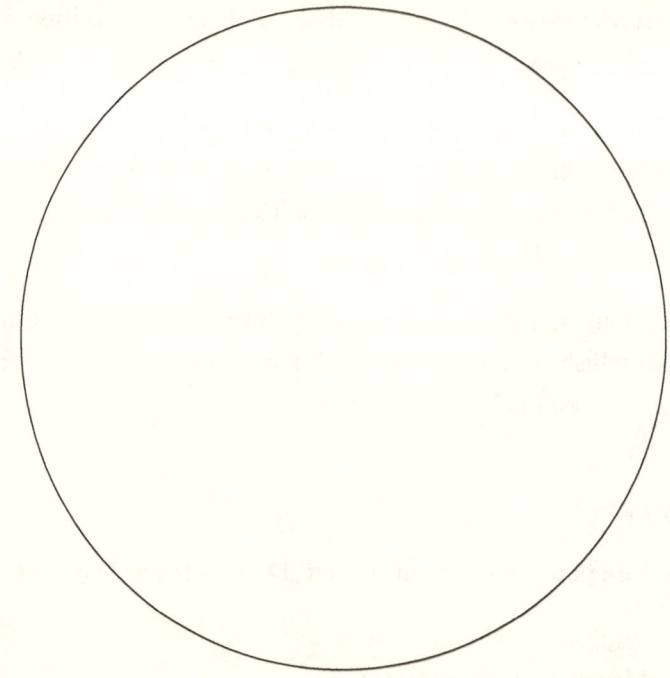

On a scale of 1-10, how satisfied are you with your current exploration of interests?

_____

Describe your perfect day. If you lived this day, how satisfied would you be?

_____

_____

_____

_____

_____

What innate qualities, attributes, talents, and gifts do your interests bring out in you?

_____

_____

_____

_____

_____

What three things stop you from pursuing your interests and hobbies every day?

1. _____

2. _____

3. _____

Can you see how NOT pursuing your interests on a daily basis could be contributing to a downward spiral of emotions?

_____

_____

_____

_____

- **Invitation:** *If you are in a committed relationship,* I invite you to ask your partner to do their own Circle of Interest. Once you are both finished, create a Venn diagram using overlapping circles to illustrate shared elements,[3] adding common interests in the area of overlap.

Building your relationships on these shared interests creates ease in companionship and can support a deeper connection.

If you spend time dating, use your Circle of Interest as you get to know, build trust in, and choose commitment in relationships. Common interests can be an important element in building a strong foundation in a relationship.

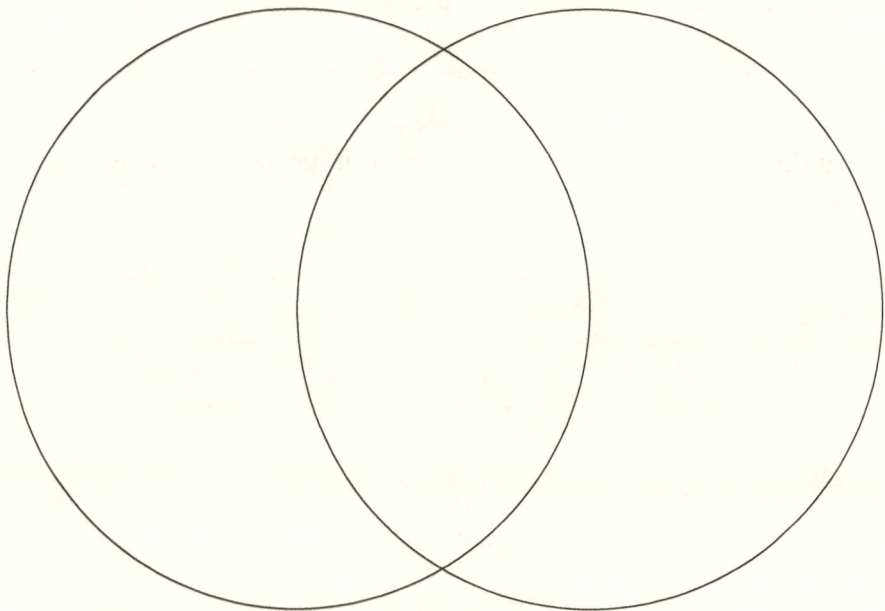

• **Be in Bermuda at least 1x today.**

ACTIVITY 7: WRITING AND IDENTIFYING BELIEFS GUIDING YOUR LIFE

Consciously or not, we all have beliefs and philosophies guiding our decisions. For some, it's science or the natural world. For others, it's religion or the culture we were raised in. For others still, it's a guru, a higher power, or a Source of Inspiration. For some, ideology guiding our lives can be a combination of all the above. Knowing what is happening in the background of our thoughts can give us valuable information as we maneuver throughout our day.

This quote by Marianne Williamson became a large part of the philosophy I raised my children with. "Our deepest fear is not that we are inadequate. Our deepest fear is that we are powerful beyond measure. It is our light, not our darkness that most frightens us. We ask ourselves, 'Who am I to be brilliant, gorgeous, talented, fabulous?' Actually, who are you not to be?"[4] This quote guided what I did as a mother. Do you know what philosophies are guiding you?

Writing helps us understand ourselves, opens our thought process, and can record impressions that we may want to circle back and refer to again and again. Over thirty years ago, I began writing in a journal. Writing every day unloaded and expelled thoughts and feelings that otherwise would have festered in the corners of my mind.

I invite you to write every day. It doesn't matter what you write. You don't need to sound eloquent. Just write whatever comes to mind. You don't need to re-read it and you don't ever have to show it to anyone. Ever. For the rest of our time together, I will be asking you to write. Please dive deep into your own thoughts.

Observing what is happening within our thoughts, our beliefs, and the philosophies informing our decisions gives us an advantage in making conscious, directed choices. Being a human is powerful. It means we have the innate ability to add or subtract information and ideology in our life. We get to observe what is happening both in our mind and the world around us and then we make conscious life choices. Writing is one of the best ways I know to really observe ourselves.

Discovery Activities:

- **Breathe before you even get out of bed. Do this for at least five minutes today.**

- **What is your number today?** _____

- **List Gratitudes**

  1. _____

  2. _____

  3. _____

- **Write a favorite quote or passage that directs your life.**

  _____

  _____

  _____

  _____

- **Write about what ideas and beliefs are informing your decisions?**

  Are humans innately good or bad? Why?

  _____

  _____

  _____

  _____

  Do you believe in free will, and what does it have to do with human happiness?

  _____

_____

_____

_____

What is unethical? Who decides what is right and wrong?

_____

_____

_____

What is the purpose of a human life?

_____

_____

_____

What do you feel about the idea that we as humans are obligated to help others?

_____

_____

_____

What is the reason for creating relationships? Friendships? Romantic?

_____

_____

_____

_____

Free write for a few minutes about your personal philosophy of life.

_____

_____

_____

_____

From your answers above and the free write you just finished, create a simple two-three sentence philosophy for your life.

_____

_____

_____

_____

- **Either go alone, invite one of your success partners, or another friend to an art gallery, into nature for a walk, or shopping at your local market.** Find three pieces of art or items in nature or anything in the market that represent your philosophy of life. Take a picture of each item. When you've finished your search, find a quiet spot and write why they represent your philosophy and then share with your friend.

- **Be in Bermuda at least 1x today.**

ACTIVITY 8: HONORING YOUR CHILD WITHIN

There's a little child within you who wants to be loved, who wants to play, and who wants to be acknowledged. Since becoming an adult, have you ever connected with the child in you?

At twenty-eight years old, while helping my grandmother move, my uncle Dave stopped by. I'd not seen him in over twenty years, yet still had fond memories of him from my childhood. Upon seeing me, he gave me the biggest hug and exclaimed, "Wendy Beth, you haven't changed one bit!" His words stayed with me and nurtured a personal breakthrough.

Reflecting on his comment, then raising and watching my own children grow from infants into adulthood caused me to realize that the core essence of WHO we are is innate and infinite.

Childhood sexual trauma, drug addiction, suicidal ideation, attempting suicide, sexual assault, multiple relationships, marriage, and bearing children had all transpired since the last time I'd seen my uncle, yet the core of WHO I was, an exuberant at times reserved child, had never gone away. The core essence of WHO each of us is, is always present.

If you suffered trauma as a child as many do, I invite you to remember a few things.

- Pain from childhood trauma can be worked through and healed.

- Trust your process. Don't force yourself to look at anything.

- Ask for outside help even as you trust yourself to heal.

- Stay in the present moment.

- Who you were as a child has always been with you and will never leave. Reconnect with that perfect, small human.

Discovery Activities

- **Breathe, before you even get out of bed. Do this for at least five minutes today.**

- **What is your number today? _____**

- **List Gratitudes**

    1. _____

    2. _____

    3. _____

- **Write your answer to the following questions.**

    What people, places, or things made you feel so content and satisfied that you lost track of time as a child?

    _____

    What is your favorite childhood memory?

    _____

    What do you believe are the two worst things that happened as a child?

    _____

    What do you consider the three best things about you as a child?

    _____

    What is one thing you appreciate most about your childhood?

    _____

    What about the child within you would you like to invite and enjoy every day of your life as an adult?

    _____

    _____

- **Do one thing from your "Circle of Interests" today that connects you to your inner child, then answer the following question:**

What did it feel like to play and connect to your child within?

_____

_____

_____

_____

- **Be in Bermuda at least 1x per today.**

ACTIVITY 9: IMMERSING YOURSELF IN NATURE: WALKING IN THE SUNSHINE

A rainy day outside or the unknown blackness of the midnight sky invokes vastly different emotions in each of us. The legendary music producer Rick Rubins says, "It is communing with nature that we move closer to our own nature . . . the closer we get to the natural world, the more we realize we're not separate."[5]

Who of us when in the forest upon hearing the pitter patter of footsteps doesn't get excited to see a mama deer and her little golden fawn? In some cultures people even connect deeply to the animals in the natural world, calling them totems, expecting messages, or guidance for their lives. Buddha said, "If you wish to know the divine, feel the wind on your face and the warm sun on your hand."

Walking outside in nature is one of the best things I did for myself on my personal healing journey. Whether by myself, with my children, or with friends, moving my body outside in the elements always made me feel better. Breathing deeply and being mindful of our environment while walking in nature allows us to experience smells, textures, colors, and even tastes that can help us connect more fully to the present moment.

I invite you to walk in nature and be in the sunshine on a regular basis. This practice can bring an elevated awareness into your daily life. Slow down and allow curiosity to carry and invigorate your imagination as you walk your way to unexpected healing and learning moments outside in nature.

Discovery Activities:

- **Breathe, before you even get out of bed. Do this for at least five minutes today.**

- **What is your number today?** _____

- **List Gratitudes**

  1. _____

  2. _____

  3. _____

- **Go for a walk and be in nature. Find a park or a woodland area, sit by the sea, or go anywhere you can walk to enjoy the natural world.**

  What are you hearing, smelling, seeing, and tasting?

  _____

  _____

  _____

  _____

  Write about being drawn to explore. Or would you rather sit and observe? Why?

_____

_____

_____

_____

Look for connections. What in the natural world reminds you of the world you live in every day?

_____

_____

_____

_____

What plant, insect, or animals in nature do you identify with or have a personal connection or feelings toward? Why?

_____

_____

_____

_____

Draw a picture of something you are observing in nature.

What about this thing inspired you to draw it?

_____

_____

What questions does the thing you drew invoke within you?

_____

_____

What does it remind you of?

_____

_____

- **Be in Bermuda at least 1x today. Perhaps today, do it in nature.**

Have you heard, "practice makes perfect?" What I've learned is that *effective* practice makes perfect. That's why a consistent exploration of WHO you truly are is so vital to your happiness. The more you practice being the real you, the more natural and free you will feel in your own skin.

Remember, small disciplined action over time brings lasting results. Be patient and mindful of your micro-movements forward in discovering WHO you are.

Something else I've learned is that when life is getting us down, doing things that nurture the truth of WHO we truly are not only informs our decisions but can change the trajectory of our destiny. Cultivating our interests can be the smallest thing like taking a walk, listening to a song, playing a game, solving a puzzle, taking a trip, or enjoying a piece of chocolate.

Oscar Wilde said, "To live is the rarest thing in the world. Most people exist, that is all." Moments of satisfaction and bliss strung together not only carry us through difficult times; they are the very fabric of our lives.

Not doing things that add pleasure and joy can leave us feeling empty, bored, and disinterested in life, negatively impacting our overall contentment. If you want to change how you feel, change what you're doing with your body and what thoughts you are allowing your mind to follow. Your heart, even if it's hurting, will open to the love that surrounds you as you live from WHO you are and choose simple moments of conscience acts from the interests that bring you joy.

CHAPTER 3 LIVING FROM WHO YOU ARE

when we know a truth
and act from it every time
confusion dissolves

Living from WHO you are opens your heart and your mind to the best and highest qualities and attributes within you. Strengths not previously noticed will begin to show themselves as you live from your epicenter. The battle within will cease. How we feel is based on what we do with what we understand and know. Living from our true self is like an arrow hitting its mark right in the bullseye. The light in us breaks open and peace fills our soul.

Awakening our true self uncovers more than just new layers of potential. It also unveils past trauma, viruses, buried talents, unwanted character traits, and ultimately the light within the core essence of WHO we are. Labels, expectations, and the opinions of others become less important and may even fall away. Freedom in our thoughts and feelings are unleashed as we live from the truth that we know, allowing it to guide and direct every decision. Remember, growth is part of our evolution and sometimes it can be uncomfortable! Especially if we're not expecting it, which let's be honest we rarely are!

Hang on. You got this!

Money was tight; it seemed there was never enough. But moving to Bozeman, Montana and being a student at Montana State University as a single mom gave me a sense of freedom I'd never experienced. Thankfully, I was only an hour and a half away from my mom. I still depended on her emotional support.

Working twenty hours a week for two retired couples who had me take care of their homes and gardens allowed me to pay my rent. Ryder sent money every month, which took care of anything Rhodes needed. And a government program for single mothers helped me with food, healthcare, and childcare expenses. Again, both Rhodes and I were blessed with a babysitter who loved him like he was her own child.

Homework felt endless. At night I'd either let Rhodes take a bath and sit next to the tub in the bathroom to study as he splashed in the water or I'd turn on the shower and let him play in the running water with his toys till the shower ran cold. He loved water time. And I was grateful for time to study.

Pressure of being a single mother, going to school full-time, and working part-time felt more difficult than usual. I ached inside and I wanted to use something to stop the pain. Pills, pot, alcohol, cocaine, and LSD had been my escape when I was hurting before I was a mother, but I could never go back to that again. Not when I had a child. *The AA program helped me before. Maybe it could help me again.*

Walking through the halls on campus, I saw a sign with a large red arrow and words that said, "Need Help?" I followed the arrow and told the person at the counter, in an almost pleading sort of way, "I've been sober for almost two years, but I'm feeling like I want to use again." He sent me to the school's counseling office, where I met Miriam, a psychologist.

"What can I do to help you?" she asked with an invitational tone.

"I can't fall apart. I have a son to take care of. I've been addicted to drugs and alcohol since I was a teenager and I survived suicide two years ago."

"Are you feeling like you want to hurt yourself now?"

"No, I have a baby. I just need some help. Something inside of me is hurting and I don't know how to make it stop, but I don't want to hurt myself."

The next time I met with Miriam we talked about the intake assessment she'd given me at our last visit. Then she asked, "Are you open to talking about your childhood?"

"Sure."

"What's a memory that really stands out from when you were a child?"

"Hmm." Closing my eyes, I thought back, then said, "One night maybe when I was four or five, I remember intently watching the blinking pink lights from a tavern's neon sign reflect on my legs. I was in the passenger seat of our family car waiting as my mom went inside. After a while, she came back. She slid into the driver's seat next to me and said, 'I just poured a drink over your dad's head and told him to get out of our home.'

"She started the car and drove until we stopped. We waited and watched, she and I and my two little brothers and our little sister. My dad went into our trailer and packed his things. I was watching my mom, while at the same time, I was watching my dad's truck slowly drive away."

Sharing this memory with Miriam invoked a longing in me, an ache from deep inside my heart. Tears formed in my eyes, but I didn't cry.

"After that, my mom got a job delivering newspapers. I remember all night long she drove, with four of us children on top of the newspaper bundles, folding newspapers and placing them in the tubes. The air coming in the window was always so cold, but she couldn't close it. The cold air kept her awake. The stacks slowly got smaller through the night as the sun began to rise. Sometimes after she'd finish her route, she'd take us to a donut shop. We all got chocolate alligators filled with whipping cream."

"Where was your dad during this time, Wendy?" Miriam asked.

"He lived in Moses Lake, Washington, I think. He loved us. Mom let him come home. We got a new house and mom got a new pink dress. She wore it when my dad brought her home from the hospital holding my new little sister." Our time was up.

The next time I went to Miriam>s office, she asked me if there was violence in my home as a child. "Some," I replied. "After my baby sister was born, something happened. My dad told my little brother to turn down the TV, but my little brother, who at the time was four years old, didn't hear him, so my dad said it again, a little louder, but my little brother was so focused on the football game that he didn't hear him that time either.

"All of a sudden, my dad flew out of the recliner and kicked my little brother in the back of the head. Then my mother came out of the kitchen, screaming, 'Don't you ever touch him again!' and before I knew it, my dad was charging at Mom. He pinned her to the wall, his hands around her neck."

Shaking my head, I looked around and reminded myself that I was in Miriam's office. "I rushed my brothers and my sisters into our bedroom so that we could hide. From the other room, I heard the 'f' word. I didn't know what it meant, but it was bad. It sounded bad. 'Fuck . . .' then intermitted with glass breaking. And 'fuck . . .' as multiple things hit the floor. I sat down at my red and white Raggedy Ann checkerboard table.

"Drawing a picture, I waited till my mother came. It was dark by then. I told her I was sorry. I didn't know what to do. I didn't know how to help. Then she said to me, 'There's nothing you can do. You took care of yourself. That's the only thing you can do.'"

Every time I went to Miriam's office, she listened as I shared a lifetime of memories carefully cataloged and put away. She asked prompting questions and then listened while I talked. I was reliving moments in time, unblocking what had been blocked for so long. After a few months of visits, during one of our sessions, suddenly behind a wall inside my brain, I saw my five-year-old self hiding behind a chair watching myself be raped. Unable to even fathom what had been uncovered, flustered, I finished the session quickly, then fled to my church's college activity building just a short distance away.

Scared and shaking, I picked up the phone. "Mom, I just got out of a session with Miriam and I saw something in my mind that I don't understand. A man was hurting me."

Her accusatory tone and question, "Who was it?" took me by surprise, shattering me further.

Shaking, I breathed deeply, then lied, "I don't know."

Then I ended the conversation. Looking around for something to hang onto, I immediately walked into my institute director's office. He was a leader from my church who was specifically in place on campus to support college students.

With tears streaming down my cheeks, I said, "I just got out of a session with my therapist. I saw something I don't understand and it scared me." I paused, unable to grasp, let alone even verbally describe to him, the horrific nature of my memory. I swallowed, then went on, "When I called my mom to talk to her about it, she sounded angry at even the idea of me bringing up something bad from my childhood."

"I suggest you not pursue the thoughts any further," he replied matter-of-factly. "Sometimes the devil fills in the blanks when we don't know all the answers." He talked some more, but I didn't hear a word he said. I never again saw Miriam.

Spencer and I met on a cool autumn Monday night at a church activity in Bozeman. He was a cool twenty-two-year-old senior, just home from a religious service mission in France, disinterested in making friends. He spent his time either in class or watching movies.

At twenty-three, I was a free, happy, high-strung, single mother to an almost two-year-old. Being a mom, working, going to college, and having fun with friends took all my time.

At first we didn't pay much attention to each other, just laughed with the group, but soon he was helping me with Rhodes's car seat. I liked his confidence and his aloofness. He didn't give a hoot what anyone else thought. Since he didn't have friends at college and he didn't like any of my friends, we quickly became just he, me, and my son. Something about him felt familiar and there was no sexual tension between us. We became best friends.

Spencer wore the dorkiest red, white, and blue hat resembling a flag. But being with him, especially driving down the road in his car, was like being next to a lake at dusk when the water looked like glass. He was the water. Calm until something, like the wind, moved him. Then he was focused, organized, and swift in accomplishing a task. I could be myself with him. He and Rhodes loved to watch Monday night football together. They, too, became best friends.

Conversing with Spencer, I learned that before his mission he'd been in love with his high school sweetheart, and they'd been sexually active until he left for his religious mission. Feelings of shame for not keeping the required agreements of chastity once he went on his mission caused him to tell his church leader about his premarital sex. The traumatizing experience and repercussions from ecclesiastical leaders had paralyzed him from even looking at a woman sexually until he planned to marry. He had no plans on marrying me. I was a single mother.

Spencer's degree was in international business. He was fluent in French. He planned on getting an MBA once he finished his bachelors. When he spoke, there was no question he knew what he wanted and where he was going. Everyone who met him liked him and would have loved to spend more time with him. The feeling was not reciprocated. He only wanted to hang out with me, but just as a friend. Spencer wasn't looking to become a father.

For my birthday in October, my college friend Lorie planned a surprise party. Unbeknownst to me, she'd decided that Spencer and I would make a beautiful couple. Lorie asked Spencer to pick up a birthday card and sign it. He'd assumed she and the rest of my friends would sign the card as well. Unbeknownst to Spencer, Lorie had picked up a bouquet of flowers for me.

Walking into the dimly lit restaurant, a group of my friends yelled, "Surprise!" Laughing and smiling, I looked to the left as Spencer handed me both the bouquet of flowers and the card Lorie had shoved into his hands. Feeling a bit awkward but not knowing what to do, we all just sat down. With everyone's eyes on me, I begin opening cards and gifts. When I got to the card Spencer gave me, I saw that in very small handwriting, on the inside cover, in the left-hand corner, he alone had written at a diagonal:

To: Wendy

Re: Happy Birthday I hope you have a great year.

I was puzzled at the inscription and the flowers but thanked him for them anyway. We all sat down to eat and had a memorable birthday celebration.

Later that night, after I got my son to sleep, Spencer was lying on his back on my living room floor. He asked me for the lip balm sitting on my desk. For some reason that I'll never know, I put the lip balm on my lips, walked over to him, then stepped one foot over his body. Straddling his torso, I lowered myself to sit on his stomach and gave him the lip balm he had asked me for, from my lips to his. He wasn't a bad kisser.

From then on, we were more than best friends, but we didn't have sex. Since previously having sex with different people, we'd both decided to commit to live the law of chastity of our religion, meaning to only have sex if we were married. As much as we kissed, Spencer never tried to have sex with me.

Being in Spencer's dorm room was my favorite place in the entire world. He kept it dark and perfectly ordered. The sticky notes on his desk were all spaced exactly the same distance apart. While cuddling in his bed, we ate barley waffles with real maple syrup. He made us air-popped popcorn with more butter than I'd ever seen eaten in my entire life. With him, I felt protected from the world. Except, a part of me felt like I was running away anytime we got too carried away kissing. I shrugged it off.

Three months after we met, Spencer surprised me when he said, "Let's talk about getting married."

My body stiffened as I consciously calmed myself. "I don't know . . ." I paused hesitantly. "There's a few things I need to tell you first." Waves of anxiousness moved through my body.

"Sounds good," he agreed. "I need to study for a few hours and I'll be back tonight. We can talk then."

All afternoon I paced and panicked. My stomach clenched. *What is he thinking? We're not ready to get married. What is he going to do when I tell him that? He's not going to want to marry me. Just breathe, Wendy Beth. Just breathe.* The afternoon ticked by like molasses on a cold, winter day as I rehearsed over and over how I was going to tell him the truth about me and my past.

Jovial and lighthearted, he returned that night, tossing me a box of popcorn. "Let the show begin," he chuckled and a twinkle in his eye.

Shaking like a leaf, I began slowly, "Well, there are three things I want you to know about me before we even talk about getting married."

"Okay, let's hear it," he said, relaxing.

Before I could change my mind, I blurted, "First, I used to drink a lot and I used a lot of drugs. I've been clean since the day I found out I was pregnant with Rhodes. Second, I was in love with a woman, and we were together for two years. And third, I'm pretty sure I was sexually abused as a child because with my counselor I saw something in a memory. But I haven't looked at it since leaving her office and I never went back." Immediately, I breathed out a sigh of relief.

Having these things out in the open between us allowed me to relax. I had so many reservations about marriage, but something just felt right with Spencer. He didn't even blink.

"I love you and I want to be with you!" he said, looking at me and smiling, completely unfazed by my admissions. "So . . . can we talk about getting married now?" he laughingly prodded.

"Yes," I said as he moved in closer for a kiss. We called our parents and gave them the good news.

In preparation for our marriage, we both sought out the ecclesiastical authorization that is required in order to be married in a temple. At the conclusion of the interview, the church leader looked at me somberly, finishing our visit with these words, "Remember that you're marrying above yourself. Don't ever forget that. You are very lucky."

His words to me were condescending and wrong. They did not feel good. But I knew as a single mother, in my church others looked down on me for having a child and not being married. He was right. I was lucky! Spencer was my best friend and we were going to be a family! Two months later, we were married.

Spencer and I read a small blue handbook about sex on the plane to Hawaii. Sexual intimacy felt exciting, but I could feel myself pulling away the very first time we made love. Our relationship had been perfect as best friends, but neither of us had any idea how to be lovers.

"I don't want to make love tonight," I admitted while we were still on our honeymoon. It wasn't because I didn't love him, but because something inside of me was running away. He said nothing, staring at me as if he didn't understand the words I was saying. The look on his face screamed his disapproval.

A cookbook by Susan Branch, called *Heart of the Home*,[1] was one of our wedding gifts. I began learning new recipes that I thought would make my husband happy when he returned home from work each night. I adopted many of her ideas of how to create a tranquil home. I put flowers in the bathroom in little vases, filled the fridge with Spencer's favorite foods, and began having Sunday dinner every week, creating traditions that our little family could count on. Making a wonderful home for Spencer and our children was my highest priority.

Thinking about our future I had a *feeling* that we should look into the army. Spencer decided to sign up under the GI Bill, a program that helped veterans pay for their college tuition.[2] The army would provide health insurance for our family and Spencer would get money to finish his bachelor's and earn his master's degree. Spencer joining the military was pure inspiration.

Married to Spencer and feeling inadequate as a wife and lover, I fell back into the self-loathing and full-blown trying to be good enough I'd dealt with most of my life. The scripture from 1 Corinthians 13:4-7, "charity suffers long and is kind, charity envies not . . . charity is not puffed up . . . charity bears all things, believes all things . . . hopes all things . . . and endures all things . . . charity never fails"[3] became my mantra. Though I wasn't great at applying it to myself, I tried. I tried to love who I was. I didn't understand that the only thing Spencer really wanted was *me*.

Basic training turned out to be the best thing that happened early in our marriage. The time apart gave me space to recenter and remember who I was and why I chose to get married. Before Spencer left, I'd become irritable and tense anytime sex was involved, which was often as newlyweds. But after six weeks apart, I missed Spencer desperately. His loving letters were an unexpected blessing.

Spencer and I reunited at his first assignment at the Department of Language Institute in Monterey, California. That night we made a bed on the floor with the blankets I'd brought. Our household items had not yet arrived and we didn't have enough money for a hotel. After reading the scriptures, praying as a family, then tucking Rhodes into bed, I went into our bedroom first. After six weeks of basic training, his arms and chest were chiseled like an Auguste Rodin sculpture. I'd missed my husband terribly.

Six weeks of waiting and wanting to make love with Spencer grew stronger and stronger. But I was paralyzed. The image from Miriam's office haunted me. Nothing I said to myself was enough to get me to act out what I was feeling in my body and my heart for my husband. In my mind there was an iron wall I could not get through. Confusion began to torment me.

Spencer worked overtime to be nice to me so that we could have sex more often. Roses were inexpensive in California and there was a shop he passed every day on his way home from work. He made sure I was never without a bouquet on our kitchen table. For this and a thousand other reasons, he was a good husband. I loved being married to him. I wanted to be a better wife.

A young army wife and mother named Andie in my church congregation was an amazing example of wifehood. We both had toddler sons and began walking together. As she talked, I learned she spent a lot of time and energy planning surprises and dates for her spouse.

I wanted to do some of the things I saw her do. I watched and I followed her example. Together we created games, sweet treats, and date nights for our partners. Though fun at times, what my husband wanted was sexual intimacy. A gulf began to form in our marriage.

Two months after I met Spencer in California, I was called to be the president of the young women's organization in my church. Curriculums were structured around the core belief that every person has infinite value and infinite potential and that they are a beloved child of God. Its core tenet was that Jesus Christ as a personal Savior could heal, lift, and redeem the individual.

Serving and guiding the youth while working with other adults opened me to leadership, teamwork, and delegating, bringing a new level of maturity into my life. Learning and working the designed program with the girls in my church, especially a young blind girl, ignited not only compassion but a belief that no matter what obstacles a person was dealing with, if there was a will, if there was diligence and persistence, there was always a divine way to succeed.

The truth was helping young people feel safe, helping them understand their worth, and teaching them Jesus's gospel brought immense joy and fulfillment into my life. I could see that the potentiality I was experiencing in myself was also present in every single young woman I worked with, regardless of what was happening in their homes. And some of them lived in distressing circumstances. Those ones I'd wanted to wrap up in my arms and bring home and protect them from the atrocities in their worlds.

Understanding that we are multidimensional beings with the capacity to not only survive but thrive in the midst of immense challenges grew inside of my soul as I chose fully and lived peacefully in my roles as mother, wife, and teacher. An insatiable curiosity for more truth in order to more fully magnify the roles I was choosing exponentially expanded within me. Except for my husband's frustration from the lack of sexual relations in our marriage, living life felt like my own happily ever after.

True Principles for Living from Your WHO Blueprint:

- Nurturing the seedlings of potential inside of your soul can be one of the most exciting and invigorating parts of living. **Discovering qualities and attributes from the roles you are currently choosing can help you see not only WHO you are, but WHO you have always been.** Remember, no one can tell you WHO you are and nothing can change the truth that is inside of you.

- In my experience, **harmonizing your daily decisions with the truth of WHO you are can bring a measure of peace,** no matter what is happening around me. If something is taking away your peace, look deeper. There are options not only inside of you but in the world around you that you just haven't seen yet. Keep looking. You will find them.

- We all spend an enormous amount of time working, do we not? **Aligning daily work with WHO you are can create satisfaction and equanimity in your moment to moment living.**

While completing activities 10-12, you will discover:

- Activity 10: Understanding and Expanding WHO You Are

- Activity 11: Harmonizing Decisions with WHO You Are

- Activity 12: Embracing What You Do and What You Want

ACTIVITY 10: UNDERSTANDING AND EXPANDING WHO YOU ARE

Congratulations on getting this far in discovering your Blueprint. You've spent time slowing down, breathing, enjoying moments, and getting to know WHO you are better. You've made a conscious choice to live and begun keeping track of what you're grateful for. Every day you're doing things that move you in a positive direction. Ralph Waldo Emerson said, "To be yourself in a world that is constantly trying to make you something else is the greatest accomplishment." He's talking about you and me.

Underneath the nurturing we either did or did not receive and the roles we live in are the attributes and the qualities of our true self. These attributes are an innate part of ourselves and bringing them to the forefront of our mind supports our growth and development. For example, sustaining my roles of mother, wife, and teacher was the truth of WHO I was. A nurturer, a lover, a believer, a seeker of knowledge, and a good listener. Over my lifetime, those roles and how I manifest in them change in different seasons and circumstances. But the qualities and attributes are always present in who I am. They are always expanding.

Extrapolating from and attaching to our core qualities and attributes and not only to the roles we choose allows us to transfer our gifts and talents to other endeavors, especially when our roles change, as they often do. Focusing on the innate and infinite characteristics supporting the role can create a trajectory of growth and evolution through a lifespan.

I think you'll notice that your intuition is at work here as you ponder three powerful words that embody WHO you are from the roles you are living.

Discovery Activities

- **Breathe, before you even get out of bed. Do this for at least five minutes today.**

- **What is your number today?** _____

- **List Gratitudes**

  1. _____

  2. _____

  3. _____

- **Set up a thirty-sixty-minute conversation with a success partner for Activity 12.**

- **Write down words that describe the roles you live and labels you currently choose.**

  _____

  _____

_____

_____

_____

_____

- **Extrapolate your Three Words**

  From all of the information you've captured in the past ten activities, choose three words or short phrases that best describe your core
  attributes and qualities. Look at the roles you live in your life and ask
  yourself what innate attribute is inspiring, bolstering, and sustaining
  your actions.

  For example: If you are the provider for your family, what inspires you
  to get up and go to work every day? Is it that you are loving? Or is it
  that you are responsible? Maybe it is both. What attribute inspires
  your action to be "The Provider"?

  Here are a few words and phrases to get you thinking:

  Amorous. Tenacious. Optimistic. Nurturer. Kind. Hopeful.
  Reliable. Drama-free. Believing. Fairness. Diligent. Busy as a Bee.
  Humble. Engineer. Musical. Princess-like. Self-Aware. Adaptable.
  Courageous. Influencer. Loyal. Confidence. Full of energy. Efficient.
  Dolphin-like. Mystic. Enchanting. Generous. Magnetic. Comedic.
  Likable. Hardworking. Sincere. Hunter. Zealous. Nonjudgmental.
  Trustworthy. Gamer. Communicator. Birdlike. Brainiac. Industrious.
  Childlike. Forever learner. Connector. Driven. Hopeful. Entrepreneur.
  Tycoon. Actor.

  This list is just a springboard for you to get started.

  In thinking about your three attributes/words, here are a couple of
  ideas to think about:

- What words would you want to filter every decision through?

- Do the words encapsulate your core beliefs?

- Is this word taking you toward your life's purpose?

- How do your words inspire you?

  One man, while creating his Blueprint, shared this about his Three Words: "*The Three Words have been very powerful. It's only been a week since I discovered them, but in one week I am making connections from my thoughts, feelings, and decisions to my three words. It's incredible. I have a new weapon to use against my demons.*"

- **Write two sentences about each of these words and describe why they encapsulate you.**

  1. _____

     _____

  2. _____

     _____

  3. _____

     _____

- **Transfer your Three Words to My Living Blueprint.**

- **Write your Three Words on your bathroom mirror.**

- **Using your Three Words as your guide, do the following:**

  - Create your ideal sleeping space based on WHO you are. Make sure when you finish there are elements where you sleep that represent who you are. You may want to declutter your space first. Take out things that do not represent WHO you are to make room for those things that do represent you. For example, if one of your words is "nurturer," you may want a soft pillow for yourself. If one of your words is "celebrator," you may want to add a book of poems about celebration. If one of your words is "wolf-like," you may want to add a small wolf figurine. You get the point. Make your space representative of who you are.

- **Be in Bermuda at least 1x today.**

ACTIVITY 11: HARMONIZING DECISIONS WITH WHO YOU ARE

Dissonance will accompany us as long as we capitulate WHO we are to the circumstances of life and the expectations or opinions of others. Making decisions from and harmonizing our daily life to WHO we are takes humility, time, and persistence. No matter what is happening, if I'm humble, if I'm open to trusting my core wisdom and the truth that I know new ways of being present, intuitive answers and logical reasoning work in tandem, moving me forward. Peace accompanies my daily journey.

Why? Because I'm not paralyzed by my thinking mind telling me I need to know everything, that I need to be perfect. I know I don't have all the answers right now and I can trust that there are infinite options in the universe just waiting to be uncovered by me. Not knowing, learning, and then aligning are part of my journey. A curious mind and an open heart are best achieved when judgment is suppressed. Both are key factors in harmonizing our life to WHO we are in the moment while enjoying the process of becoming who we were born to be.

Just being on this journey of life takes courage and you may be afraid to align your life with WHO you really are. But I'm here to tell you that getting out of your comfort zone and exploring new ideas, as well as new ways of being connected to who you are, will save your life and fortify it over and over again! You have your free will. Lean in. Let go.

Discovery Activities

- **Breathe, before you even get out of bed. Do this for at least five minutes today.**

- **What is your number today?** _____

- **List Gratitudes**

  1. _____

  2. _____

  3. _____

- **Calibrate your life to match WHO you are:**

  Including attitudes, behaviors, or circumstances, write freely about anything you see or feel out of alignment in your current life. What would you like to see change in your life in order to harmonize your daily routine with WHO you truly are.

  _____

  _____

  _____

  _____

  _____

  In thinking about your above answer, how will aligning your life to WHO you are affect your relationships?

  _____

- **Mindfully do one thing from your Circle of Interest, harmonizing at least one of your Three Words with your daily life.** For example, if one of your words is *nurturing*, do one thing from your Circle of

Interests that is nurturing either to yourself or another person. If one of your words is *intelligent,* do something that uses your intelligence.

- **Write about your feelings in recognizing and honoring this aspect of who you are with a daily activity out of your Circle of Interests.**

_____

_____

_____

_____

_____

What stops you from making decisions and living a life that is connected to WHO you truly are?

_____

_____

Ponder this question . . . we'll talk more about it in the next activity.

- **Be in Bermuda at least 1x per today.**

ACTIVITY 12: EMBRACING WHAT YOU DO AND WHAT YOU WANT

Your Three Words have the power to energize, streamline, and transform your life *if* you mindfully live from them. Remember, this is a journey of exploration. We're just looking at what has and hasn't been working while creating a Blueprint by which to move forward with. Making changes regarding what you do all day, every day that are in alignment to WHO you are takes commitment *and time.*

My husband spent most of his adult life working occupations that required a "tiger-like" personality. After discovering that he was more "bear-like," he realized that being in jobs requiring him to be a "tiger" was exhausting and, in fact, was the reason he felt depleted.

"Striving to be true," which was WHO his true self is, meant making changes in his career. He took the necessary steps in order to live authentically to WHO he was both in his career and in his personal life. In time, the feeling of depletion he'd been living with was replaced with an exuberance for his daily work life balance.

Change takes commitment to align your life from WHO you are. Please, be patient with yourself.

Discovery Activities:

- **Breathe, before you even get out of bed. Do this for at least five minutes today.**

- **What is your number today?** _____

- **List Gratitudes**

    1. _____

    2. _____

    3. _____

- **Below is a process by which to align WHO you are and what you do:**

    - First, honestly **admit** that something feels out of alignment.

    - Second, **look** for answers with curiosity. Ask for help.

    - Third, **open** yourself to new ideas. Expect an answer as you live life fully.

- Fourth, **create and commit** to a plan.

- Fifth, **apply** the answers you get.

- Sixth, **give** gratitude for the ability to change.

- **Look at and become aware of work/career/life balance.** If this part of your life is in alignment with who you are, choose something in your life that is out of alignment with who you are for this activity. (Consult with a trusted professional trained to support you when making big bold changes).

What would you like to see more aligned with who you are? What is out of alignment in your life?

_____

_____

If applicable, **admit** you want something else. Be humble and honest. What needs to be adjusted in order for you to truly live from who you are?

_____

_____

Curiously **look** for answers, and ask questions. Where might you look then find your answer?

_____

_____

Open yourself to new ideas. **Be still** and just listen to your intuition for a few minutes. Write down any thoughts that come to you.

_____

_____

Apply the answers. Write down the *very next step* you might want to make in order to create the change you're looking for so that you can live a more aligned life.

_____

_____

Begin to **Create and Commit** to a plan that allows you to live from who you are. Make it as simple or as complex as you desire.

_____

_____

_____

_____

What resistance are you experiencing as you think about any adjustments or changes to living fully aligned to WHO you are.

_____

_____

What strategies have you employed in the past to overcome your resistance to change?

_____

_____

How will you know when this one thing in your life has sufficiently shifted? What will you feel, see, or experience differently?

_____

_____

What will be the greatest part of overcoming any resistance and shifting this ONE thing in your life?

_____

_____

Draw a picture of this change that has already happened and the fruit of your work fully realized in your daily life.

```



```

- **Have a thirty to sixty-minute conversation with a success partner about this one change you want to make.** Then, I invite you for the remainder of your Living Blueprint journey to make your commitment accountable by sending an emoji every day to your success partner upon completing your desired plan.

  How did you feel about the conversation you had with your success partner? Were you able to fully disclose the desired plan of action and your plan to change?

  _____

  _____

  Give gratitude for your answers. What are you most grateful for in this process of change?

  _____

  _____

- **Be in Bermuda at least 1x today.**

STEP 2 –PGS BLUEPRINT

CHAPTER 4 DEVELOPING YOUR PERSONAL GUIDANCE SYSTEM

learning and healing
are often synonymous
both come in layers

Centered and grounded in WHO you are, the next element of your Living Blueprint is to understand and then follow your Personal Guidance System. Think of your PGS like the GPS of your car. Thoughts, feelings, values, and attitudes work together, navigating your conscious and unconscious behaviors and ultimately creating your life. Are you satisfied with what you're currently creating?

If there's more you want out of your existence, understanding, designing, and following your PGS can change the trajectory of your life. Guided by a Source of Inspiration of your choosing, and the five most important desires you have-running programs on the motherboard of WHO you are-you can focus your life and achieve what you are dreaming about. I know this is true because I have been doing it and I am doing it, one step at a time, for over thirty years.

Agency, the ability to choose for oneself, is an inalienable right that we can fully embrace as we learn and follow our PGS. Remember, you have the power to change the programs and viruses running on your Personal Guidance System and live from WHO you are. The conscious use of your free will toward what you want, know, believe, and value will help you act in remarkable ways toward your goals.

Mental flexibility allows us to see *and then learn* options previously never considered in overcoming obstacles, solving problems, and healing personal trauma. Learning experiences are available all around us, helping us move forward as we open our minds and hearts to new opportunities.

Remember, that curiosity is the first step in learning and overcoming; both take time, so be patient with yourself. For me, I had to learn how to do that.

Before our first year of married life came to a close, sexual abuse memories from my childhood broke wide open, oozing their poison into our marriage. Paralysis throughout my body pushed me into flight and freeze mode whenever Spencer touched me. The rational part of me was trying to stay present with my new husband. My brain yearned to please Spencer so that we could create a happy family. Yet my body felt paralyzed and numb.

No matter what I did, every morning I woke up to the same image playing in the theater of my mind. It was a horror movie of me watching myself across the living room on the floor. My skinny, bare, five-year-old legs were bent with a fully grown adult man in between them. My face was hidden behind his body. A dissociated sensation shifted to darkness, and a feeling like I couldn't breathe overtook me.

One day in the kitchen of our military housing, while preparing my husband's roast beef sandwich for lunch, I snapped. "Spencer, can we talk about what's going on with our sex life?" Then I softened a little, hoping he would hear me. "I'm so confused. I know I love you; I just don't know how to be with you. And I feel angry . . . all the time."

Polite but dismissive, he replied, "I'm sorry you're hurting. I don't know what you want me to do about it. I can't fix it. Let's just have fun together. Why do we have to talk about this?"

Without thinking, I reacted by throwing the pound of sliced rare roast beef over the top of his head where he was seated. It hit the wall behind him, stuck for a moment, then slid down the wall, leaving a bloody trail like the tears of my broken heart. Spencer only looked straight at me, his eyes wide. He said nothing.

Communication, when it came to our sex life, always ended in a stalemate. Talking made sense to me because my brain was trying to run away. Verbalizing my thoughts kept me present with him. I thought if we talked more, it would solve our problem. There was something that was trying to get out, to be resolved. It made me feel crazy not to be able to express it while trying to continue sexual relations in our marriage. Spencer, on the other hand, didn't want to talk at all because he didn't know how to fix what was hurting me. We got nowhere.

My budding belief in a God and His Son Jesus was the only place I found peace, especially as I sat in the pew each Sunday and took the sacrament[1]–a ceremony symbolizing Christ's atonement, with bread and water imparting divine grace, even for me. At church, in a class designed for women, I devoured anything preached about creating a happy home or a successful family. Then, the following week I executed what I'd learned on Sunday. Rituals learned at church became my lifeline.

Books opened my mind to new ideas. Praying, then searching for answers lent me to reading and studying religious texts like The Book of Mormon,[2] The Bible,[3] and Jesus the Christ by James Talmage.[4] The portrayal of Jesus's loving kindness, His ability to heal, and His trust in an all-powerful Father inspired me to want to be like Him. To trust as Jesus trusted.

Ayn Rand's character, Howard Rourke, in The Fountainhead gave me a human prototype of the ideal man (or woman, in my case), embodying the virtues of independence and integrity.[5] I wanted to be like Howard Rourke, willing to do anything for what I believed.

George Orwell's *1984*, though grim, especially in its conclusion, gave me hope.[6] The character Julia's rawness when it came to sex and the freedom in her thoughts to be with the man she loved inspired me. Her words, "When you make love you're using up energy, and afterwards you feel happy and don't give a damn about anything" were what I hungered to experience with Spencer. Yet, disassociation from my body plagued me during intimacy.

Walking everyday alone or with my children relieved building tensions in my brain. Writing in my journal before anyone else woke up gave me an escape, a place to center myself and a place to cry into. The pages of my journal were a place to voice thoughts I couldn't say out loud to anyone. No one knew how much I was hurting.

Despite talking, praying, reading, walking, writing, and taking care of my husband and children, being touched sexually by my husband continued to send shockwaves through my body and mind. For Spencer's sake, I put on a brave face while lovemaking as often as I could. If I cried before we had sex he would hold me and he never forced himself on me. Mostly, I just cried myself to sleep afterward. My heart started to shut down even though I knew I loved my husband.

Looking at my behavior, I realized I'd either run away from any relationship involving men and sex, or I'd been sexually traumatized by men over and over again. The patterns were clear. Whether the men were nice or not, once we had sex, I ran—until Spencer. But now, married, I chose not to run away. I wanted to honor the commitment I'd made with Spencer. I wanted to create a happy marriage and family; I just didn't know how.

Spencer's first assignment in the US Army was a one-year, unaccompanied tour to South Korea. Despite our sexual issues, neither of us wanted to be apart. After two months alone, he asked me and our children to meet him in Asia. Feeling trepidation at traveling with a four-year-old and a one-year-old alone but wanting to support my husband and his needs, I decided to join him. We left once our expedited passports arrived.

Stepping off the plane in Seoul was like stepping into another world. The smell of dried fish and vinegar floated on the humid air. We lived outside Camp Humphreys, a military airstrip in the small village of Anjeong-ri.[7] There, amongst hundreds of people, every inch of spare dirt was used to grow daikon radish, cabbage, and other vegetables. The rice paddies were flooded as fathers and mothers worked barefoot, knee deep in water with babies wrapped to their backs. It was one of the most beautiful, picturesque things I had ever seen.

For me, the possibility of war with North Korea always lingered in the air. Reports about shots being fired across the Demilitarized Zone or DMZ in local newspapers deepened my anxiety.[8] Peace for me came when two leaders from my church, also known as apostles, made an apostolic promise: "If the Korean people will faithfully attend the temple in Seoul, North Korea will not attack."

Their words penetrated my heart. After that, I was not afraid because of the abiding peace I felt when they spoke. And every time I attended the temple, it was full of members who also believed in their words. I felt safe.

Monstrous piles of garbage built up on corners of the village streets surprised me about Korean life. It was putrid and reeked foul odors, yet no one else seemed to notice. Soon it was springtime and I watched in wonder as brambles of rose bushes reached their sinewy vines around the white plastic bags, covering the waste completely. It was astonishing. Within just a few weeks, heaps of refuse disappeared in the foliage of brightly colored, springtime blooms. Instead of the smell of garbage, the sweet smell of roses filled the air.

Looking at the roses, I thought about my own mind and the images I fought every day. The visual was powerfully symbolic. *How do I get rid of the garbage in my mind, regardless of how I've covered it up?* The question never left me.

Being immersed in a culture not of my own once again opened me to the unknown, a place of discovery and peace, not unlike Hells Canyon and the midnight sky years before. Gratitude bloomed in me for each new learning experience, even as I was reeling from stress in my mind. More than once I found myself crying in agony at not being able to feel anything positive when we made love. My brain was a roller coaster.

At my church, Namguan, a kind, beautiful Korean woman, befriended me. We could hardly communicate with each other since I spoke no Korean and she spoke very little English. But she and I had a heart connection.

"You and children go Buddhist temple with me?" she asked.

"Yes, I would love that." I'd never been to another religious temple. I was intrigued and believed the precepts of my own religion about truth being one great whole.

"Ask my husband," she said, pointing to the man next to her. Her husband, a soldier in the US Army and I discussed the details for our excursion and made plans for the next day.

We met at the bus station in the early morning hours. The calm countryside felt moist. There was a light fog floating above the ground. Billowy fingers of white touched the emerald landscape. As the bus drove through the countryside, I noticed Korean cows were skinnier than cows in America. Further down the road, fruit trees caught my eye as every piece of fruit was covered in a brown paper bag tied with a string. *Maybe that's how they protect their fruit from pests. Maybe they don't use chemicals.*

Arriving at the Buddhist Temple,[9] my toddler in arms, I stepped off the bus. Immediately, Rhodes ran up to a large fountain and used one of the ladles to scoop water out of the pond. He poured it back into the water and out its little spout many times over. Watching him figure out how things worked was a simple joy in my everyday life.

Walking toward the whitewashed Buddhist temple, everyone took off their shoes and moved into the innermost part of the temple. We did the same. Reverence permeated the room. As I looked up at the Buddhist prayer wall, where people placed papers and symbols of loved ones, it reminded me of a prayer roll in my own LDS temple. *Hmmm, there are similarities in our religions.* I smiled to myself.

Namguan, now also barefoot, came over to me, touched my arm, then pulled me to follow her. I obliged as we made our way to the furthest backside of the temple. She pointed out a wooden antique Buddha with a green apron carved around its midriff. My eyes went wide as my mind expanded with the realization that ideas and truth were bigger than just one religion. Neither she nor I had the language ability to exchange words to communicate what we were feeling. But looking into each other's wet eyes, we smiled.

Both the Buddhist temple and my own temple in Seoul brought temporary peace to my troubled mind. *What if differences in ideology were actually opportunities for deeper communication and connection across the human family?* This idea sunk deep into my soul as we returned to our homeland, the United States of America.

We settled on Fort Lewis Army Base at the foot of breathtaking Mt. Rainier in Washington state. Almost immediately, I reached out to The Fort Lewis Army Family Advocacy Center for marital support. Time abroad had opened my mind to my own pain like a pandora's box when it came to sex. Spencer fully supported my desire to seek help for my sexual issues.

Chaplain (Major) Andros in the US Army, a jolly man, about fifty-five years old and also stationed at the army base just happened to be a sex therapist and marriage counselor. He told me to just call him "Chaplain." In our first session, he, like Miriam, my counselor in college five years prior, asked me to answer a battery of test questions.

Upon reviewing my answers, the first thing the chaplain wanted to talk about was the memory I'd seen in my mind's eye in Miriam's office. Verbalizing it was almost impossible and I was unable to articulate the word rape, even though intellectually I knew that's what was happening. I told him my memories were completely unrealistic.

"I don't believe what I'm seeing. It just can't be real, but it's destroying my marriage."

Chaplain asked me questions and listened to me for over three hours in our first session. I shared with him that another family member had been sexually inappropriate with me, as well as not being able to say no to sex in my teenage years. Another separate memory had sat dormant in my mind my entire life. Until talking with the chaplain this memory too, had never been given air to breathe.

A hulking shape had entered my childhood bed in the night, filling me with terror as the shape lay on top of me. The feeling that I was being smothered reverberated from the center of my body, mostly as I was falling asleep and waking up. I didn't say anything else. I didn't want to talk about it.

At the conclusion of our conversation, he unequivocally told me that I was experiencing PTSD: Post Traumatic Stress Disorder.[10] "Your childhood sexual memories and the trauma you experienced in high school are wreaking havoc in your current sexual experiences with Spencer." He likened the trauma I'd experienced as a small child and a teenager to soldiers being in battle. He said my brain was trying to keep me alive from a war my brain and body had fought and never won–only survived.

Going to great lengths, Chaplain tried to put all the puzzle pieces together for me. He told me that being high and drunk throughout high school was my brain's escape from what had happened to me as a child and what continued to happen as a teenager and young adult.

"It's a miracle you're still married *and* alive for that matter," he declared.

For the first time, I felt heard and seen, witnessed and understood.

He proceeded to outline a strategy to support me staying married, which I'd asked him to do. He said I could reprogram my thoughts. "See yourself as a gift to your husband. A beautiful gift. Nothing is being taken from you,

Wendy. The trauma is no longer happening. It's in the past. You can reframe your thoughts. It's just going to take time."

I didn't have an opinion one way or the other about what he was saying. I just wanted to do whatever it took so that my marriage and our family could be happy. I kept listening. His words seemed plausible.

"You're 100 percent in control of what is happening in your sex life," he added.

I wanted to believe him, I just didn't know how to let go of the fear and trepidation I felt any time sex was involved.

Fortunately, therapy calmed the stress in our marriage. Chaplain talked with Spencer, who seemed somewhat less agitated at being married to what Chaplain called "a survivor." At the same time, I could see Spencer's body language and knew by the tone of his voice that he had resigned himself to having me as a wife–one damaged and difficult. Seeing Spencer dissatisfied pushed me to work even harder to accomplish the things that Chaplain was teaching me. I wanted my husband to be happy.

About three months into therapy, Chaplain suggested I write a letter and share my feelings on paper with the person whom I had seen in my memory. Wrestling with the idea at first, I finally chose to write a loving, open, and honest letter. Instead of burning or destroying it, I sent the letter detailing my memories because I thought it would help my healing process. Orlo's words years before, *"the truth will set you free"* helped me move forward in my decision. The letter outlined what had happened and put the responsibility of my destroyed sexuality on them. I imagined all the sexual images from my childhood and the feelings associated with them leaving my brain and going back to the perpetrators front pocket. I ended the letter with my love and forgiveness for them.

Hurting and wanting to talk to my mom, I called home the week after I sent the letter. Her voice was cold as ice, just like it had been when I called her from college after running out of Miriam's office. I started to feel that cold wash over me. Unfortunately, the letter had been shared with her.

"Who do you think you are? I thought you had changed. Your lies continue just like when you were younger." She told me I'd fabricated everything. Her words obliterated my heart as she added, "You're crazy, my dear daughter."

For weeks I was shattered. All the work I'd put into rebuilding my relationship with my mother was destroyed. Her reaction to my memories was agonizing. I felt absolutely crazy–even more than before. Once again, I became an untouchable in my family.

Taking care of my children was almost impossible. I taught our oldest child who was in kindergarten how to make peanut butter and jelly sandwiches. At least when I couldn't get out of bed, the children had something to eat. Thankfully, both children loved to play together. I cried off and on all day for weeks.

Chaplin suggested I create a new extended family for myself. Heavenly Father and Jesus became my family.[11] And I opened my heart more fully to friendships, creating a "chosen family" from the people who loved and supported me daily.

My walking partner and dear friend Andie from California just happened to have moved less than an hour away and became more like a sister to me than ever before. Her upbeat, positive attitude about life and her connection to her own family gave me hope that my family could someday heal the pain we were going through.

Chaplain and I met every week. He urged me to purchase the book, *The Courage to Heal: A Guide for Women Survivors of Sexual Abuse*.[12] Terrified my life was falling apart again and my addiction would take back over, I studied the book and the scriptures every day. Fortunately, ending my life was never on the table, even on my worst days. I had made the decision to live in 1989. Still, I was not okay. In my journal I wrote:

Inside me, swell within me,
like the waves of the ocean,
like the pains of childbirth
sadness and sorrow from what depths
I do not know, but the waves they come
uninvited, relentless, crashing,
tears leak from my eyes and,
my face cannot hold the pain.
My soul is groped with anguish,
falling, falling, crying, crying
inside my body thrashes, and
then the feelings subside
pulling back to the sea as
my body prepares
for its next contraction.

Even as it was difficult to be intimate with Spencer, my life was in support of him, his career, and his needs. We tried to be playful, going on dates and spending quality time together. He tried to be supportive, giving me flowers and beautiful handwritten cards expressing his love. But it didn't make the deeper difference we needed. When our sex life waned, Spencer became distant from me and our children. Often, even our friendship got lost in his sexual frustration.

A pattern developed in our marriage. When we were sexually performing as a couple, to Spencer's satisfaction, he was present as a husband and father. If not, he withdrew dramatically. "You are my wife. You are supposed to have sex with me!" were words I heard him yell only once, but lived with every second of every day.

Fortunately, his temperament never leant to violence or promiscuity. He was absolutely loyal to me. But living in a vicious circle of him being available to our children and me, if we had sex, and him being passive-aggressive and an outright jerk when we didn't, was an absolute nightmare. In this hell, I turned more and more to Jesus. He was my lifeline.

For the next three years, my life became an obsession to heal, to be good enough. I ate ideally and exercised diligently, trying to create a perfect body. Our home was as clean and organized as any temple. Creating a place of refuge where our children were safe became my mission. Everything I did was to protect them from what had happened to me. A portrait of Jesus was always on our wall. I believed His presence was protecting our family.

My refrigerator and freezer were perfectly organized, while my cupboards were color-coded. A person could have eaten off my floors—and not just in my kitchen, in my whole house! Dust bunnies were afraid to hide under the beds. Everything in our house became just like Spencer's sticky notes in college: immaculately ordered.

Motherhood was where I found joy *and* success as I followed Spencer in leaving the military, earning his MBA, and eventually joining a corporate executive program. During this time, we had two more children and my experiences with the metaphysical world increased.

First, Briggs Durant joined our family. His deep blue eyes, set within his alabaster face, were a stabilizing universe all of their own, piercing me with constant affection. He was nocturnal, waking up around the midnight hour for the first three years of his life. Nightly feedings turned into a ritual of apples and peanut butter in toddlerhood, which I welcomed. His presence in our family was a force of nature. He made me laugh.

A dream before Brigg's first birthday was prophetic and the first of many that opened me to my spiritual gifts. In the dream, my toddler was crawling on the edge of a swirling drain. Other mothers were screaming at me to grab my child. But, as his mother, I knew Briggs was safe. Reacting the way they expected me to act, the way they were reacting, would actually be detrimental, even lethal to my son's life. In the dream, I simply watched over my son with love as he enjoyed playing at the water's edge.

Two years later at my aunt's house for Sunday dinner in Provo, Utah while using the restroom, I heard a voice call, "Mom." I looked around to see who'd just spoken to me even though I knew I was alone in the small bathroom. I saw no one. Three months later, while standing in my kitchen, having recently relocated to Rocky Hill, Connecticut, I heard the same voice say the same thing, "Mom."

Now knowing I was five months pregnant with our fourth child and remembering them talking to me in Provo, I realized the voice was the child I was carrying. Twice more my child spoke to me, saying the same thing, "Mom."

Huxley Owen entered the world with chocolate brown eyes, fetching cheeks, and an exuberant smile even as a newborn. Immense gratitude filled my soul once I knew that my baby was healthy since I'd fallen twice during my pregnancy.

Born in the middle of the night, the day after Christmas, our new baby was welcomed home and showered in love by eager and excited siblings. Huxley's insatiable appetite to learn and experience everything the older children were doing from as early as toddlerhood upleveled our family's atmosphere of learning and love.

The truth was living from my own Personal Guidance System and trusting my Source of Inspiration–Jesus Christ–as a partner and a parent was a process of forward motion for our entire family. As I learned new ways of being myself and my innate gifts of nurturing and teaching my children, my own brain reprogrammed as theirs were being informed. Absorbing anything that would help me teach my children, heal my mind, and open my heart was absorbed into my life.

Slowly and sporadically, I noticed small, micro-healing moments. Spencer and I had glimpses of success in our intimacy as I trusted him and myself. In those moments, we were a blissful couple and a happy family. At the same time my heart was ever expanding into motherhood, Spencer decided he wanted to have a vasectomy. I wanted to support my husband's choice. But I also wondered, *what if God wanted us to have more children?*

True Principles for Your Personal Guidance System (PGS) Blueprint:

- **Your Personal Guidance System is designed to take you to a joyful life.** That's its purpose. Like the navigation system in your vehicle, the programs in your brain are directing your journey.

- **A PGS is programmable and can be updated as you use your agency to do so.** Taking responsibility for the ideas, values, and beliefs you choose helps you move forward especially when times are difficult.

- Choosing five programs to focus on while letting all other distractions fade out of your life may take time and practice. Remember this. Focus creates results.

- Healing treatments in **your own healing toolkit are personalized just for you that make your life more pleasurable.** As you look at your life, be honest about what you need to do or learn in order to heal and move forward in your life. A walk outside, a therapy session, time with a friend, a massage, or taking time to just rest are little moments of support strung together that over time will make life better!

- **Document your learning and healing moments by writing them down.** Writing down what you are learning can validate and celebrate your success in a moment to moment playbook. It's not narcissistic to acknowledge the good you are experiencing, learning, or doing. The more you reinforce what you want, the more they become the programs running in your life.

- **Miracles are available for anyone open to experiencing them.** And each of our stories, our lived experiences shared can bring hope to a world that is bursting with cynicism and doubt. **Miracles can be the simplest thing to the grandest gesture.** Unlock miracles in your life by simply giving possibility to their existence and looking for them.

While completing activities 13-16, you will discover:

- **Activity 13: Focusing Programs Running on Your PGS**

- **Activity 14: Creating Your Personal Healing Toolkit**

- **Activity 15: Documenting Learning and Healing Moments**

- **Activity 16: Looking For and Opening to Miracles**

ACTIVITY 13: FOCUSING PROGRAMS RUNNING ON YOUR PGS

Many of the beliefs, attitudes, and unconscious to-do lists currently stored on your PGS were programmed long before you had capability of making choices as a child.

But today, as a rational adult, you are in control of your decisions–when you become conscious of that ability. Your PGS is programmable. Once you fixate your energy, time, talents, and everything you have on what you actually want, progress is inevitable. Focus creates results.

Unconscious beliefs, emotions, cultural concepts, family traditions, religious precepts, lived experiences, past dreams, addiction, trauma, expectations, desires, reactions to trauma, and obligations are just a few of the possible programs and viruses running on your PGS, instead of what you actually want. Once you are aware of what programs are currently running (and running your life), you choose what to keep and what to delete.

Victor Frankl, a concentration camp survivor, said of this of free will: "The experience of camp shows that man does have a choice of action. There were enough examples, often of a heroic nature, that apathy could be overcome, and irritability suppressed. Man can preserve a vestige of spiritual freedom, of independence of mind even in such terrible conditions of psychic and physical stress."[13] In every moment, you get to choose how to react to what is happening.

Discovery Activity:

- **Breathe, before you even get out of bed. Do this for at least five minutes today.**

- **What is your number today?** _____

- **List Gratitudes**

    1. _____

    2. _____

    3. _____

- **Set a timer for two minutes, then brain dump into the conversation box below what thoughts, dreams, and goals go through your mind in a day. Just start writing everything you think you want . . .** This is how we become conscious and aware of what we actually want, versus what we spend our time thinking about.

- **In the above conversation box that you just filled in, circle ONLY the five most important things you want.**

- **Write them here.**

  1. _____

  2. _____

  3. _____

  4. _____

  5. _____

- **Set a timer for two minutes, then brain dump into the conversation box below what stops you from getting what you want . . .** This is how we become conscious and aware of what barriers and obstacles we are facing every day.

```




```

- **Put a square around your #1 biggest obstacle or problem that stops you from accomplishing what you want. This is a virus.**

- **Write your most persistent virus here.**

_____

How does this specific virus affect your life every day?

_____

List reasons for wanting these five programs running your PGS.

_____

_____

_____

_____

In the boxes provided, write as many components you can think of that will support these five programs running optimally in your life. Spend two minutes on each program.

My #1
```



```

My #2
```



```

My #3
```



```

My #4
```



```

My #5

[   ]

- **Transfer these "Five Wanted Programs" to My Living Blueprint.**

- Write about what you anticipate feeling as you begin focusing time, energy, and resources on these five programs.

_____

_____

_____

_____

How will your life be different as your PGS becomes centered on your top five programs while letting go of the distractions . . .everything else in the brain dump box.

_____

_____

_____

_____

- **Be in Bermuda at least 1x today.**

ACTIVITY 14: CREATING YOUR PERSONAL HEALING TOOLKIT

In 2022, *Time* magazine published "Alternative Treatments," a special edition sharing many choices supporting an individuals' well-being. I appreciated this inclusive invitation: "New solutions are critical to helping both people with hard-to-treat medical issues and those who just want to feel a little better."[14] To their point, physical, mental, emotional, and spiritual wellness begins with each of us.

Whether the tool you choose is going for a walk, writing, a hot shower, meditation, a needed prescription, an orgasm, or an AA meeting[15] (or all of the above), knowing what you need at any given moment and giving that thing to yourself in order to bring peace into your soul amid life's ups and downs is not only attainable but every individual's responsibility.

Running up and down the Grand Canyon was a gold medal moment for me in my early thirties. Soon after, on a simple weekend run, I fell not once, but twice. I wasn't really hurt, but I was scraped and bloodied up and down the right side of my body. Thinking I needed a little less contact sport, I began practicing yoga, setting running aside.

Yoga became a healing modality I chose to practice almost every day. Being on my mat gave me a feeling of peace. Learning to listen to my body and practicing balance postures led me to severely lessen my intake of processed sugar. I noticed that when I ate too many sweets my balance wasn't as good.

Twenty years later, I picked up running again. As my legs gained momentum on a slightly down-sloped dirt trail, and my foot hit the ground, the memory of me falling came rushing back to mind—a traumatic incident I hadn't thought about in years.

For the next few weeks, I consciously practiced and reminded myself to be present while running, focusing on my balance and making sure I wasn't losing my footing on tricky parts of the trail. Over time the fear that I would fall again dissipated. Running once again brought a feeling of joy and freedom into my daily life.

Whatever healing treatments you choose to employ, make sure they are of your choosing and they bring peace, pleasure, and satisfaction into your life.

Discovery Activity

- **Breathe, before you even get out of bed. Do this for at least five minutes today.**

- **What is your number today?** _____

- **List Gratitudes**

    1. _____

    2. _____

    3. _____

- **Set up a thirty-minute phone call with a success partner for Activity 16.**

- **Write about any healing moments in your life where the wounds, burdens, and stress of life diminished or were removed completely.** These can be from conventional or nonconventional healing modalities that improved your physical, mental, or spiritual health and well-being, from your earliest memory in childhood to the present day.

_____

_____

_____

_____

Looking at what you have just written, what in the past for you has been your *greatest source of healing*?

_____

_____

_____

_____

- **Make a list of all healing tools you haven't used before but might like to try. List as many as you can.**

  (A few examples are: AA 12-step program. The Path of Enlightenment in Buddhism. Writing. Jesus and His miracles. Yoga. Conventional Medicine. Bubble baths. Snuggling. Massage. Body Work. Creating Art in Nature. Breath-work. Science/Medicine. Meditation.)

  _____

  _____

  _____

- From the list above, what are the five methods you would like to consistently use in your everyday life in creating your unique healing tool kit? Maintaining these activities on a regular basis is preventative in keeping you out of crisis.

  1. _____

  2. _____

  3. _____

  4. _____

  5. _____

- **Transfer your "Healing Toolkit" to My Living Blueprint.**

- **Commit to your Healing Toolkit.** Anytime you are feeling less than fantastic, exuberant, or awesome, (a 7 or below on our "How Am I Scale") I invite you to use one of your treatments from your tool kit. Are you willing to commit to choosing these healing treatments?

  __YES

  __ NO

- **Share your healing tool kit with a success partner. When you are feeling down, ask them to remind and recommend these particular healing modalities to you.**

- **Write about any preparatory work you will need to do in order to be able to turn to any of these five healing treatments in a moment's notice.** For example, if one of your tools is "attend a yoga class," do you know where you will go, do you need a membership, etc.?

  1. _____

  2. _____

  3. _____

  4. _____

  5. _____

- **Be in Bermuda at least 1x today.**

ACTIVITY 15: DOCUMENTING LEARNING AND HEALING MOMENTS

Learning and healing moments are often intermingled in our daily lives when we are aware and open to new experiences. Curiosity to all truth in the universe while opening our mind to options previously never considered can be lifesaving. Even if it feels like all avenues for solving a problem have been explored, I invite you to open yourself to more.

Remembering what has worked in the past and looking for successful patterns is a great tool when times are difficult. Past victories and success in learning and healing build trust in one's self and can become foundational principles in your PGS toward future decision-making.

Celebrating your moments of willingness to take whatever time is required in order to understand yourself and perhaps brainstorming with a success partner can lead to revolutionary new solutions. Staying focused on WHO you are helps keep you centered and grounded on your unique journey and limits confusion as you see more clearly, understand more deeply, and follow your own unique PGS.

Discovery Activity

- **Breathe, before you even get out of bed. Do this for at least five minutes today.**

- **What is your number today?** _____

- **List Gratitudes**

    1. _____

    2. _____

    3. _____

- **Remember and write down the greatest *learning* moments in your life.** These are moments where you had an epiphany, a stroke of genius, or learned something that affected your decision-making capability.

    _____

    _____

_____

_____

Look at what you have just written. What was the catalyst for learning? Was it pain or was it a desire to learn? What prompted those learning moments?

_____

_____

_____

_____

How observant are you in the world around you? What do you see?

_____

_____

Are you able to experience small learning moments or do you gravitate to more earth shattering awakenings in order to open your consciousness to deep learning?

_____

_____

_____

_____

What is the biggest decision in your life that you are currently searching for answers to?

_____

_____

_____

_____

What are the things you need to learn in order to make this decision?

_____

_____

_____

_____

_____

Spend a bit of time researching and learning about what you just wrote above. Take notes below.

_____

_____

_____

_____

_____

- **Spend time doing one thing from your Healing Toolkit. Look for the learning and healing potential.** Write about your experience.

_____

_____

_____

_____

- **Be in Bermuda at least 1x today.**

ACTIVITY 16: LOOKING FOR AND OPENING TO MIRACLES

Have you ever thought about small, everyday happenings being one of life's greatest blessings, maybe even miracles? For example, one day I was babysitting my grandsons. As I took a box of animal crackers out of their bag and offered them a snack, my oldest grandson said, "Grandma, don't ya know, animal crackers take away all your problems?"

To which his smiling little brother, who wasn't quite talking yet, gave me a two thumbs-up in confirmation of what his older brother had just said. That moment was a miracle I held dear to my heart.

Today, years later, every time I see a box of animal crackers, my heart warms with love for not only perfect grandsons but for their conscientious parents teaching them positive ways in which to deal with life's problems. Not only did my grandsons communicate their thoughts with me through words and hand signs, but their love and their purity were conveyed to me in their shining eyes.

Then that moment in time was stored on the hard drive of my mind, coming back into my consciousness every time I walked by a box of animal crackers in the grocery store, bringing a smile to my face. Extraordinary, is it not?

Thich Nhat Hanh said, "People usually consider walking on water or in thin air a miracle. But I think the real miracle is not to walk either on water or in thin air, but to walk on earth. Every day we are engaged in a miracle which we don't even recognize: a blue sky, white clouds, green leaves, the black, curious eyes of a child—our own two eyes. All is a miracle."

Small, seemingly insignificant moments can be eye opening, life affirming, and can easily get lost when we're distracted. When we notice the everyday miracles, it opens a doorway to the extraordinary.

Discovery Activities:

- **Breathe, before you even get out of bed. Do this for at least five minutes today.**

- **What is your number today?** _____

- **List Gratitudes**

    1. _____

    2. _____

    3. _____

- **Look for miracles** throughout your day. Capture them here.

_____

_____

_____

_____

Write about miracles you have experienced in your life from your childhood to the present moment.

_____

_____

_____

_____

- **Have either an in-person or a virtual conversation about miracles with your success partner.** Here are some possible questions you could discuss:

Are there miracles either of you have heard about that have caught your interest?

_____

_____

_____

_____

Define "miracle."

_____

_____

_____

_____

What miracles have either of you experienced?

_____

_____

Do you see a preparatory action on a person's part in order to experience the miracle or do they just occur or both?

_____

_____

_____

_____

From your perspective, what is the purpose of miracles?

_____

_____

_____

_____

Do you or could you see yourself as a miracle? What does that mean to you?

_____

_____

_____

Thank your success partner for their time. Continue looking for miracles and capture them here.

_____

_____

_____

_____

- **Be in Bermuda at least 1x today.**

Remember, there is an infinite ocean of love available for you as you learn to live from your Personal Guidance System (PGS). Programs, ideas, and actions that are love filled allow the love inside of you to connect to and expand exponentially to all that is love. Subsequently, when we shut down love or choose to follow thoughts or actions that are absent from love, our own relationship to love diminishes.

For me, sexual trauma was a virus absent of love that wreaked havoc in my life. It informed my actions and my reactions and hurt my relationship mostly with myself and others. It took time, but today that virus has been deleted and a healthy sexual program has been added, one that is based on love and adding vitality, satisfaction, and joy to my life.

You can make a kind and conscious plan toward what programs you want running your life and which ones you want to delete. Only then, from a place of compassion do I invite you to take consistent, disciplined action toward change. In doing this, your actions will spring from love. And from the inside out you will see that you are becoming the person you were born to be.

CHAPTER 5 TRUSTING AND FOLLOWING YOUR PERSONAL GUIDANCE SYSTEM

faith and believing
open to the transcendent
miracles occur

Your Living Blueprint, as I trust you may be realizing, is discovered and designed from small, everyday occurrences *and* from the most unexpected, sometimes extraordinary experiences. Time can heal, and it can open us to new opportunities if we let it. Unique moments in time can open your mind and heart to parts of yourself you may not have recognized, believed, seen, or even known existed in the past. Believe them! Honor them!

Curiosity and an open mind to the unknown will teach you things you never knew you didn't know. They did for me. Here are a couple of questions to consider as you're thinking about your Personal Guidance System. Who or what has inspired you in the past? What is something you would like to know about yourself that you may have forgotten or do not yet know? How does your Source of Inspiration connect with you?

Tears streamed down my face more than once as I watched and rewatched in horror with the rest of the world the terrorist attack at the World Trade Center in September 2001. Thinking about the children, parents, friends, and families in the wake of such a tragedy was unimaginable. I was in shock as my heart ached and my mind reeled.

Spencer was on a business trip to the East and all planes were grounded. I began praying that he would return home safely to our family in Peoria, Arizona where we had just recently purchased our first home. Days passed as the world waited on pins and needles for survivors to be rescued. Spencer was still not home, but at least I knew he was alive. Thousands were not so lucky.

On Friday September 14, 2001, the president of the United States gave a press conference.[1] His words, interspersed with shocking footage of planes hitting the towers combined with the wreckage in Manhattan and the demolished Pentagon, broke my heart and my mind wide open.

As my eyes took in the alarming images on the television and my ears heard the president's voice, my brain somehow associated the damage I was seeing on the screen to what Chaplin and *The Courage to Heal* had taught me about being a sexual abuse survivor, "a war the brain and body had fought but never won–only survived." In those moments, I understood and internalized that the brains, hearts, and bodies of children, like mine, who are abused emotionally, mentally, physically, or sexually carry trauma with them. How could they not?

For years, I'd been living inside of the pain, running and unable to escape. It was bizarre, but something triggered in my brain as if unlocking the pins of a secure vault. For the very first time since being five years old, I felt innocent instead of guilty. I understood that a child's sexuality is perfectly intact when they are born, whatever that may be. That I or any child abused had done nothing wrong, just like the victims of this terrible act. Every child was innocent, exactly like the people who'd been targeted and died in those buildings.

Self-loathing, dishonesty, addiction, defiance, suicidality, perfectionism, and anger had pummeled me and left me ragged and destroyed. Years of intense work healing myself had created structure and order, allowing me to let go of some of my self-destructiveness. However, feelings surrounding my sexuality still reminded me of the ugly, thick black smoke rising into the atmosphere along with the twisted rebar and broken-up concrete that represented a battered heart and broken personality.

As the president spoke, I quickly realized that I needed to write down what he was saying so that I could not only remember but integrate what I was feeling and experiencing. "You can choose to be stronger because of this. Love is stronger than hate. The light of hope is bright."

Those words sank deep into my mind and were a balm to my own shattered heart. As a child, a perfect little girl, I'd been terrorized by being raped and sexually abused and no one in my family would acknowledge what had happened to me. To add pain to misery, they told me I was crazy. And the worst thing of all was I believed them! For years, I'd told myself I was crazy. Every day.

As I listened, the man on the screen sort of faded out and his words were what I needed to hear my "mother" and my "father" say in order to soothe my inner child's anguished soul. His message trickling into my brain was healing a lifetime of pain and abandonment.

"Pray for wisdom," he continued. He then admonished the American people to use prayer to help us through the days ahead. "We have so much to be grateful for. Nothing can separate us from the love of God. God bless America."

As he said, "America," my brain replaced it momentarily with, "Wendy." *God bless Wendy.*

Riveted, I listened further as the president said that we as a people would rebuild everything that had been destroyed. I believed him. Not only for our country, but also for myself. He said we would be stronger than before. Electric sensations went up and down my entire body.

My own healing breakthrough did not take away from the anguish I was feeling for all the victims and the ones they left behind. But a puzzle my brain had been trying to put together for eight years was delivered in that unexpected package, and I was changed for the better. I was not the same person who had sat down an hour prior. I was still reeling in shock, but something tangible had changed inside of me.

Getting up from the table and looking around, I saw my four, perfect, innocent children playing. Toys, art supplies, and pieces of children's clothing were scattered everywhere, my house was an absolute chaotic mess. And my house was never a mess. In eight years of marriage, it was the first time I didn't rush about making everything perfect. In fact, it felt freeing to see everything lying about the floor. And since Spencer was still stranded on the East Coast, everything didn't have to be ordered and in its place before he got home from work.

Then, walking into the bathroom, I turned my head toward our mirror on the wall. For the first time in my life, I saw all of me, not just my darkness, but also my light. I saw myself as a strong, beautiful, and graceful woman. I saw who I was, my true self. After eight hours, my ability to see all of me began to fade. But in my journal I wrote:

> *I saw a woman in the mirror,*
> *her poise, her beauty astonished me,*
> *her eyes so bright, full of light*
> *her smile was warmth and love,*
> *she was in control,*
> *she glowed from the inside out,*
> *she was tall, strong, and beautiful.*
> *She had no fear, she was happy,*
> *in love and confident*
> *a lover, and a mother.*
> *God gave her gifts*
> *a teacher, a guide.*
> *She was not self-destructive.*
> *Ignored, hurt,*
> *put down, or victimized.*
> *She was taken care of,*
> *and paid attention to.*

While writing, I understood that I'd spent my life depriving myself and trying to be enough. In my journal, I asked the question: *How can I protect myself from myself?*

I wrote as the answers came. I could:

Smile at myself in the mirror
Enjoy time with myself
Do nice things for me
Encourage myself
Breathe easy
Open my arms and embrace me
Stop hurting myself with negative thoughts

Later in the day, after I could no longer see all of myself, I felt a bit frantic at having lost that ability. It had been such a powerful, healing moment for me. However, I'd experienced a part of myself I'd never seen, which meant that she was *in* me. She was who I was. And somehow I would learn to access that part of myself all the time. I was her and she would be the person who could connect to Spencer sexually. Then he would be happy, and our children would have the father they needed. We would be a happy family.

Escaping the Arizona heat with my children, we often spent our afternoons in the public library. One day while browsing the bookshelves, I was intrigued with a new book about yoga–a group of principles of combining physical, mental, and spiritual practices toward well-being. I had fallen twice running and was looking for a new form of exercise. I checked it out and immediately began studying the sun salutations. Each day I practiced the prescribed twelve rounds next to our pool while my children played in the water next to me.

A daily yoga practice began to open my eyes to dissonance in my mind, heart, and body. The first thing I noticed was that when I ate too much sugar, I had a difficult time holding a balanced posture. Next, I could see that when I pushed myself too hard on my yoga, I was also pushing myself and my family too hard in our daily routine. Practicing yoga began to harmonize who I was in my core essence and my behaviors more succinctly than ever before. Moving on my mat gave me invaluable information about where I was in my healing journey. Somedays I was moving forward, somedays I felt stuck.

The next year, Spencer wanted to move again. I supported his decision, packing everything and even having a birthday party for Briggs the day we left town. We sold our home in Arizona, settling into a new purchased home in West Hartford, Connecticut. Spencer continued on with his career, our children began their activities, and I continued supporting our family. The move taxed my mental health. I was exhausted. Within a few months, I began therapy again.

Christine, my new therapist, met with me every week. She, like my therapists from drug rehab in high school, Miriam in college, and Chaplain while in the military, asked me questions about my childhood, my family of origin, and my daily activities. She also asked a lot of questions about my children, my marriage, and my husband.

She was impressed that I was successfully navigating life and even more impressed at the rigorous way at which I approached being a wife and mother. She worried about the schedule I lived and the lack of time I spent on myself. She encouraged me to find an outlet and she invited me to try an antidepressant. She said medication could stabilize my emotions and help me gain coping skills in my marriage.

I balked, but finally agreed. For the next year and a half, I not only began experimenting with different medications, but I also began drawing lessons. The prescription leveled out my emotions and calmed my anxiety and drawing helped me to see the world differently, from a new perspective. Instead of one giant mass of experiencing everything at once, I was able to compartmentalize my brain and separate my emotions from what was happening in the moment.

Separating negative space and positive space, slowing down, creating one-line drawings, and playing with color pastels increased my ability to see more of what was hidden in my daily life. Moment-to-moment choices were made more carefully.

More than once Christine advised me to leave my marriage. "Your husband is unwilling to take accountability for his part in the problem or step up with the children. This is not just about you." I heard her words but did not believe her. Leaving Spencer was not an option. I knew if I healed my sexuality, he would be happy.

More than once I inquired about my own sanity, and my own ability to succeed. Every time my inquiry was met with, "This is not just about you, Wendy. You have a lot going on in your life, in your family history, in your marriage." Every time she said those words, she validated my mental health. I felt seen. I felt sane.

While working with my therapist and with a strong home yoga practice in my daily routine, I decided to venture out and try a meditation class offered at a studio where I occasionally practiced with other yogis. During my first class, as the lights went out and my eyes closed, I panicked.

When Shankara, the facilitator, began going up the chakras[2]—also known as energy centers or vortexes that go up the spine in the body—I noticed that the space between my root chakra at the bottom of my pelvic floor up to my ribcage felt dead. I could feel nothing. In my mind's eye, the space was as black as the midnight sky, instead of the bright colors of red, orange, and yellow that Shankara was telling us the vortex were supposed to be. After class, I waited in line as Shankara patiently answered every person's question.

Once everyone was gone, I began. "That was really scary for me. I felt like I might go crazy when I closed my eyes. I couldn't follow you into the mediation. And my lower three chakras are black! I couldn't feel anything, Shankara. I want to be able to meditate effectively. Do you have any ideas?"

Even with his bright blue eyes and blond curly locks, he looked at me gravely. "You need to hire a healer to come into your home. One whom you trust and can take you through this process and be with you all the way. That way when as you say, 'you feel like you're going crazy,' your healer will be there to bring you back." He paused, a little concerned. "Just know that healers in that capacity are very expensive."

"Thank you so much. I will talk with my husband, Shankara." I had a lot to process.

When I got home, I told Spencer what had happened. "Do you think we can afford to hire a healer?"

"Of course, Wendy. Find one." Spencer telling me to find a healer did not surprise me. He wanted me to do anything that would support the sex life he expected to have. We went to our beautiful light blue room with lace curtains and knelt at the side of our bed. I spoke our evening prayer, humbly asking for help. While drifting off to sleep and thinking about the events of the evening, the thought occurred to me, *Wendy, you know the greatest Healer that ever walked on the earth. His name is Jesus.* Soon after, I fell asleep.

Early the next day, before the children woke, I prepared to get on my mat for my daily one-hour yoga practice. I'd decided to take myself to the edge of what I'd felt in the meditation class and then trust Jesus to comfort me if I needed His help. After years of studying about Him and His miracles, I believed He would come to me if I needed Him. I did not doubt it.

As I moved my body through the sun salutations, I let my mind go. Moving into the unknown, dark, thick waves of emotion began to move through me. The movement in my body somehow caused tears to fall, which then turned to crying. But I kept moving. I did not stop. Tears fell for the entire one-hour practice. Still, I could feel something happening inside of me.

It was good. In fact, it was amazing! Kind of like the feeling you get when the sun begins to shine after a heavy thunderstorm. At that moment, I was not blocked. The light, that I knew had been there all along, was shining through.

I was moving through the sludge in my brain. Fear was not stopping me. I realized my desire for freedom was bigger than my fear. So much bigger.

Getting off my mat, I went about my day, accomplishing all my responsibilities as a wife and mother. My husband and children could see no difference in me. But I could feel something shifting. The next day I repeated the exact same steps. Then again, the next day. On the third morning, I was getting tired, but I got on my mat anyway for one hour, again. This time, on the third day, I broke through.

The process each day had been controlled, just like I'd experienced in my therapists' offices in the past. During those visits, I'd released emotions, through words and tears. But now on my mat, I was releasing bigger emotions, and the movement in my body was triggering their release. I felt freer than I ever had.

At the end of my practice, I could not see Jesus, but I could feel Him. And sitting on my mat, my mind, my heart, and my body felt absolutely clear. I couldn't see myself as I had in the mirror after 9/11, but I could feel. And I felt as free as a bird.

Later that year on a cool, New England Saturday morning while stirring scrambled eggs over our kitchen stove for my family's breakfast, a directive from outside of me came into my mind. "Prepare to see me in the temple."[3] It was Jesus's voice.

Immediately, I began to prepare. I felt a need to fast and I began praying in my heart constantly. Reading the scriptures helped me stay centered and buoyant. I did not doubt myself or what I had heard. I knew that if I did not doubt, I would see Jesus in the temple.

As I bathed my children, the water coming out of the faucet reminded me of the living water that Jesus had been to my soul for so many years. Each droplet glistened and shone with His light. He was my best friend, and I knew He would meet me.

On Tuesday morning when I woke up, Spencer offered to take part of the day off and drive me to the Boston temple. When we arrived and went inside, I could immediately feel Jesus's presence. He was there. A magnetic pull drew me toward something I could not see.

As my husband and I continued walking slowly into the temple toward the gathering area and sat down, I noticed the lights in the room were celestially bright as if light was coming from a place other than the electric fixtures. It was His light. He was everywhere.

Never before had I been so absolutely spiritually present, robust, and strong all at the same time. As we continued through a beautiful ceremony of teaching and prayers, I expected and believed that I knew when and where I would see Jesus. Yet, when the appointed time came, He was not there.

Devastation hit my entire being. I burst into tears, walking around the room like a wounded animal looking for Jesus. My surroundings were obsolete. I was frantic. My eyes were wild, darting up and down the walls, looking for places I could have missed Him. A faux balcony in the architectural design kept pulling my eyes upward. *Is He there? Is He hiding from me?* I could feel Him, I just couldn't see Him. He'd told me to meet Him and I knew I'd done my part. *Why can't I see You? I didn't doubt.*

Spencer, along with a room full of people, were watching me. I'm sure they thought I was having a psychotic episode. Had I been the one witnessing myself, I might have thought the same thing. But I wasn't. I was completely sane.

Spencer told me he'd meet me in the car and left the room. A woman then came up to me and asked if there was something she could do to help me.

"Yes," I said. "I need to talk with someone in charge."

"Let me check and see." She walked away and a few minutes later came back. "Follow me," she said with a smile, then showed me into a room. Sitting down, I waited. Shortly after, a man dressed in all white entered the room.

"What brings you to the temple today?" I was still teary but looked at him as he spoke. He asked a few more questions about my family and was a very kind human being.

After answering him, I said, "Jesus told me to meet Him here and I am prepared to see Him. I can feel Him, but I cannot see Him. I believed every word that He would meet me here. He told me to prepare . . ."

In the middle of my sentence, Jesus appeared before my eyes within the same space as the man who'd just sat down asking me questions! No longer could I see the man, but only Jesus filled my entire line of vision. He was multidimensional. His features and His form were clear, distinct, and pure radiant light as if I was looking into the center of the sun. I could feel what I was seeing in every cell of my body and my being. There was no end to what I was seeing; I could see forever.

Heat that felt like a supernova permeated every cell of my body. Recognition that I would disintegrate in an instant was clear except that a change was happening in my body, allowing me to remain fully intact and present, looking into the eyes of Jesus.

Infinity without measure was revealed before my eyes. Diamond white light spanned as far as I could see. Eons of spiritual matter moved through me as the understanding that there was nothing Jesus did not or could not see about me. He knew me exactly as I was and He loved me perfectly. Everything that ever was or ever would be was known to Him. His power was infinite. And He loved me. *He loved me.*

An absolute awareness and sensibility of my weakness, frailty, and human-ness came to my mind in an instant. *You're not smiling at me* was a conscious thought I had, and before it was finished, the corners of His lips turned up. He smiled at me. I was transfixed with His presence and His power, after which what permeated and remained in every corner, crevice, and wit of my being was His perfect, infinite, Loving Kindness.

An understanding that the clothing I wore or anything I possessed was absolutely irrelevant and inconsequential to my worth. I felt no judgment. He didn't tell me to change or do anything different. He was with me and He loved me.

Basking in His love, I became aware of my surroundings, noticing that the man who'd been talking became visible to me once again and his form, like the sand in an hourglass, disintegrated before my eyes into a pile of matter.

As I stood to leave, everything was permeable. I left the temple and met my husband in our minivan. I sat down in the passenger seat and laid my head back.

"He was there," I breathed reverently. "He was there."

"I'm glad for you, Wendy Beth."

Lying my head back, I went to sleep all the way home. When we arrived, Spencer dropped me off and went back to work. My children met me at the door and we went into my bedroom. I shared with them the events of the day. They smiled, then asked if they could continue watching their cartoons and playing their games on my bed. For them, it was just another day. For me, I would never be the same again.

The truth is, after being with Jesus, Loving Kindness for everyone and everything like I now knew Jesus loved me was paramount in my life. My children, husband, loved ones, neighbors, animals, even insects. Spiders that had caused me anxiety in the past were released into the outdoors. Anything that had life in it felt connected to Jesus. And being like Him and trusting His love was my north star.

Learning and trusting my Source of Inspiration and following my Personal Guidance System took time (years, in fact), and healing came in ways that I would've never imagined for myself. But not only did I know what I'd experienced to be real, it was through this breakdown and breakthrough that I truly learned to trust my Personal Guidance System.

After seeing Jesus, I did not go to another well-meaning therapist looking for the truth. So far, that had only added to my sexual trauma by counseling me to be a "gift" to my husband when I didn't have the capacity. Nor did I seek approval from my husband who didn't understand, nor my family members who denied any wrongdoing. I didn't even need to spend thousands of dollars on a healer to sit beside me and bring me back from "crazy" if I went too far.

Jesus and His perfect loving kindness was my answer, my truth, forever. Still, it would take everything I had to really, truly listen, trust, and follow my truth no matter what.

True Principles for Your Personal Guidance System (PGS) Blueprint:

- You have innate gifts and a highest and best self. How you connect with and trust this part of you is completely up to you. **Connecting deeper with yourself and learning your innate gifts will bring clarity to your life.** More than once I've shared my experience with others and they in turn have been able to experience new, amazing parts of themselves. There is no wrong or right answer here. Be open to the best parts of you!

- **Identify, understand, rely upon, and trust your Source of Inspiration.** Whether you're being navigated by moral principles, a deity, science, the natural world, religion, or a guru, I invite you to ask, how does your Source of Inspiration make your life better? What healing capabilities does it possess? Does your Source of Inspiration require you to give up your dignity or your free will?

- As you **deepen your connection with your Source of Inspiration,** you'll experience a sense of stability that will center not only your undeniable life in every moment but your potentiality for peace. Feeling connected to a Source of Inspiration is stabilizing and empowering.

- **Harmonizing your highest self with your Source of Inspiration can make life easier.** A Source of Inspiration gives you another centering point to ground from, to know what you need to heal and progress forward in your own life-to help you find answers to the heart and soul questions that have kept you up at night, that you've been seeking answers to for far too long.

- If you do not currently have a Source of Inspiration you follow or if you do not trust the one you are turning to, I implore you to keep looking. One is available for you. Open your heart and mind to the truth that is in the universe we live in and you will find the answers you are looking for.

While completing activities 17-20, you will discover:

- **Activity 17: Believing the Truth of WHO You Are**

- **Activity 18: Identifying Your Source of Inspiration**

- **Activity 19: Deepening a Connection with Your Source of Inspiration**

- **Activity 20: Harmonizing PGS with Your Source of Inspiration**

ACTIVITY 17: BELIEVING THE TRUTH OF WHO YOU ARE

In our deepest, truest essence we are noble, empowered beings connected to love. Ralph Waldo Emerson said, "Every man is a divinity in disguise, a god playing the fool." The light within us allows self-actualization, encompassing our fullest potential. It recognizes the parts of ourselves still progressing and has no judgment or negative feeling toward our darkness. Our highest self understands that WHO we are is in the state of becoming.

I love Matthew McConaughey's response to the question, "Who's your hero?" He replied, "It's me in ten years. So I turned twenty-five. Ten years later, that same person comes to me and says, 'So, are you your hero?' And I was like, 'not even close. No, no, no.' She said, 'Why?' I said, 'Because my hero is me at thirty-five. So you see, every day, every week, every month, and every year of my life, my hero is always ten years away. I'm never gonna be my hero. I'm not gonna attain that. I know I'm not, and that's just fine with me because that keeps me with somebody to keep on chasing.'"[4]

Up until my 9/11 experience, I didn't know, let alone chase my higher self. I was oblivious to the fact that I even had one. Since seeing the best part of me, I have talked with many people, some who've never experienced their higher selves and others who do frequently. The difference? Awareness, education, and being open to connecting to the hero, the highest and best part of ourselves.

Discovery Activity:

- **Just breathe, before you even get out of bed. Do this for at least five minutes today.**

- **What is your number today?** _____

- **List Gratitudes**

  1. _____

  2. _____

  3. _____

- **Write your thoughts:**

  When have you experienced the best part of you? Capture your thoughts about these moments.

  _____

  _____

_____

_____

Write down the attributes that best describe your best and noblest self.

_____

_____

_____

_____

Do you feel separated from this part of you? Write about what program could possibly be running that's keeping you from seeing and being in touch with this part of you all the time.

_____

_____

_____

_____

What gifts do you possess? Circle your greatest gift.

_____

_____

_____

- **Mirror Meditation**

  Caution: mirror meditation can be detrimental if you allow a virus like negative self or self-loathing run. Delete or at the very least pause any unwanted programs and only focus on your highest and best self when doing mirror meditation.

While listening to one of the songs you added to your playlist in Activity 2, be with yourself in front of a mirror. Let go of expectations and just be with you for a few minutes. Try not to look at your hair or your clothes or even your face. Look in your eyes.

Say these words as you are looking in the mirror. "I see you, [say your name]..." Then add whatever else feels appropriate.

Allow all the best parts of you to emerge. Imagine them in you, with you, witnessing you, loving you. Draw and write your thoughts about what you felt while doing the mirror meditation. What did you see?

- **Write the good, positive, and amazing things you experienced with yourself during the mirror meditation.**

_____

_____

_____

_____

_____

_____

- **Encapsulate "Your Greatest Gift" into one sentence, then transfer it to your Living Blueprint page 357.**

_____

This process is one I repeat after my personal meditation often. Mirror meditations allow me to connect with myself, through my eyes, and instantly tell me if I am out of alignment with my Personal Guidance System or my Source of Inspiration. The mirror, _when used correctly,_ can be a great teacher because no one knows us better than ourselves.

- **Be in Bermuda at least 1x today.**

ACTIVITY 18: IDENTIFYING YOUR SOURCE OF INSPIRATION

Free yourself of judgment as you explore your connection to a Source of Inspiration. Who or what helps us in experiencing our best self and guides our decisions is absolutely personal to each of us. Trusting who or what is guiding your life is one of the greatest blessings you will ever have. If you already know your Source of Inspiration, I invite you to give gratitude for it. Not everyone has your experience. Many feel lost and unguided.

For some individuals their Source of Inspiration is a deity or a religion. Children, ancestors, a hero, or another person who has passed on are many people's Source of Inspiration. For others a set of ethics, morals, or science navigates decisions. Others are inspired by the creation of art, the process of making music, or the connection of human beings. Each is perfectly unique as is our guidance system.

Delia Evans's fictional character Kya in, *Where the Crawdads Sing*, lived through horrific circumstances because The Marsh, her Source of Inspiration, taught her how to survive.[5] Though not a true story, the principles taught are absolutely true and can guide a person trying to understand and choose a source by which to be guided by. Many people, including myself, look to the natural world for answers. If that's you, you're not alone.

As you read in my story so far, Jesus is my Source of Inspiration. Looking back over my life I know He knew and loved me and was with me long before I knew He existed. For as long as I can remember, He has met exactly where I am.

Today my experiences with Him guide every aspect of my life. As much as I wish I could give others the assurance I have in Him as a Source of Inspiration, I have learned that every person must be open to finding and experiencing their own witness, in their own time, in their own way. Even parents cannot give their knowledge to their children. That is gained by each of us. Let's find out what or who is your Source of Inspiration.

Discovery Activity

- **Breathe, before you even get out of bed. Do this for at least five minutes today.**

- **What is your number today?** _____

- **List Gratitudes**

    1. _____

    2. _____

    3. _____

- **Ponder the definition of "inspiration" from Merriam-Webster:** *inspiration* //: a divine influence or action on a person believed to qualify him or her to receive and communicate sacred revelation, the action or power of moving the intellect or emotions.

- **Let's write.** Using the above definition to prompt your own thoughts, what is your understanding of "inspiration" in your life?

    _____

    _____

    _____

    _____

- When do you feel inspired? When was the last time inspiration moved you to action?

    _____

    _____

    _____

    _____

As a child, what or who inspired you, and how did it/they do it?

_____

_____

_____

_____

When you need help or want to make a decision, who or what is the first thing you turn to? And the next? Write about your process in receiving and using inspiration.

_____

_____

_____

_____

Be still for a few moments, then ponder this question,

What or who is my "Source of Inspiration?"

_____

_____

What does your Source of Inspiration feel like?

_____

_____

_____

_____

What are the attributes of your Source of Inspiration?

_____

_____

_____

_____

Does your Source of Inspiration possess healing capabilities? If so, what are they?

_____

_____

_____

As you understand yourself today, what or who is/are your source(s) of inspiration?

_____

_____

_____

- **Transfer your "Source of Inspiration" to My Living Blueprint page 357.**

- **From your Circle of Interests in Activity 6, choose an activity, then engage in that activity with a curiosity for _inspiration_ from your Source of Inspiration as defined by you above.**

  o For example, if being outside is in your circle, then be outside and look, listen, and wait for inspiration. Slow down and just be with the clouds. If science, music, or a particular religion inspires you, engage in an activity open to inspiration today.

- **What did you notice?**

_____

_____

_____

_____

- **Be in Bermuda at least 1x today.**

ACTIVITY 19: DEEPENING A CONNECTION WITH YOUR SOURCE OF INSPIRATION

The family and the culture were born into has a great deal to do with how we view our Source of Inspiration and what we believe. "The hidden rules, subtle nuances, and private rituals and dances that define every family's microculture might not be easy for an outsider to perceive at first glance, but they are there."[6] You know them and your brain knows what you were taught as a child to believe. However, today you get to decide what and/or who your Source of Inspiration is.

A dear friend, while working a 12-step program[7] in order to be free of heroin, learned a powerful lesson I'll share with you. He'd been born into a religious family and he'd carried the idea of a deity based on what he'd been taught as a child. It was impossible for him to trust in that being.

One day his sponsor suggested creating a new image of Deity, one that supported him, loved him, and was willing to help him be free of his addiction. My friend made a conscious decision of who he believed Deity was and began trusting and turning to Him. From then on, my friend referred to his higher power, his Source of Inspiration, as *My Jesus*. It was a very different version of what he was taught growing up. He has been sober for many years.

Building your relationship with your Source of Inspiration takes effort and time. If you want your Source of Inspiration to move your intellect and your emotions, open your heart, be willing to act, and live in humility to direction. Don't force yourself to believe anything. We trust when we trust, not before.

Discovery Activity

- **Breathe, before you even get out of bed. Do this for at least five minutes today.**

- **What is your number today?** _____

- **List Gratitudes**

    1. _____

    2. _____

    3. _____

- **What does your *"ideal relationship"* with your Source of Inspiration feel like or act like? How does it play out in your life?**

    _____

    _____

    _____

    _____

    What do you need to do in order to have the above relationship?

    _____

    _____

    _____

    _____

You must have some evidence that your Source of Inspiration is reliable and trustworthy. When you trust, you can rely on it and further choose to make a commitment to be guided by it. Why do you trust your chosen Source of Inspiration?

_____

_____

_____

_____

Do you easily trust your dad? Mom? Write down your feelings and thoughts regarding your parents today.

_____

_____

_____

_____

Do the above thoughts and feelings correlate to how you feel about a higher power? If you are having trouble trusting a Source of Inspiration, could other relationships be biasing your ability to trust?

_____

_____

_____

_____

How does your Source of Inspiration communicate with you? In your body? With your ears? With your eyes? In your heart?

_____

_____

_____

_____

How do you communicate with your Source of Inspiration?

_____

_____

_____

_____

What do you do with ideas, thoughts, and feelings your Source of Inspiration brings to you?

_____

_____

_____

_____

What, if any, healing capabilities does your Source of Inspiration possess?

_____

_____

_____

_____

Are you currently engaged in a daily practice of seeking, asking, offering gratitude to your Source of Inspiration? Write about how you can improve your communication and your relationship to your Source of Inspiration.

_____

_____

_____

_____

- **Spend time embraced by, and embracing, your Source of Inspiration. What do you notice?**

_____

_____

_____

_____

- **Be in Bermuda at least 1x today.**

ACTIVITY 20: HARMONIZING PGS WITH YOUR SOURCE OF INSPIRATION

Remember, your PGS is like the GPS of a vehicle. Ideally, it's taking you where you want to go. But sometimes viruses get into the system. What then?

For all of us, understanding, trusting, and acting in alignment to what we have learned and know to be true takes time and experience. It is a skill we learn over a lifetime. Timothy Galloway, author of *The Game of Inner Tennis* says, "If we let ourselves lose touch with our ability to feel our actions by relying too heavily on instructions, we can seriously compromise our access to our natural learning process and our potential to perform. No teacher is greater than one's own experience."[8] Does that mean we have to try everything in order to know if we should or should not do something? Of course not.

However, if your Source of Inspiration is the natural world, yet you rarely go outside looking for your answers and direction, then there's a good chance peace and satisfaction will escape you. If cultural, religious, or familial dogma is the basis for your beliefs and values, yet you do not live what you believe is true, sadness and even guilt may follow decisions made against your own ideology. My point is, know who you are, and live what you know.

Confusion, frustration, and a constant wanting and a hunger for something more can be filled and alleviated when we trust and follow our PGS. Distractions, past trauma, procrastination, overload, addiction, or anything else that gets you out of sync with your PGS are like unwanted programs and viruses running on the GPS of your car, sucking energy and slowing progress. They take up space, waste time, and cause upsets in our lives.

If you're dealing with any addiction, attuning your Personal Guidance System can be part of your answer to freedom. It has been mine. It seems impossible to me today that I was once addicted to alcohol, speed, marijuana, nicotine, caffeine, sugar, perfectionism, and other people's approval. None of those things have any hold on me today. I am free. Your Living Blueprint is a complimentary program to any 12-step addiction recovery program, but they are not interchangeable. Please add a 12-step recovery program if you are battling an addiction.

Discovery Activity

- **Breathe, before you even get out of bed. Do this for at least five minutes today.**

- **What is your number today?** _____

- **List Gratitudes**

    1. _____

    2. _____

    3. _____

- **As you contemplate and respond to the following questions, be mindful of you and your Source of Inspiration and how you work together.**

  Between any stimulus and your response there is a gap allowing you to choose. How do you make a decision as to how to act or behave?

  _____

  _____

  _____

  In contemplation of a *really big* decision, what criteria goes into allowing forward movement when you feel unsure or afraid?

  _____

  _____

  _____

  _____

  List a few incessant distractions you just can't seem to get over in creating the days and/or the life you want.

  _____

  _____

  _____

  _____

- **From Activity 13, write down the number one virus or obstacle that is creating unrest and dissonance in your life.**

  _____

How would you like your Source of Inspiration to help you overcome this virus or obstacle?

_____

_____

_____

Write down the opposite, or what would make this better; i.e. the correction or the deletion process that needs to occur for this virus to stop slowing your progress.

_____

_____

_____

What would life look and feel like without this virus running in your life?

_____

_____

_____

Is there a complementary healing tool from your toolkit that will either heal the issue, alleviate discomfort, or allow you to deal with the virus better until you are fully free from this issue?

_____

_____

_____

Spend time today engaged in a chosen treatment from your healing toolkit to alleviate discomfort from your most persistent virus.

What healing treatment did you choose?

What did you notice?

What do you find yourself thinking about when you have nothing else to think about, when your mind is free to just be? Do you ever feel guided by your Source of Inspiration?

What are the first thoughts that fill your mind in the morning when you wake up? What about before going to sleep? In these quiet moments, do you feel guided in your thoughts by a Source of Inspiration?

Can you consult with your Source of Inspiration in deleting the virus? How exactly would your Source of Inspiration help you eliminate this distraction?

_____

_____

_____

How do you and your Source of Inspiration work together to help you move forward, heal, or let go of guilt or shame when you have done something you feel is wrongdoing or wrong thinking?

_____

_____

_____

_____

What obstacles do you foresee getting in your way of working harmoniously with your Source of Inspiration?

_____

_____

- **Write the plan of how you and your Source of Inspiration are working together in harmony as if it is already happening today.**

_____

_____

_____

_____

_____

- **Refer to Day 12 when executing changes in your life.** Write exactly *what* you will implement and *how* you will implement the above plan.

_____

_____

_____

_____

- **Be in Bermuda at least 1x today.**

Remember, learning, designing, and following your PGS takes time. Be patient with yourself. Often we think *there just isn't enough time* to do the things that are most important. I'm here to share with you, that's just not true, and I invite you to delete that program from your thinking.

There is enough time. There is space and occasion and moments enough for you to understand you and for you to figure out how to work harmoniously with your Source of Inspiration so that you can create the life you were born to experience joy in. You are worth whatever time it takes to learn and then learn to follow your Personal Guidance System.

STEP 3 – BIO BLUEPRINT

CHAPTER 6 UNDERSTANDING YOUR BODY'S BIOCHEMISTRY

biochemistry
is not only to survive
but for pleasure too

Your brain, your cardiovascular system, your happy hormones, your sexual response system, and so many more networks in your biochemistry are working toward not only a base existence but a satisfying and fulfilling life. Dr. Daniel G. Amen in his 2023 *Wall Street Journal* bestseller, reported that Alzheimer's is expected to triple between now and 2050, depression has risen 400 percent since 1987, half of American adults are pre-diabetic or diabetic, 60 percent have hypertension or prehypertension, and 73 percent Americans are overweight.[1] Staggering statistics.

BIO, the third element in creating a Living Blueprint, is about learning to listen to your body and giving it what it needs to thrive. Optimizing a meditation practice, hydrating the body, getting adequate sleep, utilizing the sexual response system, fulfilling nutritional needs, incorporating a daily movement and exercise program, exploring social connections, and laughing every day are in and of themselves pretty simple practices. But when choreographed into the daily tapestry of our lives, they can make the dance of our daily existence exquisite.

As we mature, understanding and nurturing physical developments and changes with our biochemistry will enhance our overall well-being, boost our energy and productivity, reduce illness, and promote longevity. Friedrich Nietzsche said, "There is more wisdom in your body than in your deepest philosophy."[2] Nurturing your BIO while following your PGS harmoniously on the foundation of WHO is an elixir for resilience.

Resilience, our ability to recover from adversity, is inherent in each of us to varying degrees. Have you ever noticed that at different times of your life you feel more resilient than others? Adam Grant on his Instagram posted, "Scars are more than evidence of trauma. They're proof of resilience."[3] Of course, circumstances certainly play a role in our level of resilience, it's true. But the choices we make influence the many systems of our biochemistry, impacting our ability to thrive and be resilient, especially in stressful circumstances.

Using what you already know and looking for answers in the toughest circumstances when life has kicked you in the guts is not easy or a given. Lots of people don't do it; they stop trying. They settle. But you are here, which means you are not settling. I am proud of you for not giving up!

For me, developing resilience came as I chose to be in nature, moved my body, developed my talents, prepared nutritional food, nurtured my loved ones, had fun with family and friends, trusted and connected to my source of inspiration, accepted help, worked on goals, prayed, and just kept going even when I wanted to quit. These are just a few examples of the things that nurtured my biochemistry.

These activities, along with the new habits I was developing thanks to my naturopath strengthened my biochemistry, so that I could deal with and move through incredibly difficult situations, especially those that had nothing to do with my own choices. They were just part of my greater destiny. I invite you to discover in yourself and wear like a badge of honor your own resilience as you design your Living Blueprint.

When was the last time you enjoyed a long afternoon nap? Or maybe a really great workout, or took time to prepare a nutritious meal just for you? Honestly, I was wired to work, and work hard. For me, it took my body breaking down to learn how to nurture my body's beautiful biochemical systems and let them do what they were designed for, keeping me alive, and supporting my happiness. What is your favorite way to boost your feel-good hormones naturally?

The New England trees were naked when Spencer quit his job. After eleven moves for his career and five years in a corporate executive program, to say I was devastated that he was changing our plans once again was an understatement.

"I'm just another number in a sea of employees," he said. Since he was the one working while I was at home with the children, and it was *his* career, following him and supporting his happiness was my priority. I was sympathetic to his pain.

We put our home up for sale and made plans to move from Connecticut to Idaho so that we could live closer to his family. In the back of my mind, I hoped that living near his parents might help him be a more attentive father. Although relations were still strained, I wanted to be close to my family too. I missed them. He moved to Idaho and began searching for a job while I remained in Connecticut.

While waiting for the house to sell and for our children to finish the school year, I got an unexpected gift: a new member to my chosen family. Genie, a young woman just out of high school, needed a safe place to land for a short time. She was smart, articulate, and loved to talk once we got all the children to bed. She brought a spark of light, newness, and laughter to our home–and she knew how to use the computer, a device we had owned for years, but I was scared to touch. I thought I would break it. Our children from Rhodes, who was thirteen, to Huxley, who was now four, loved spending time with her playing video games on the computer, something I as their mother had no idea how to do.

Moving from an East Coast school system to a West Coast school system caused me concern regarding possible gaps in our children's education. We decided I would homeschool the children the following year. Throughout the spring and into the summer, I studied the Connecticut Board of Education standards and the Idaho school district's curriculums, creating individualized academic plans for each child.

Once we moved to Idaho, Spencer continued to look for work, but he discovered that finding a job was more difficult than he'd had anticipated. After eight months and with our savings spent, money was tight. We didn't have a spare dime to our name.

While grocery shopping for our family, an acorn squash caught my eye. It sounded delicious to me, but no one else liked squash and I decided not to spend money on something only I would enjoy. Returning home from the store, a friend surprised me with a large black garbage bag of produce she'd just picked up from her parent's farm. Opening the bag, I saw ten acorn squash! From then on, I knew we'd be okay. In my prayers, I offered gratitude for such a bounteous blessing.

Nine months after walking away from "being just another number in the corporate machine," Spencer began his new career in consulting. He became a road warrior, traveling three and half weeks per month, which was hard, but at least we had money coming in. Life felt a lot less stressful and Spencer loved all the new and different places he got to see.

Anxiety from moving, leaving my home and friends in Connecticut, dealing with unemployment, being short on money for months, Spencer's extensive travel schedule, and homeschooling our four children by myself began to take its toll on my health. I had a deep awareness that something was physically wrong with me. Pain in my stomach never went away.

Coldness flowed from the core of my body through my limbs into the tip of my nose. Even buried in my down comforter, I couldn't get warm. After several weeks of doing everything I knew to feel better, I began to worry. "Spencer, I'm not well and I'm not getting better," I said in a moment of vulnerability. "I'm exhausted. We don't have the money for me to go to the doctor and our COBRA insurance deductible is too expensive to use unless it's a catastrophic emergency."

"I have an idea," he said gently. "How about you travel with me when my clients are close enough for us to drive as a family? You're working so hard. I know you aren't ready to see a doctor yet, and you wouldn't be telling me this if you weren't worried. But I can help you with the children at night when I finish working if you're with me. Then, during the day you can help them with their homework. You can watch them play in the hotel pools and rest while they swim." His idea sounded exactly like the respite I was looking for. This was the best we could do. He was surviving too.

Spencer made reservations at hotels with complimentary morning buffets, allowing us to eat healthy breakfasts. The children loved making their own waffles and I didn't need to prepare food upon first waking, allowing me even more rest time. One hotel we visited in Montana was designed like a jungle and had eight hot tubs with two water slides for the children to play on. They had so much fun getting their homework finished, then laughing, splashing, and playing together for hours. Seeing them laugh was contagious, and even as sick as I was, I laughed too.

Homeschooling my children was better than I'd ever imagined it could be. Slowly they, like Spencer, were feeling more freedom. Their wings spread before my eyes. At night Spencer brought groceries depending on what everyone wanted to eat. We cooked in the hotel kitchenette together. For the first time in years, it felt like he and I were working together as a team coparenting our children. Still, I still wasn't getting better. I could hardly eat anything and what I did eat made me nauseated, every time. I was losing weight I didn't have to lose.

Looking at my children, I wondered what would happen to them if I died. There was no one to take care of them if I wasn't there. Upon returning home from one of our trips, I prayed with the most urgent pleading I'd ever prayed, especially for the sake of my children:

"Father, thank you for our little family. Thank you for Spencer's help with the children and for his job. Thank you for helping me homeschool my children. It is one of the greatest joys of my life to teach them. I need your help more than ever. I'm sick and I can't go to the doctor yet. Please help me until our insurance isn't so expensive. My children need me. If I'm not here, I don't know what will happen to them. Please don't let me die."

Several weeks later, Spencer had a client in Canada. We stayed home in our rented house on the cul de sac surrounded by ponderosa pines. After a day of teaching, mothering, and cooking, it was time to rest. Once I got all the children to bed, I tidied the house, then checked on each sleeping child. Climbing the stairs, I went to my bathroom to brush my teeth and wash my face. A gaunt but peaceful version of myself met me in the mirror. I walked to my bed and dropped, weary from exhaustion.

Later that night, I had a dream that I was drowning in a lake. I felt like I was dying. All of the sudden, a dark angel stood over me next to my head. Its posture was looming. I could not breathe.

Immediately, a brilliant angel of light, larger than a tall man, appeared next to my bed close to my feet, facing off the dark angel, who then immediately disappeared into thin air. He just vanished. As I caught up with what was happening, I noticed in the angel of light's hand a scepter the same brightness of light as they were. The being was neither male nor female but a perfect mixture of masculine and feminine energy and the color and likeness of a diamond. The angel said nothing, then touched my stomach in the place that was hurting me.

Something, I don't know what, began to be pulled out of my abdomen, kind of like a ball of yarn slowly being unwound. *Please get it all. Please don't leave any of it inside of me.* When the angel of light was finished pulling, the end of it-whatever "it" was-slipped out, making a wet sound of *PLIP* as if Dr. Seuss had designed the whole thing himself. Immediately, the angel of light dissipated before my eyes.

For the rest of the night, I laid in a bubble of bliss that felt identical to the warmth and freedom being with Jesus had in the temple the year before. Pure peace and love permeated every cell of my body. I floated in my heart and mind while lying stationary on my bed. The next morning as I descended the stairs, Huxley, the baby of our family, greeted me.

"Mom, will you read with me?"

"Of course, let's sit down."

Lowering myself onto the chair, my child crawled into my lap. Lying back into me, instinctively I held myself taut so that I would not hurt from the pressure of my child's little body on my stomach as I had in previous months, then quickly noticed that the pain in my stomach was completely gone! I pulled my child closer, humbled and in gratitude. *Thank you, Father.*

Delighted to be out of pain, my temperature still would not regulate. I felt like I was freezing to death, I was always tired, and my skin was drier than it had ever been. As soon as our health insurance kicked in three months later, I went to the doctor. Blood work revealed my thyroid was not working. Our new physician prescribed levothyroxine and I began taking it immediately. Within several weeks, I began to feel warmer in my core.

Finances stabilized and I reached out to Cheryl, a registered nurse, trained in holistic medicine, who'd worked with our family on various health issues over the years. I was hoping to find answers other than a prescription medication for my thyroid. The antidepressants had supported my healing process, but I had eventually found natural treatments that gave me the same benefits. I hoped I might be able to do the same with the thyroid issues I was experiencing.

Cheryl had always been the softest, yet most knowledgeable woman I'd ever met when it came to healing the body. She smelled like essential oils and her hugs were filled with love. A deep concern for my well-being traveled through the phone line. For almost an hour, Cheryl and I spoke about my life and I shared intimate details that she didn't previously know. That included talking about my sexual trauma, my daily routines, my miracles, and my relationship with Spencer.

"Wendy, do you want to keep killing yourself? Or would you like to learn something new today?"

Her question was matter-of-fact, free of judgment. It penetrated all the distractions and walls in my brain and went straight to my heart.

"Yes, Cheryl, anything that will help me heal so that I can take care of my children and my husband."

"Is there ever a time when you are not in flight, fight, or work mode? When do you rest? When do you stop working, Wendy?"

My mind raced. I couldn't think of a single time since becoming a mother I'd ever stopped working. Not even once. "I honestly don't know; I can't think of one."

I could hear her flipping through her reference books. She continued, "Once in the morning, once in the afternoon, and once before you go to bed, I want you to go to Bermuda."[4]

"Go to Bermuda? What does that mean, Cheryl?" I asked.

"Three times a day, lie on your back and put your feet on the wall specifically at a seventy degree angle, making sure to keep your legs straight, but don't lock your knees. Stay in that position for twenty minutes, doing absolutely *nothing*. No reading, no talking, nothing. Just be with Wendy for twenty minutes, three times a day in Bermuda."

"Okay," I said, a bit confused.

She added, "Wendy, when any part of you is faced with a threat-whether that be conscious or unconscious, physical or emotional-your sympathetic nervous system[5] is automatically shifting into fight and flight mode. In fact, what I'm hearing from you is that you're in your sympathetic system most of the time."

As she spoke, I could feel the truth of her words opening my mind, touching on a lifetime of running away, surviving, and fighting for not only my life but my children's lives as well. She then shared about the other part of my nervous system: the god state or my parasympathetic nervous system.

"This part of your nervous system brings a state of calm to your body, allowing you to rest, relax, and repair. The trick is to have the correct balance between these two parts, Wendy. And currently, sweet lady, this is not happening in your body. Ideally, I want to see you in your parasympathetic system ninety percent of the time and in your sympathetic system ten percent of the time. If you go to Bermuda three times a day, over time, you'll harmonize your nervous system."

Before our conversation ended, she gave me prescriptives regarding my water intake, sleep patterns, nutritional supplementation, and my relationship with Spencer. After writing down what she wanted me to do, I finished the appointment feeling confident that I could change the trajectory of my health.

Later that day, I went to Bermuda for the first time in my life. As I placed my feet up on the wall, they began to tingle. The longer I was there, the more sensation I felt in my feet and ankles.

"Mom, what are you doing?" the children asked.

"I'm going to Bermuda."

"Can we do it too?"

"Of course. Each of you find your own wall space and you'll need to be quiet till the timer goes off. Okay?"

The longer we remained in Bermuda, the more disinterested they became, and soon I was left alone to finish my practice. As I brought my feet down, I could feel a sense of calm in my whole body. The feeling was cumulative.

LIVING BLUEPRINT

Within a few days, I began to notice the hypervigilance, my default before Cheryl, was shifting to a more peaceful, more present state of mind.

The next week, after helping my children settle into an outdoor sibling activity on the trampoline, including water and fudgesicles, I went to the freezer and pulled out one for myself. Taking off the wrapper, I walked upstairs and laid on my bed. I put the iced chocolate in my mouth and took a lick with my tongue. Its coldness shocked me as I reveled in the chocolate sweetness melting into the break I was allowing myself to take.

Lying there, listening to my children play, laughing together in the backyard, I realized that for the first time since becoming a mother, I was resting with and for myself. For nearly fifteen years I had been going nonstop: working, healing, studying, and trying to create a happy family and a peaceful home life for my husband and for my children. That day I decided-and allowed myself-to just rest.

Adding more water to my diet, as per Cheryl's recommendation, came soon after implementing Bermuda. Consciously, I had lowered my water intake over the years because it made me need to pee all the time, and I didn't think I had time for that while taking care of my children. Drinking my water and going pee when I needed was a simple act of self-care.

Wanting to be more present in every movement, I purposefully carried a lidless cup full of water everywhere I went, especially to and from the car. I refilled it as needed from a water bottle I also carried with me. With a lidless cup full of water, falling back into "hypervigilance" mode and hurrying anywhere caused me to spill my water, sometimes all over my clothing. My open cup ritual kept me focused on drinking, and it slowed me down to a pace that kept me in the present moment.

Doing more than one thing at a time was something I'd perfected since becoming a mother. But as I slowed down, I realized that it did not support me experiencing joy in the tasks I loved doing. Making dinner, talking on the phone, and helping children with homework was absolutely possible,

172

but it pulled at too many parts of my brain, preventing me from actually experiencing pleasure in the moment. That day I stopped multitasking-and I never went back! Experiencing the moment mattered more than getting everything done.

Over time I realized that I accomplished just as much, and with all the changes I was making, my body relaxed. I went from existing on four to five hours of sleep to needing at least eight hours of sleep every night. Taking naps, even removing my clothing and getting under the covers so that I could really get a good afternoon nap became my norm, not the exception.

While learning to heal my body, one of Spencer's clients, who owned a large farm, offered him the job of becoming their full-time business manager. With his new position, he created his own company, worked less hours, and was home more. Over time, his new venture allowed him time to begin creating his vision for a more balanced work/home life. Spencer's dream of owning his own company was finally coming true!

Early one morning, while he was playing basketball and a few months into Spencer's new position, I received a phone call. Spencer was in the emergency room. When I arrived at the hospital, he was in excruciating pain. His wrist bones were gruesomely contorted and the ER doctors were unable to get his pain under control for hours. In our entire marriage of thirteen years, I'd never experienced this side of my husband. Vulnerable.

In the hospital, Spencer was broken, yet so gracious in his pain, as the nurses and I attempted to help him. Once the swelling went down, an orthopedic surgeon put his wrist back together with two plates and seven screws. For the next six weeks, he required full-time convalescent care. I was his girl.

Nurturing Spencer was not only instinctual, it was joyful. As I assisted him in showering, dressing, and performing other tasks he usually did for himself, for the first time in our marriage, I felt safe enough to be vulnerable with him. He was no longer angry at me. Slowly he and I traveled deeper into our hearts and the truth of our relationship. His entitlement regarding sex dissipated as I helped him day and night. Love was present in every moment.

As I cared for Spencer, we grew closer than we'd ever been as husband and wife. In fact, I thought we were making progress toward a real, authentic relationship. But once he stopped taking the medication, was out of pain, and didn't need my help anymore, life went back to the way it had been before the accident. He was aloof and distant. I was surprised and saddened. But also hopeful.

The truth was, after thirteen years of healing and overcoming my sexual trauma, through learning new ways of being present in my body and constantly reframing my thought patterns, nurturing Spencer had allowed my own sexuality to blossom. With a healthy body and a strong mind, being *a gift* for my husband's satisfaction was no longer enough.

The realization that intimacy in a relationship was in fact a consensual choice between two adults who wanted to enjoy each other versus one person just trying to please the other opened in my mind—my own pleasure mattered, for me. Not only in the bedroom, but in every aspect of my life.

Understanding that my physical body was a gift, I began experiencing life's abundant opportunities of pleasure, fulfillment, and satisfaction. Snowboarding fresh powder under blue skies in the winters and kayaking in the waters of North Idaho during the summers became integral parts of my and our family's life. At forty-two years old, my body was strong, and for the first time since being a small child, it was open to experience what it was born to feel: physical joy!

True Principles For Your Biochemistry Blueprint:

- **Consistent meditation like Going to Bermuda can calm anxiety and support you in living a more mindful life.** Choose walking, eating, eye gazing, or sitting meditations based on your particular needs.

- **Consider carrying a lidless cup for a type of meditation to help you slow down and be more conscious of each and every choice.** Rushing about and doing too many things at once lowers our ability to experience the cues our body is giving off. When we slow down, our ability to make mindful choices based on our long-term desires is more accessible.

- **Get adequate sleep consistently to improve brain performance, mood, and health.** It allows the body to rest and repair itself. In an analysis of random controlled trials, "improving sleep was associated with better mental health regardless of the severity of mental health difficulty or the presence of comorbid health conditions," Scott et al. (2021).

- **Your physical body requires adequate hydration to perform vital functions like maintaining temperature, disposing waste, and lubricating your joints.** The complexity of the human water regulatory network, which includes the central nervous system and several organ systems as well as significant inter-individual variations, makes it difficult to define across the board hydration requirements for all individuals, (Armstrong & Johnson, 2018). Hydration needs are based on multiple factors, two of those being body mass and activity levels.

- We learn about sexuality from our families, friends, and the culture we were raised in. "One society's perversion may be another society's accepted sexual practices," Carroll (2004). **Positive self-awareness regarding sensuality and sexuality cannot only increase mood, reduce stress, and make life more fun. It can also open us to a whole new world of physical pleasure and fulfillment.**

Consult a professional practitioner as you make changes and dive deeply into nurturing and caring for your physical body.

While completing activities 21–24, you will discover:

- **Activity 21: Optimizing Your Mediation Practice**

- **Activity 22: Hydrating Your Body**

- **Activity 23: Getting Adequate Sleep Regularly**

- **Activity 24: Utilizing Your Sexual Response System**

ACTIVITY 21: OPTIMIZING YOUR MEDITATION PRACTICE

Meditation aids in concentration, peace, mindfulness, and experiencing the present moment. It can help stimulate the parasympathetic nervous system, or "the peaceful state" as Cheryl called it. Deepak Chopra says, "Meditation is not a way of making your mind quiet, it is a way of entering the quiet that is already there. Stop, take three breaths, and smile. To make the right choices in life you have to get in touch with your soul."[6]

Meditation might at first seem daunting and too much to add to your day. But you've already been doing a form of it in breathing before you get out of bed and every time you go to Bermuda! As you focus on your breath, a feeling in your body, an image in your mind's eye, or a simple mantra, you become present in the moment. Prayer is also a form of meditation that you may want to explore, if you haven't already.

There are powerful breathing exercises like "breath of fire" and "alternate nostril breathing" that you can look up on the internet and find a plethora of easy examples to practice.[7] These breathing techniques open up the thought process and quickly clear the mind in preparing for everyday meditation. Building on your morning "just breathe" and going to Bermuda every day will support a solid meditation practice. Final note: If you are new to meditation, be patient with yourself. Try for one minute longer each day.

Discovery Activities

- **Breathe, before you even get out of bed. Do this for at least five minutes today.**

- **What is your number today?** _____

- **List Gratitudes**

  1. _____

  2. _____

  3. _____

- **Write your thoughts.**

  Write about meditation techniques you've used in the past, how you felt, what you experienced, etc. If you've not tried meditation, think of questions you have that you'd like to answer.

  _____

  _____

  _____

  _____

  How would you like to see meditation improve your daily life experience?

  _____

  _____

  _____

  Go to the Internet or the library. Spend time researching mediation in whatever direction you feel your curiosity taking you. Here are a few topics to get you started: *meditation, reduce stress, blood pressure, hypertension, yoga nidra, mantra, sleep meditation.* Take notes about what you learn.

_____

_____

_____

_____

_____

_____

From what you already know, and from the notes you've taken, how would you like to implement a meditation practice into your life?

_____

_____

- **Transfer the above to line 1 of BIO on My Living Blueprint.**

Do you have any reservations or concerns following through with your meditation action plan? If so, what are they? If not, what do you need to do in order to follow through with your plan?

_____

_____

_____

What are three benefits you would like to experience from a daily meditation practice?

1. _____

_____

2. _____

_____

3. _____

_____

How will you ensure your meditation practice is a success?

_____

_____

What obstacles or opportunities may get in the way of you executing your plan to meditate?

_____

_____

How will you overcome these obstacles?

_____

_____

Are you willing to commit to this daily meditation practice?

_ YES

_ NO

Will you track your progress? If so, how?

_____

_____

Would a reminder or alert on your phone help you when it's time to meditate?

_____

- **Be in Bermuda at least 1x today.**

ACTIVITY 22: HYDRATING YOUR BODY

"Mental alertness, staying cool, reducing pain in muscles and joints, preventing constipation, and sweet-smelling breath are just a few of the benefits we receive when we're getting our optimal daily intake of water. In addition to impairing mental and/or physical performance, dehydration may also have detrimental effects on cardiovascular health."[8] Getting hydrated matters!

To support my daily intake of water, I do pre-measuring of my water in a three-gallon jug, and I enjoy using a water decanter on my bathroom sink. Doing this shows me how much water I've drunk on any particular day. I also order heated lemon water before I order my meal when I am dining at a restaurant. Having a pitcher of water next to my bed reminds me to drink both when I wake up and before I go to sleep.

Life gets busy and staying hydrated can get lost in our mountain of responsibilities. Creating routines that become part of our normal, everyday activities makes drinking water a lifestyle choice rather than just another thing we have to do. Do you know how much water you've drunk so far today? What do you need for your biochemistry to be fully hydrated and have the water it needs to function optimally?

Discovery Activities

- **Breathe, before you even get out of bed. Do this for at least five minutes today.**

- **What is your number today?** _____

- **List Gratitudes**

  1. _____

  2. _____

  3. _____

- **Currently, circle the hydration program that you follow.**

  - Fully hydrated, feeling great!

  - I grab a bottle of water a couple times per day.

  - My coffee has water in it, so I'm all good.

  - I'm dying of thirst!

- **Let's learn how much water you need.**

  Everybody is different and there are many theories telling us how much water we need. Spend time searching the Internet, calling a nurse at your doctor's office, or asking your physician exactly how much water your body and its unique needs require. Take notes below.

  _____

  _____

  _____

  _____

  What is the one thing you will do that will support you in being hydrated? What if you drink more water, add electrolytes, and make time to use the restroom more frequently?

  _____

  _____

- Transfer the above to line two of BIO on My Living Blueprint.

  What do you need to do to implement this practice into your daily living? For example, do you have a water bottle? Do you want to measure your water so you're incredibly clear about your consumption?

  _____

  _____

  What will change in your daily routine in order for you to drink the amount of water that *your* specific biochemistry needs?

  _____

  _____

  _____

  _____

  What are three benefits you are seeking as you become fully hydrated?

  1. _____

  2. _____

  3. _____

- **Spend time preparing whatever you need to do in order to implement your hydration plan into your daily routine.**

  What obstacles will get in the way of you executing your plan to hydrate every day?

  _____

  _____

How will you overcome these obstacles?

_____

_____

Are you willing to commit to this daily hydration practice?

_YES

_NO

How will you track your progress?

_____

_____

Will you utilize a visual or auditory reminder? If so, what?

_____

- **Be in Bermuda at least 1x today.**

ACTIVITY 23: GETTING ADEQUATE SLEEP REGULARLY

Like every other element in your Living Blueprint, sleep needs are uniquely yours. Loise, my dear friend, has slowly gone blind over her lifetime. Today, she loves to sleep. She told me once that she especially likes to sleep because at night she can see beautiful colors like the rose-hued couch she once owned and the dark brown earth with green vegetation. When she dreams, she dreams all the things she could see with her vision. Knowing Loise helped me to understand at a deeper level that sleep means something different for everyone, and we all need our unique dose.

For me, realizing I was terminally tired after I went to Cheryl changed my sleep habits. Cheryl helped me to see that I had to slow down and sleep more if I wanted to heal my body. Today, my morning ritual of just breathing before I get out of bed ensures that I check in with my body to see if I am rested. Becoming conscious of our sleep patterns takes time, but it is so worth it in the long run. Being rested feels divine.

Recently, I was listening to a podcast by Dr. Andrew Huberman, a research scientist at Stanford University. He shared that early morning sun exposure helps set a timer in our brain so that sixteen hours later in the day we are ready to go to sleep.[9] After learning this, I have been experimenting with how this works for my Biochemistry.

Changes in our habits do not need to be huge; they just need to be relative to what we as individuals need. Then we need to be consistent in our application. What do you need for better rest?

Discovery Activities

- **Breathe, before you even get out of bed. Do this for at least five minutes today.**

- **What is your number today?** _____

- **List Gratitudes**

    1. _____

    2. _____

    3. _____

    How restful is your sleep? How many hours of sleep do you get every night?

    _____

    _____

How many hours of sleep do you need? Do you know? When you wake, do you feel rested?

_____

_____

List a few incessant distractions that keep you awake at night or wake you in the morning, disrupting your ideal sleep.

_____

What thoughts are keeping you awake at night?

_____

What are the first thoughts that fill your mind in the morning when you wake up?

_____

Write the obstacles you face in getting the sleep you need.

_____

Spend time researching possible solutions to your sleep disruptors. Take notes here.

_____

_____

_____

Ideally, what would a good night's sleep look like for you?

_____

_____

_____

What is the first adjustment you will make in order to get the sleep your body needs to function optimally?

_____

_____

- Transfer the above to line three of BIO on My Living Blueprint.

  How will you overcome obstacles in getting adequate sleep?

  _____

  _____

  Are you willing to commit to making adjustments in order to get adequate sleep?

  _YES

  _ NO

  How will you document your progress? Will you use a sleeping app, a calendar, etc.?

  _____

  _____

- **Be in Bermuda at least 1x today.**

ACTIVITY 24: UTILIZING YOUR SEXUAL RESPONSE SYSTEM

Sexuality is so much more than just having sex. What if we viewed sexuality as a creative energy, a passion, and a yearning to be fully alive–an enthusiasm and zeal toward our own existence and pleasure? Maybe it is a longing to connect with ourselves first and then others. Still, the topic of sex can be confusing and polarizing.

Our families, religion, cultural programming, trauma, and social media often define what sexuality is or isn't for us personally. But you can be abstinent and still be fully alive sexually, utilizing your sexual response system.

Dancing naked alone or with a partner, Kegel exercises, and tantric breathwork are three actionable items that can support your sexual Blueprint. Janell Carrol, author of *Sexuality Now*, a textbook used in human sexuality college curriculums, writes, "Human sexuality is grounded in biological functioning, emerging in each of us as we develop, and is expressed by cultures through rules about sexual contact, attitudes about moral and immoral sexuality, habits of sexual behavior and patterns of relations."[10] Sexuality is a complex interplay of our nature, our nurture, and our decisions.

As I shared in my storytelling so far, my own sexuality was all but erased, crushed into a ball so tiny and dormant it could sit in the tip of my little toe. And even that was contaminated by sexual trauma. That seemed my destiny for years.

But my decisions to study, reprogram, and then practice living what I wanted my sexuality to be and feel like healed me. Today, I accept my bisexual feelings as part of my personality. And, after fifty-five-plus years of experience with my sexuality, I choose to live the Law of Chastity. This has brought peace and protection into my life. For which I am so grateful. You can have clarity and vibrant feelings about your own sexuality too. Be patient; it will take time and healing . . . maybe even years. But you can do it. You were born to experience joy in pleasure.

Discovery Activities

- **Breathe, before you even get out of bed. Do this for at least five minutes today.**

- **What is your number today?** _____

- **List Gratitudes**

    1. _____

    2. _____

    3. _____

- **Circle the five words you associate most with your sexuality:**

    safe sex body shape powerful hanky-panky coupling lovemaking horny sensual trauma lover naughty confidence pair self-pleasure carnality whoopee beautiful shy intercourse smooth breeding dalliance lust mating coition luxurious love dreamy off-limits self-indulgent delightful frigid palatable fleshy bold secret joy hopeful shut down kinky twister candle warm cold

    Look at the five words you circled. What do you notice?

    _____

    _____

    _____

    _____

    On the continuum, where do you experience your sexuality?

    Me 100% |---------------0-------------| *In Relationship 100%*

    Are you dealing with sexual trauma from your past? If so, how is that going?

    _____

    _____

Do you enjoy looking at your body? Are you comfortable with others looking at your body?

_____

_____

_____

In your opinion, what is the purpose of the sexual response system?

_____

_____

Have you ever danced naked in front of a mirror, pleasured your body in gratitude, or given yourself a foot massage? What was your experience?

_____

_____

Write about anything or any time when you feel fully alive sexually.

_____

_____

_____

What were the attributes of these moments? Were they loving, hot, safe, primal, peaceful, etc.?

_____

_____

_____

What is your personal definition of sexual pleasure?

_____

_____

How can you best utilize your sexual response system in bringing more pleasure into all aspects of your life?

_____

_____

_____

_____

What is one thing that you would like to see yourself more fully embrace when it comes to utilizing your sexual response system? Spend time researching. Take notes here.

_____

_____

_____

_____

_____

In one sentence, what is the #1 thing you would like to do in order to utilize your sexual response system toward your happiness?

_____

_____

- **Transfer the above to line four of BIO on My Living Blueprint.**

- **Will you commit to doing the #1 thing to nurture your sexuality?**

  _YES

  _NO

  What obstacles do you foresee in following through with your sexuality blueprint plan? How will you overcome them?

  _____

  _____

  Is there any preparatory work to be done in order to follow your plan?

  _____

  _____

- **Be in Bermuda at least 1x today.**

Documenting what you already know, researching how to nurture your specific needs, then making a commitment to live what you know, even if it's as simple as walking one hundred more steps than yesterday, will change your life. You can do it. And you can keep doing it every day!

Remember to not compare yourself to anyone else. Deleting the program of comparison will free up valuable time and allow you to honor your unique body by giving it what it needs based on WHO you are, what you want, and where you are going in your life.

Take time to create space that is conducive to your goals. For example, if your body needs fourteen cups of water per day, help yourself toward success. Get a gallon jug and measure your water out every morning. Keep your jug in your line of vision all day long. Then record your success at night. If you can see your water, you are much likelier to drink.

The Yes/No question at the conclusion of each activity is like a switch you are flipping in your brain. Commitment to your intention of nurturing your Biochemistry means ambiguity and floating around in the minutiae of your daily life slowly disappears. Self-mastery, not perfectionism, and a healthy body are in the making.

CHAPTER 7 NURTURING YOUR BODY'S BIOCHEMISTRY

widening the gap
between a stimulus and
response is power

Architecting the life we deeply desire is a natural and an innate tendency; even as children, we build and construct things that interest us from our imaginations. Nurturing your body by living from your BIO Blueprint can help you move forward with strength and resilience to make decisions that will create the life you want. One step at a time, you can do it!

If you feel overstressed and paralyzed from a mountain of "to-dos" or maybe even from the trauma you've survived, you're not alone in feeling debilitated. Life can be so hard. But guess what? Your brain and your body have the power to get past all that. It knows your Blueprint of wholeness already–it's wired inside of you.

Still, there's a gap between what we know and what we do. A space where our agency comes into play and where any stimulus meets our response. Being present in order to make conscious choices to nurture your Biochemistry from moment to moment is one the best things I know for widening that gap so we don't go into immediate-and sometimes unwanted-reactions to current circumstances. Widening the gap is personal power.

―――――――――――――――――――――

Out of the clear blue sky my mother called and told me a family member wanted to talk with me. Spencer was out of town at the time and I was ecstatic to hear from this particular relative. Intrigued, I sat down on the living room sofa as we began our conversation. Ever so quietly, as if someone might hear him, he began to share. I was completely unprepared for what happened next.

Memories from his childhood and his teenage years began to spill from his pained soul. Sentences I could barely hear with my ears and mentally could not fully comprehend with my mind dropped like the anchor of a ship on a turbulent sea. My heart followed.

He relayed sexual exploits that had happened not only to him but by him. He told me that he had told his mother some of what he was telling me. "Was there penetration" was her only response. My brain shifted like the plates of earth under the ocean floor as he shared graphic, sexual details specific to individuals he had witnessed or been a party to growing up.

As he spoke, my brain grappled to stay present. What was happening? *Is this true? Is he lying? Is he crazy?* After the letter I'd written to our family member, a decade prior, I'd worked hard to put all my own memories in an imaginary box on a shelf, trusting that Jesus was holding them for me, which He was. With one conversation, the pandora's box busted open.

Later that night after my children were asleep, still dazed, I naively picked up the phone and called several other family members implicated in our conversation. Asking them specific questions about what had been shared with me, they began to relay the same or similar details and unknowingly, added more particulars to the menagerie of information I was already processing.

Swirling in my mind were the images of my own rape and molestation added to all that I had learned that day from four different conversations. The puzzle Chaplin had painstakingly attempted to fit together for me, many years before, and this new information crashed into place. A sinewy web of lascivious sex acts, over decades, and throughout generations came into focus. I was sick.

Subsequent phone calls with other close and distant relatives revealed that at least four generations had been infected with incest as well as additional sexual abuse from individuals outside our family line. Not only had I been sexually assaulted, but many others had been sexually assaulted as well, and no one, not one single solitary person, prior to my phone call had acknowledged what had happened to me, to them, or to our family. Individuals and couples had ignored, pretended, or straight up lied for my entire life about sexual misconduct, then called me a liar or cut me out of their life when I brought it up in the sent letter.

The next morning before five a.m., I woke up with a dark, heavy cloud crushing my chest. I couldn't breathe. I begged Jesus to lift it from me. Immediately, the darkness hovered six inches above my body. I could breathe! I bolted to my closet, put a dress on as quickly as I could, then ran downstairs for my car keys. After writing a note for the children explaining that I would be home by noon and instructing my teenager to make breakfast, I drove straight to the Spokane Washington Temple, a thirty-minute drive from my home. Once I arrived, I jumped from my car and ran through the double doors. Inside, I felt safe.

While in the temple, my mind slowed down and the sticky, slimy truth that I was born into a generational incestuous family became crystal clear. Contemplating the absence of love in actions from humans spanning decades that had hurt countless lives infuriated me. There were lies upon lies that had been told to protect other lies.

Other people's choices had all but destroyed my sexuality early in childhood. The plague that had affected our family felt one thousand times more common than I'd ever known. As I proceeded through the temple ceremony, the befouled weight that I had carried into the temple washed off my soul like a car slowly moving through a carwash. The images in my mind dissipated and I breathed freely and deeply. As I sat in the temple, I felt God's love for me and for the perpetrators. I could not deny that they too had once been victims. [1]

Orlo's words the winter after my attempted suicide came back to mind: "Ye shall know the truth and the truth shall set you free." *Had she known?* I didn't know.

The gift of the revelations, the conversations, and the memories shared was that I finally knew the truth. Once and for all, I knew I wasn't crazy. In fact, I was completely sane and alive by the grace of God.

Creating a safe space in the woods as a young girl had been instinctive, then protecting my own children had been the same. Now I understood why I'd been so hyperattentive, not allowing my children to have sleepovers at friend's houses, teaching them about conscious sexual choices, and giving them a structure in religion they could hang onto, no matter what. Nurturing was the heart of who I was. Being their vigilant protector was the role that was forced upon me. Over time, my heart healed another deep layer. Mostly.

My roles as wife and mother stabilized me. Creating our family's homestead filled the minutes, hours, and days as I learned to live with the knowledge of my family's disease. With time, more secrets were uncovered from additional family members, offering more opportunity for healing. More than once I wondered, *will this ever end?*

Spencer and I had just recently purchased my dream home. Grinding my own grain, making sourdough bread, preparing large family meals, and working in my gardens brought feelings of gratification and pride. Tulips, daffodils, roses, peonies, daylilies, and a cornucopia of other flowers bloomed throughout the spring and summer. To our plum trees and Asian apple trees, we added blackberry bushes, raspberry bushes, and a massive vegetable garden.

Fresh lilacs, from the gardens, placed in small vases in the bathrooms and the kitchen filled our home with their sweet fragrance, making it even more a place of respite and comfort. The children all decorated their rooms with their own tastes and colors and the big family room turned into the TV room. My mornings became a walking meditation followed by my yoga practice. I was happier than I'd ever been in my life, even with the knowledge I now lived with every second of every day.

Consciously choosing to create my life and moving in the direction that I wanted to go did not erase the truth that I was a victim of incest and multiple assaults. Nor did it take away the fact that I had been born into a family infected with systematic sexual dysfunction. However, using my agency to find healing for my mind, heart, and body was the antidote. It was up to me to live in love, no matter what! And I did!

Two years later, Spencer approached me and said, "I've got the opportunity of a lifetime. Wendy, I think I figured out a way to buy the farm." He was talking about the lovely farm upon which he'd worked as their business manager for the past six years. "All I need is two investors and the bank will loan us the rest of the money we need." He wanted the deal so bad he could taste it! I wanted it for him.

The deal would include growing, harvesting, packing, then selling 1300 acres of onions, peppers, cucumbers, asparagus, and a bit of winter wheat. Spencer was the financial mastermind of the deal. His partners were the growers. With their experience in the fields growing the crops and Spencer's knowledge in the office, he felt confident they would be successful. He had a five-year plan, then he'd retire.

The deal took six months and it was tenuous, but he got it done and we moved our family to Granger, Washington, smack dab in the middle of farming operations. I missed my dream home, but the new farm home was a beautiful place to live. The home was already in place and included a large farm-style kitchen, a patio, a fenced yard, and an indoor pool with a diving board. Amid the dust from all the farming trucks, it was an oasis for our family.

Owning the farm was very different from creating our little homestead. I had nothing to do with operations and often felt trapped in a life I hadn't really understood in following Spencer toward his dream in buying the farm. Mornings, before anyone else woke up, I meditated and swam naked in the pool, twisting and turning in the watery blue abyss. Being in water as the sun came up every morning gave me an extra feeling of freedom in a place where I wasn't sure I belonged.

Nineteen years of preparation had gone into Spencer finally owning his own business. And, after so many years of Spencer traveling, we were all together again. We played in the pool, built fires by the Yakima river, and spent copious time together as a family. We had our family photos taken in our asparagus fields gone to seed. I began to relax.

One night my baby brother Johnny called me in the middle of the night. He'd been drinking and told me he just needed someone to talk to. He was gay and said he felt close to me because of my relationship with Sage. He said, "You understood how I feel, sister. I'm so sorry, Wendy. I'm sorry. I wish I was a better brother. I wish I was a better uncle." He said this over and over again on the phone until he passed out. He often dealt with suicidal thoughts and shared those with me too. We talked about going to London when my children were raised, and he was finished with hair school. We had a plan!

While at the farm, after years of practicing yoga alone, I was overjoyed that my youngest child Huxley wanted to practice with me. "Mom, can I do yoga with you? I found a yoga app I think you'll like."

It wasn't until I began practicing with my child every day that I realized in fifteen years of a home yoga practice I'd never allowed myself time for *savasana* at the end of my practice–a time of quiet relaxation and reflection typically part of the very end of a yoga practice. After that, I never missed *savasana* again. [2]

At the end of our second year's growing season, Spencer came to me, somber. "We lost two million dollars in the pepper crop," he admitted, his face screwed up in pain. "I have been trying to figure out how to tell you."

My stomach dropped, then began to tighten as I looked deeper into my husband's eyes. "Oh, Spencer, I'm so sorry. Do your partners know?"

"No, I wanted to tell you first. I've been trying to figure some way out of the hole we're in and I'm still working on it. I just needed you to know what the numbers look like so far." He was devastated.

Traveling for Christmas that year was a conscious choice as a way to get away from the stress of what was happening at the farm. However, to add insult to injury, I fell while snowboarding. Seeing stars, I asked the ski patrol to take me down the mountain. I had a concussion. Spencer took me home.

The next few weeks I spent in a darkened room being waited on by my family. As I lay in bed, Spencer would tell me what was happening at the farm. Slowly, we learned that it had been an incredibly hot summer and pepper crops up and down the state had burned up. As hard as he tried, losing two million dollars was catastrophic to the business deal with our partners. The bank assigned a consultant to work with Spencer and they transitioned him and me out of ownership.

Three months later, as my brain injury was still healing, I watched Spencer graciously work with the bank as his dream of owning his own business slowly slipped through his fingers. His concern for our oldest son, an employee at the farm, counting on money from his job to prepare him for the next school year, was noble. I witnessed that even in his deep pain, he was making sure that not only our child, but all his employees were taken care of during the transition. My heart ached for him.

He and I had been through so much, so many battles in twenty years that no one saw. "Do you want to start a new business?" I asked. "Maybe I should go back to school and get my PhD?" We talked about traveling overseas. We didn't have answers, but we were open to whatever was best for our family.

Usually, I wouldn't have let anyone know about my pain, but losing the farm was too big to hide. Everyone in our life knew what was happening. Myra Faye, a friend dying of cancer, gave us gifts she didn't realize she was giving. The last few days of her life I had the beautiful opportunity to sit at her bedside with her family. As her physical body slowly shut down, I felt her spirit rise. Who she was, her infinite self, filled the immensity of space in her bedroom. In those moments, I basked in the love that she was and that I had felt when she was fully alive in the physical realm.

Losing millions of dollars seemed inconsequential when compared to a family losing their mother. Her love and who she was palatable.

Her son had flown in from another state and we grew to know each other at her deathbed. In our quiet conversation, I shared with him what was happening in our family and with our farm. He offered to help my husband look into a training program for administrators in the skilled nursing field in which he was a leader.[3] I shared this information with Spencer and conversations ensued. Within a short time, Spencer decided that Utah was the best place for him to begin his new career. I wasn't sure why, but Utah felt absolutely like the right choice to me as well.

Spencer and I planned a white water rafting trip down the Deschutes River for our family.[4] Rhodes had fallen in love and married his sweetheart, Emberly. We were excited to spend quality time together with all of our children and bond as a family in such a stressful time of life. We made dinner reservations at a beautiful mountain-top restaurant the night before our river run.

As we made our way along the mountain roads, an overcast evening enveloped the fog hovering in the valley. The yellow lights of the lodge gave off a romantic glow. Looking over the valley, my body felt strong, my heart was full, and my mind was clear. I was on top of the world, even as our financial world was crumbling.

The next morning, all of us jumped into the transport, towing the rafts behind us in order to put in upriver. Our river guides were capable and jovial as they guided us into our boat. Together, we rode Wapinitia, Box Car, and Surf City class three and four rapids. We dove in and out of rapids, digging in when our guide called for us to do so and resting when he yelled for us to stop. Splashing water at each other, we laughed and played all day long in the warm, Washington sun.

The truth was with all our shortcomings in our relationship, Spencer and I were still successfully navigating one of the biggest losses in our lives together. And although everything was absolutely not perfect, our family together was perfect.

Not unlike the rapids and the undercurrents of the river, our life was swirling with unseen pain, trauma, and turbulence that no one else could see. Years of learning and healing had gone into being together at that moment. The heaves, crashes, and swells of the river easily could have collapsed our raft. But the expert guides versed in navigating the hidden rocks were guiding our adventure just like my Personal Guidance System was guiding me. Working as a team created a marvelous moment in time and a fun adventure.

That day we rode the rapids of the Deschutes river the same way we were navigating life– as a family with guts and gusto! I had no idea what was next, but whatever was coming, I knew my mind, my body, and most importantly, my heart was up for the task.

True Principles For Your Biochemistry Blueprint:

- **Fulfilling your nutritional needs is a form of self-love.** Creating a diet that is balanced with proteins, fats, carbohydrates, vitamins, and minerals will help your body from the inside out.

- Moving your body changes your state of mind. **Exercise is one of the most important factors in supporting and improving your brain function and well-being.**

- Laughter activates and relieves stress response. What makes you laugh at the drop of a hat? **Laughter enhances your intake of oxygen-rich air, stimulates your heart, lungs, and muscles, and increases the endorphins that are released by your brain.**

- Did you know that people who feel connected to others are happier and experience a sense of belonging? **Social connections can lighten your mood and make you feel happier.** Humans are designed for connection and social interaction is good for your brain.

While completing activities 25–28, you will discover:

- **Activity 25: Fulfilling Your Nutritional Needs**

- **Activity 26: Activating Daily Movement and Exercise**

- **Activity 27: Exploring Friendship and Social Connection**

- **Activity 28: Enjoying Life and Laughing Every Day**

ACTIVITY 25: FULFILLING YOUR NUTRITIONAL NEEDS

Food, like the oxygen we breathe and the water we drink, is essential for our survival. And, like both, when contaminated or consumed incorrectly, can be harmful. We would never consider drinking an entire shiny, new, horse trough full of ice-cold water. Nor would we consciously spend time outside breathing toxic and polluted air.

Yet, everyday many of us eat food that is damaging to our bodies and detrimental to our well-being, often unconsciously. Dr. Daniel G. Amen, author of *Change Your Brain, Change Your Life* and a leading neuroscientist in the United States has said, "Food is a powerful drug. You can use it to help mood and cognitive ability or you can unknowingly make things worse."[5] Stopping before you put even one bite of food in your mouth and asking yourself, *"Is this beneficial or harmful to my well-being?"* is a good start in becoming conscious of your personal eating habits and whether or not you are meeting your nutritional needs. Slowing down when eating is a great second step to mindfully creating a successful eating plan.

Supplementation is not always necessary. But if you need more nutrients than your food can provide or if you want to supplement for any reason, please, please inform yourself. All supplements are not created equal. Many are known to be low quality and full of fillers. Take the time to know what you are putting in your body as well as its source.

Circumstances, family traditions, economic situations, what is taught in the public schools we grow up in, and our health care system typically don't support the best health practices in fueling our bodies with nutrient-dense calories. Today, that becomes only part of your story. Now, as a conscious adult, it's time for you to take control of what nutrients you are putting in your body.

Food, like air and water, is our direct connection with our environment. These three things bring what is around you inside of you and fuel your biochemistry, ultimately propelling your level of energy, clarity, satisfaction, and well-being. Eat well to live well!

Discovery Activities

- **Breathe, before you even get out of bed. Do this for at least five minutes today.**

- **What is your number today?** _____

- **List Gratitudes**

    1. _____

    2. _____

    3. _____

- **Set up an appointment to spend thirty-sixty minutes with a success partner for Activity 27.**

- **Write your thoughts.**

What does "live to eat" mean to you?

_____

_____

_____

What does "eat to live" mean to you?

_____

_____

_____

When thinking about food, how would you define your relationship? "Live to eat" or "eat to live"? What makes you think what you wrote?

_____

_____

_____

_____

As a child, what were your family's eating practices on a typical day? Fast food? Family dinner around the table?

_____

_____

_____

Today, what are your daily eating practices? Planned, grab and go, or peaceful, sit-down meals?

_____

_____

Ideally, what would your daily eating practices look like? Write out what you would like your diet to consist of.

_____

_____

_____

_____

_____

Ideally, what would you like your daily eating plan to look like? Draw a picture here.

Do you have any issues with food? Do you eat too much? Do you eat too little? If yes, do you know why? Have you addressed the underlying reason why or why not?

_____

_____

_____

_____

What information do you need in order to be able to implement the above improvement into your daily nutrition routine? Spend time researching what you want. Take notes here.

_____

_____

_____

_____

_____

_____

How much money do you budget each month for food and supplements? Do you need more or less? Is the above amount enough for your needs? Do you spend too much or not enough?

_____

_____

_____

_____

Are there supplements that would fill nutritional gaps? What do you want to add or subtract to your daily routine?

_____

_____

_____

_____

Are you currently engaged in a practice of preparing and enjoying nutrient-rich food? If so, what does that look like and what is one improvement you want to make? If not, what would your ideal food plan and prep look like?

_____

_____

_____

_____

What obstacles will get in the way of you feeding your body nutrient-rich food and supplements every day?

_____

_____

How will you overcome these obstacles?

_____

_____

Define in one sentence the #1 thing you want to improve upon regarding your nutritional intake.

_____

_____

- **Transfer the above to line five of BIO on My Living Blueprint.**

  Are you willing to commit to your #1 change in your nutrition practice?

  _YES

  _NO

  How will you track your progress?

_____

_____

What preparation do you need in order to follow through with your goal?

_____

_____

_____

- **Be in Bermuda at least 1x today.**

ACTIVITY 26: ACTIVATING YOUR DAILY MOVEMENT AND EXERCISE

What do you love to do that gets your body moving? Swimming, hiking in the mountains, yoga in a studio, or playing basketball at the gym? In my humble opinion, what you do is less important than enjoying yourself while you do it! Why? Because, if you enjoy doing something, if you are excited to do it, then you're much more likely to continue doing it! Moving your body matters. In many cases, you can even change or elevate your mood.

Walking is one of the greatest tools I have used to deal with my anxiety, depression, and destructive thought patterns. Getting out of bed and going outside clears my mind, energizes my body, and opens my heart. Smelling the fresh morning air, seeing the vibrant or not so vibrant vegetation, and listening to the sounds of nature, traffic, and other people talking stimulate my senses. I can't think of a single time in thirty-plus years of walking to exercise that I didn't feel better when I returned from my walk than before I left.

President John F. Kennedy made an observation, "Physical fitness is not only one of the most important keys to a healthy body, it is the basis of dynamic and creative intellectual activity. Our growing softness, our increasing lack of physical fitness, is a menace to our security." [6]

Discovery Activities

- **Breathe, before you even get out of bed. Do this for at least five minutes today.**

- **What is your number today?** _____

- **List Gratitudes**

  1. _____

  2. _____

  3. _____

- **Brainstorm.**

  Write down all your favorite ways to move your body.

  _____

  _____

  _____

  Write any and all ideas that would improve your body movement that you haven't tried but would like to.

  _____

  _____

  _____

  What stops you from trying these new activities?

  _____

_____

_____

Consider what you want your body to feel like in one year. What are the things you need to be doing today to have your body feel the way you want it to feel as you age?

_____

_____

_____

What is the one thing that you believe would be the most beneficial in activating a body movement program?

_____

_____

_____

Spend time researching the thing you want to improve upon. Write your findings here.

_____

_____

_____

_____

- **Let's discover what may be sabotaging your exercise success.**

  Write down the #1 obstacle that impedes you from moving your body and exercising toward your fitness goals. Is it time? Is it a scheduling issue? Are you in pain?

_____

_____

Hold that thought. Spend one minute centering yourself and getting very quiet.

Now ask: _Why am I letting this obstacle stop me?_ Listen. Just wait. The answer is within you. Just write down the answer that comes to your conscious thought.

_____

_____

Now ask: _What do I need to do in order to correct this and move through the obstacle?_

_____

_____

Looking at the above answer, what will change as you give yourself what you are asking for?

_____

_____

_____

Do you have any physical limitations holding you back? If so, what can you do to modify your plan that's effective and still stretches your vision toward a fit, strong, healthy body?

_____

_____

Write your #1 measurable, actionable step that you will do to begin your body movement exercise practice.

_____

_____

- **Transfer the above to line six of BIO on My Living Blueprint.**

  Write down what you will do when you come up against ANY obstacle in moving your body and exercising.

  _____

  _____

- **Remember: make sure your plan is sizable enough that it challenges you only as far as you can be consistent in its application.**

  Will you commit to making the necessary changes to move your body in a way that will support you being healthy?

  _YES

  _NO

  How will you document your progress?

  _____

  _____

  What visual or auditory reminder will you use every day?

  _____

- **Be in Bermuda at least 1x today.**

ACTIVITY 27: EXPLORING FRIENDSHIP AND SOCIAL CONNECTION

We are hardwired to connect with others, even if you're an introvert like me. Susan M. Johnson, family psychologist of the year in 2016 said, "Having a positive sense of connection with others is the best, and perhaps the only, viable way of helping human beings find a place called 'safe and sound.'"[7] We all need social connections.

Still, if our past connections have been painful or trauma-filled, it can be difficult if not impossible to trust others or reach out and really connect, especially when we are feeling vulnerable or not our best selves. I know things happen in life that cause us to not feel safe or even want to be with others. But all of that can be reprogrammed and overcome in time. I promise! Today, let's spend time with one of your success partners either in person or on the phone and see what you notice when it comes to connecting with others.

Discovery Activities

- **Breathe, before you even get out of bed. Do this for at least five minutes today.**

- **What is your number today?** _____

- **List Gratitudes**

  1. _____

  2. _____

  3. _____

- **Spend time with a friend or close associate, ideally in person,**

  Practice the following exercises:

First, share with each other the two worst things that happened during that week.

Next, share with each other the three best things that happened in your week.

And lastly, share with each other one thing you appreciate about the other person and one thing you appreciate about yourselves.

Continue the conversation naturally.

If in person or on video, sit quietly across from each other, and for one minute look into each other's eyes. Say nothing. Just be present with each other. See what you feel. Then simply share what you notice with each other.

Thank your success partner for their time.

- **What did you notice:**

about your connection from when you first began the exercise and when you completed the exercise?

_____

_____

regarding your ability to feel safe, be honest, and vulnerable?

_____

_____

when it came to being true to yourself, were you?

_____

_____

What would you like to see change in your social connections?

_____

_____

Do you have too many friends or too few?

_____

_____

What are your ideal amounts of social interactions? What would improve in your life if you had your ideal amount of social connection?

_____

_____

_____

What is the #1 thing you are willing to put into action regarding having the social connections and friendships you desire?

_____

_____

- Transfer the above to line seven of BIO on My Living Blueprint.

  Will you commit to doing the #1 thing to enjoy balanced social connections?

  _YES

  _NO

  What obstacles do you need to be aware of in cultivating friendships and nurturing social connection and how will you overcome them?

  _____

_____

_____

- **Be in Bermuda at least 1x today.**

ACTIVITY 28: ENJOYING LIFE AND LAUGHING EVERY DAY

When was the last time you had a really great belly laugh? What makes you laugh till you cry? You've heard the saying, "laughter is the best medicine." Well, this story from 1964 shows that choosing laughter has a significant effect in our lives.

"A doctor by the name of Norman Cousins was diagnosed with a degenerative disease. He was in constant pain and was given a poor prognosis of only a few months to live. With his strong beliefs in the power of human emotions and his dire prognosis, Cousins decided to take his treatment into his own hands. Along with his treatments, he watched humorous movies and television shows to induce laughter consistently. His laughter markedly reduced his pain . . . Cousins' humor-induced treatment saved his life and allowed him to live and prosper for nearly twenty-five additional years."[8]

Your sense of humor is unique, and figuring out what makes you laugh is part of the fun! Did you know that January 24 is Global Belly Laugh Day? It was established in 2005 by a yoga teacher, Elaine Helle. Mark Twain once said, "Humanity has unquestionably one really effective weapon—laughter. Power, money, persuasion, supplication, persecution—these can lift at a colossal humbug—push it a little—weaken it a little, century by century, but only laughter can blow it to rags and atoms at a blast. Against the assault of laughter nothing can stand." Take time today to laugh!

Discovery Activities

- **Breathe, before you even get out of bed. Do this for at least five minutes today.**

- **What is your number today?** _____

- **List Gratitudes**

  1. _____

  2. _____

  3. _____

- **Choose one of the following:**

  o **Watch a funny movie**

  o **Read funny memes**

  o **Talk to a friend who makes you laugh**

  o **Listen to a comic**

  o **Talk to a small child**

  Specifically, what was it that made you laugh?

  _____

  _____

  In your life, what makes you laugh on a consistent basis?

  _____

  _____

As a child, what made you laugh? Write down a specific time when you couldn't stop laughing.

_____

_____

What positive effects do you imagine you would experience if you spent time laughing and enjoying your life every day?

_____

_____

_____

What simple activities bring enjoyment and laughter into your daily life?

_____

_____

Have you ever laughed, even when you were sad? What did that experience *feel* like?

_____

_____

What happened in the moment that made your state change from sadness to laughter?

_____

_____

What do you want to incorporate into your day that will support you in laughing each and every day?

_____

_____

What obstacles get in the way and stop you from laughing every day?

_____

What is the #1 thing you can do to keep laughing, everyday?

_____

- Transfer the above to line eight of BIO on My Living Blueprint.

  Will you commit to enjoying a bit of laughter each and every day?

  _YES

  _NO

  Find a joke or a comic that makes you laugh. Either draw it or Print it off and paste it here.

  _____
  | |
  | |
  | |
  | |
  | |
  | |
  | |
  | |
  | |
  |_____|

- **Be in Bermuda at least 1x today.**

Obstacles are opportunities to better understand your relationship with yourself, your Source of Inspiration, and the world around you, especially when it comes to your BIOchemistry. For example, if you continually sabotage goals, you might want to ask yourself why. Maybe you're picking activities you don't actually enjoy. Maybe you're following someone else's plan instead of listening to your own wisdom.

Consistently exploring your thoughts and feelings regarding your specific changing biochemical needs and then making a commitment to your plan every day will bring positive results over time.

Part of our Biochemistry's job is to protect us. If you're feeling stuck, maybe thank your brain for doing its job in safeguarding you. Perhaps, it's giving you time to think of more options and help you make better decisions that will benefit you in the long run. Remember, there may be more options than you can see at the moment.

You have systems and chemical reactions embedded within to help you move out feeling stuck and in paralysis, heal physical *and* emotional wounds, feel peace, and experience pleasure. Your body naturally produces serotonin, oxytocin, endorphins, and dopamine for your well-being and joy. You were born to succeed.

STEP 4 –TRU BLUEPRINT

CHAPTER 8 LEARNING WHAT AUTHENTICITY MEANS

suffering is born
in fraud and dishonesty
peace abides in truth

Alive, the fire inside of you is ignited. You've taken the challenge to move your life in a dramatically new and powerful way. Commitment to living from your Blueprint is showing up in the choices you are making and in the healing and learning you are experiencing. Let's keep going.

Have you ever noticed the imaginary "truth-telling line" inside yourself? We all have one. On one side of this line is what we share with others. These are the thoughts, feelings, ideas, and parts of ourselves that we feel safe enough to be completely honest about. And then on the other side of that "truth-telling line" are those things we keep hidden to ourselves. These, we tell no one.

Until now.

Element number four is TRU. It stands for Tell the Truth and Be Authentic. Bessel van der Kolk in the book, *The Body Keeps Score*, says, "As long as you keep secrets and suppress information, you are fundamentally at war with yourself...The critical issue is allowing yourself to know what you know. That takes an enormous amount of courage."[1] I know from my own experience that this is 100 percent true.

Ignoring something we know to be true, perpetually breaking promises, private toxic relationships, or not talking about something that we think others would look down at us for can stop us from moving forward and creating the life we want. According to the CDC, self-harm thoughts and acting on those thoughts is a secret millions of people deal with every day.[2] Do you have self-harm thoughts? Do you know anyone who does? Telling the truth can affect our life in a dramatic and positive way.

Bringing to light what we've buried in the deepest parts of ourselves can actually act as a stepping stone toward profound personal progress. Energy used to keep secrets, hide failures, and ignore addictions or other problems can be used to heal and overcome adversity. It certainly was the first step for me. Being honest no matter what allows me to overcome the biggest obstacle of my life (fear), over and over again.

Things we think we can't talk about, that we keep buried inside, and are afraid to share are like cancer. In time, they grow destructive, hard to control, and lethal. If you believe a thought, a memory, or a feeling can't be shared, I invite you to ask yourself, why? Brené Brown says, "If you trade your authenticity for safety, you may experience the following: anxiety, depression, eating disorders, addiction, rage, blame, resentment, and inexplicable grief."[3] For me, peace has been the by-product of telling the whole truth and being authentic no matter what the consequences.

Telling the truth and acknowledging who you are and what you want, then actively taking accountability for your decisions in order to achieve your desires leaves nowhere else for the results of your choices to land except on you. Which is exactly where they belong because as adults we are accountable for our lives.

Merriam-Webster's simple definition of authenticity is the ability of an individual to act according to one's personality, spirit, or character, to be true, not false or imitating.[4] Being authentic doesn't mean being a jerk; it means not pretending. It means being 100 percent honest with yourself first, then others.

How will you know if you are telling the truth in the deepest parts of you and living an authentic life? In my fifty-five years of life experience, what I have noticed is that a person living authentically experiences peace, especially when circumstances are not ideal. This includes peace for themselves, and peace toward others, especially amid differences. When we are 100 percent honest with ourselves, the battle within ceases. Peace abides those who tell the truth and live an authentic life.

Losing the farm was too painful for Spencer to discuss. Once leaving Washington, we just moved on, renting a home in Orem, Utah. With our children now in college and high school, I enrolled in BYU Pathways, a three-semester, higher education program designed for non-traditional students. At its completion, I enrolled in the Art Illustration and Design program at Utah Valley University.

Spencer became an administrator in training, learning how to manage skilled nursing facilities. A job in another state was offered even before he finished his AIT training. After over twenty-two moves, three homes, and one multi-million dollar farm deal gone bad all in twenty-three years of marriage, I found I couldn't relocate again.

"No, I'm sorry," I said to him. "I cannot move our children once more. They just got settled. It's too much for them."

For the first time in twenty-three years, I set a boundary. I did not support something Spencer wanted to pursue in his career. Alone, he proceeded to secure his job, and then left for Iowa. Weeks would go by without him talking to our children. "Please call them. They need you," became my daily plea.

The summer after Spencer left, he and I planned to meet on the Oregon Coast in Neskowin.[5] Spending time as a family and enjoying our first grandchild together was important to both of us. We both loved our family dearly.

Becoming a grandmother was an unforeseen gift of parenthood I'd not truly understood until I held the newest member of our family in my arms.

Holding him, I forgot about all the pain in my marriage. Everything about my first grandson brought joy into my heart amid the storms of life. He was absolute joy and perfection.

At the ocean, Spencer and I barely spoke. As husband and wife, we were strangers in our own family. After a week of sun-filled beach time, nightly fires, digging holes in the sand, and cuddling our new grandson, we prepared to leave. While packing the car, I felt inspired to visit my baby brother Johnny in Seattle. I wanted him to know my children. The fact that he was gay did not deter me; I wanted them to know my baby brother and love him unconditionally, as I did.

The sun was setting over Elliott Bay when I arrived with my three youngest children. The golden hour light painted our faces as we walked our dogs to a park on Capitol Hill. Holding the gate open so that we could all enter first, my baby brother followed up in his gentle yet regal way. He carried himself like a prince.

We headed to his favorite Mexican restaurant. His manners in making eye contact and smiling at the hostess made me feel connected to my brother. He knew how to treat people with respect. Later, we all enjoyed a café devoted solely to chocolate. And even though they burned our s'mores, time together with my little brother felt euphoric. Johnny and I giggled as his male cocker spaniel tried to hump our male Labrador. We saw the situation as hopelessly, humorously ironic.

Returning home, already in college full time, I began selling a product for a multi-level marketing company in order to help myself become financially self-reliant. A potential client showed interest in my product. After a long telephone conversation, he asked, "Why are you with a man who would choose to live away from you? Why do you not value yourself more?"

"We just have a really hard time in our marriage," I replied defensively. "I love him and I want our family to be together. Everything I've done since becoming a mother has been to create a happy family."

"Well, he's living in Iowa and you're here, raising your boys by yourself. Doesn't seem like a happy family to me!"

Inwardly, I cringed.

Our telephone conversations continued for several weeks. The man would ask me the simplest questions. "What did you eat for breakfast today?" Or, "How are your children?" His inquiries were not monumental, but he seemed to care about us. I felt *seen* and valued. He adored his own children. Turmoil in my mind and heart ensued the more we conversed.

Lying to Spencer by not telling him what I was experiencing with another man felt wrong in the deepest part of my soul. Even though my connection was over phone calls, every conversation felt contaminated even as it was feeding the pit of loneliness in my heart. The peace I'd felt in my own soul, even as the turbulence with extended family and in my marriage raged for so many years, slowly faded and was replaced by an even deeper level of sadness. Being dishonest with my husband was unbearable.

Gripping my phone with one hand and touching my belly with the other, I shared with Spencer my emotional connection with another man. I assured him that our connection was never physical. Even so, he was hurt and furious. For several weeks, we discussed the issue only because I didn't know how to give up my other connection. Finally, exasperated Spencer gave me an ultimatum, "If you ever talk to him again, I will divorce you!"

Breaking up my family was not an option. Our conversations ended and the loneliness I felt in not being validated every day by another person consumed me like a black hole. Breathing was laborious.

That month, out of the blue, I was invited to a four-day relationship workshop for individuals and couples. Normally, I would've declined because of the time it meant away from my children, but under the circumstances, the invitation felt serendipitous. Upon arriving, the space, though in dire need of updating, felt warm and inviting. "The Rose" was being played over the speaker, reminding me of my mother and her beautiful singing voice.

A polished assistant in a bright colored shirt sitting in a director's chair by the front door surprised me with how sad he looked when I first saw him. As the night progressed, Nick and I became friends quickly. He shared with me that he was happily married and that he adored his four children. His eyes lit up as he talked about his beautiful wife. I ached to create a relationship like his.

During one of the small group sessions after sharing some of my story with Nick, he said, "Wendy, the best thing you can give your children is to show them how to be happy by actually being happy yourself." Nick didn't pull any punches. "You remind me of my mom. I understand her better after hearing your story."

That night, Nick became my cheerleader. Some of the most loving people I'd ever met attended that workshop and I learned something about self-love I'd never thought of before.

Expecting someone to fill my heart when I didn't love myself was never going to make me happy. I'd known for years that Jesus loved me, but I'd spent most of my life with an undercurrent of self-loathing, never believing that I was good enough, needing others to validate not only my existence, but my self-worth. I left that workshop understanding that feeling seen and loved was my responsibility.

Loving me meant treating myself the way I wanted to be treated by others, the way I treated my children. Learning to say no when others wanted something from me and spending more quality time with myself were actions I began to practice consistently after the workshop was over. Overcoming my tendency to follow thoughts of being bad, less-than, evil, ugly, and unworthy continued at a whole new level.

The most important thing I learned how to do was to turn inward every single time I sought validation from an outside source or another person. Looking outside myself for love became my cue to turn inward for the love I was seeking. And I was diligent in my endeavor. I didn't forget very often. Within three months of this practice, every time I looked in the mirror I appreciated the woman looking back at me. I was falling in love with myself.

A few months after the workshop ended, I had a dream about Nick. His eyes, staring straight at me, jolted me awake. In the dream, Nick had a terrible wound. It affected his face, and I could somehow see that the wound protruded out the back of his skull. The ragged, torn flesh was put back together with hundreds of surgical staples. It was ghastly.

I was so upset by the dream that I wanted to text him to see if he was all right. Overthinking, I hesitated. *He's going to think you're out of your mind, Wendy!* Lying in my bed, I agonized over whether I should reach out. But I knew my dreams always meant something.

Finally, I decided I had to text him, even if he thought I was crazy. I typed: "Are you okay? I just had a dream about you." Then as succinctly as I could, I shared what I'd seen in my dream. I hit send.

To my surprise, he replied immediately. "Thank you, I'm fine."

After that night, Nick started calling me "sister" and ending every text with a red heart and a hands in prayer emoji.

Later that spring, at the conclusion of another self-development class, Nick asked if we could talk for a moment. Looking up into his bright eyes and his confident smile, I noticed that he, too, was sprouting a few gray hairs, but that it only added to his charm and attractiveness. With a strong voice and his ever-present positive attitude he asked, "Do you remember the night of your dream?"

"Of course," I replied.

"Well," he said soberly, "The moment you sent it, I was sitting in a parking lot, in my truck, with a gun to my head. I was going to kill myself."

I gasped, my eyes tearing up. Nick was one of the most successful and happiest men I'd ever known. *How could he feel like that*?

We talked for a while. Then I stopped and looked into his eyes. "Nick, promise me that if you ever feel that way again, you *will* reach out to someone."

"I promise," he said. I believed him.

Several weeks after Nick's confession, while walking out of yoga, I was surprised to see my mother's name on my caller ID. Answering my phone, I heard her say, "Johnny is dead. We're not sure what happened. It sounds like drugs."[6]

Anguish tore through my heart with the memory of my impromptu visit the previous summer.

Feeling inspired to go to Seattle, I jumped on the next plane. Upon my arrival, Johnny's fiancé and his best friend greeted me with open arms. He shared some of my brother's personal possessions with me and invited me to stay in their home. I felt honored. They also invited me to a friend's celebration breakfast so that I could meet my baby brother's work associates and friends. Being with them filled my heart with peace because I knew my brother had died with people whom he loved and who loved and accepted him.

Drawing a portrait of my baby brother was healing for my soul. His presence felt close as I prepared the rendering to give my parents for his funeral to be held in Montana. I finished it just in time. While in attendance, plethoric tensions with extended family members infected every interaction.

Hugging my nieces and nephews lifted my spirits while the sticky truth of ignored, unresolved, and unhealed generational familial incest hung like a weight, drowning all hope of safe family interaction connection. I wanted to flee from individuals unwilling to tell the truth about being victims, per-petrators, and victims turned perpetrators. I left after hugging my parents good-bye. Heartbroken, I believed I would never see anyone in my family again in this lifetime, yet I was infinitely grateful that my baby brother knew I loved him before he died.

Me and the portrait I drew of my baby brother

Returning from Johnny's funeral, my own baby, now seventeen years old, was asked to speak and sing at a graduation event for his youth group. Our child openly shared about missing Spencer and wanting answers to life's most difficult questions. My heart, already shattered from Johnny's funeral, cracked as I listened to my child share kind, vulnerable, and heartbreaking words to all who were listening. And Spencer was there, via a live video app.

Arriving home that night, I called Spencer. "Please call Huxley. You heard what I heard. It's been weeks since you had a conversation together. We have to do something. Please help me, help our child, Spencer."

"When I call, it just goes to voicemail, Wendy. I leave messages and they don't get returned. I've tried. If you'd stop talking about all this shit, everything would be okay."

My husband's words stunned me into silence. I'd heard them before, but at that moment, any further desire to engage with him, support him, or be with him evaporated into nothingness. I knew I'd never beg him to be a father to our children again. He didn't see them or their pain. We were objects to him. He was stuck and, worse yet, he was unwilling to change. I was done being his scapegoat. In fact, I was done being *anyone's* scapegoat ever again.

Year after year, I'd tried to make everything okay in our marriage, reading self-help books, going to my own therapy, and covering up his disregard for our children. Day after day, feeling alone and abandoned, I tried to make everything look okay to everyone on the outside while dying on the inside. Our children were suffering and I was absolutely alone as their mother. They needed more; I needed more.

My head was spinning. The idea of creating a family with Spencer felt like a pipe dream. My own lonely prison was a place I'd locked myself into while trying to create my perfect life. My marriage of twenty-four years was an institution that was suffocating the life out of me. Only worse, supposedly it was for eternity.

Reeling in the pain, I knew I had a decision: to leave and live . . . or to stay and continue to die a slow death. The decision was mine. Two things brought light to my thoughts. Jesus's atonement was my hope and He loved me perfectly, and the love between me and my children was real. These two things were my truth and they held me. His love was perfect and the most powerful force I'd ever experienced. His love was big enough for me to experience joy, too, no matter what it took.

Promises to my husband were abdicated to an instinctive understanding that I was born to have joy. Showing my children that I could be happy and create peace in my most intimate relationship mattered not just for me but for them also. If I wanted them to be happy in their relationships, as their mother, I needed to show them what unity in a relationship looked like.

Seven days later, I walked into the Provo, Utah courthouse and did what I'd told myself I would never do. I filed for divorce. Stepping up to the counter, my arm rose, gripping the carefully organized papers. They were perfectly signed and dated. The young man at the counter held a silver self-stamper and placed it on the first page. It read: "Filed May 15, 2017," in blood-red ink. I was starting over.

Once I returned home, I walked to my bedroom, took off my clothes, and crawled into bed, crumpling into my covers. The sheets were cold and crisp, contrasting the heat in my burning heart. I'd held the picture of our *ideal* family for so long. Now the shattering of my dreams was starting inside my ribs. With my next exhale, I let my tears go. I felt drowned in them. My heart melted as if it were under a branding iron, pulsating streams of white hot steam throughout my body. The cavity inside my chest pressed open from the inside out. *This must be what open heart surgery without anesthesia feels like.*

Decades had been devoted to being a wife and mother, following my Personal Guidance System, and overcoming my sexual trauma. I'd been working tirelessly to create a relationship with Spencer so that we could be a happy couple. It was the bedrock of everything I did. But we weren't. And I couldn't do it alone anymore. I sobbed, thinking that we'd never learned to co-parent our children, that we'd never enjoy being grandparents together again.

Under the covers, through snot and tears, I screamed my broken dreams to a God that I'd been praying to for years. "I was obedient! You told me you'd protect my children. And you haven't. Their hearts are broken. Spencer is absent from their lives. We're nothing to him. You told me to love, to forgive. You told me those things make a happy family, and they don't. Nothing worked. I failed and I don't even know what to believe anymore."

Surrendering into the abyss of my pain, I could see all the possible ways I could end my life. Thoughts of closing my eyes and never waking up rolled through my waves of anguish. But not attaching to any of those dark thoughts, I fell deeper and deeper into myself.

Underneath the searing, scathing sensations, through the red-hot burning hole inside my chest, I went all the way to a place deep inside of me that was very quiet and held absolute stillness. In that place, I rested until the moon was high in the sky.

When I emerged from the covers, the scriptures I'd studied and read to my children for twenty-seven years caught my eye. Reaching out, I couldn't touch them. Nausea filled me. The religious practices and rituals I'd lived every day to create my dream felt like a waste of my life.

Telling our children about the divorce was the hardest. I felt their anger, their sadness, and their support. While telling Briggs, he said, "Mom, if you need to walk away from Dad, us, everything, and everyone else in your life to be happy, I want you to do that." Huxley cried as I shared with him words I never wanted to speak.

Our hearts were breaking. This was never supposed to happen to our family. After telling our children, I asked Spencer if we could go to family counseling to support our children. He said, "Absolutely not!"

Time previously spent trying to connect to Spencer, feverishly obeying religious doctrine, and wanting to be loved and supported by our families was redirected. I spent my time focused on earning my bachelor's degree, supporting my children in their endeavors, searching for a new life partner, capitalizing on my art abilities, and trusting Jesus's love to hold me. I didn't know how, but I had faith that somehow everything would work out. It had to.

Months later while doing homework, I came across a research paper about authenticity. It defined "authentic living" as a consistency of one's true self, thoughts, beliefs, values, and outward behaviors.[7] The article came to life for me as I remembered years of disowning parts of who I was in certain relationships, and how I was now learning to be true to myself in every moment. The cost of me pretending everything was okay in my closest relationships had been high. I'd learned a person could die from a broken heart. I wondered, *if I'd known all of this information, would I have been able to save my marriage?* I didn't know. *Maybe.*

Later that semester, Huxley called and asked if we could talk. I sensed my child was distressed. I continued to sit in my chair while inviting Huxley to go to Bermuda, a practice my children were accustomed to. I listened as words fell from a pained heart wanting to be honest with me.

"I like girls, Mom, but I've always liked boys better. In fact, there's a boy I like right now. I'm going on a date with him tomorrow night."

The idea had never occurred to me that one of my own children would be attracted to the same sex. I thought about my baby brother, now gone, and my mind automatically went back thirty years to the phone call when my parents had learned about Sage and me. The words, "You are nothing! You are disgusting! Change your name! You are evil!" descended on my brain like an avalanche. The long-buried pain of wanting my parents to love me unconditionally rose up in my mind like a thick, black fog on a cold winter's morning.

With the memories swirling in my head, I looked at my child willing to tell me the truth about his deepest feelings. All I could see was the beautiful, innocent human I'd given birth to, loved, taught, enjoyed, and raised for eighteen years. I thought about the voice I had heard calling out "Mom" to me four different times before giving birth to this human in the flesh and our connection beyond time and space. Everything about my child in front of me was perfect.

An infinite overwhelming warmth, like the feelings I'd experienced from Jesus in the temple, overtook me. That harsh memory from my past was instantly erased from my mind. Pure, unconditional love for my child was all that remained.

One year later, Huxley, now an accomplished ballroom dancer, was competing in Blackpool, England at the World's First and Foremost Festival of Dance. I decided to spend the money I'd earned from painting murals in a client's home to go watch the competition, then travel to Croatia and Bosnia with my child.

With a one-month window in between the end of my semester's completion and when I would meet Huxley, I decided to explore, study, and practice my drawing with masterpieces from the Renaissance. Packing up my household belongings and then putting them into a storage unit felt like a smart financial move in order to save two months' rent and utilities. I would find a new place to live when I returned later in the summer.

The night before I left for Europe, I had a sleepover in my king-size bed with my youngest children. They were my best friends. Although we were all adults, we cuddled, laughed, and talked about our upcoming adventures: new jobs, world travel, and dancing. All of us were giddy with excitement. Rhodes was working as a special education teacher, and he and Emberly, his beautiful wife, were waiting for the arrival of their second baby, due shortly after I would return from my travels.

Divorce had shattered all of our hearts, but we were navigating the turbulent waters of our pain. We were living a very different life than what I'd ever imagined as a mother, but we loved each other fiercely. I'd spent their entire lives nurturing, loving, and giving my life to them. They in turn had loved me back. I felt confident in my children's ability to succeed while I was also exploring my own life. They were all flying. They had the skills needed to create lives of sustenance, meaning, and peace. Now, as their mother, I could fly too.

While waiting to board a Boeing 737 to the Charles de Gaulle Airport in Paris, France, my phone rang. It was Nick.

"I just went to a psychic!" Exuberant, Nick shared, "She told me she could see huge, angel wings coming out of my back, wrapping around the whole world. And that there were one million angels behind me, just waiting to help me share my message!" He sounded like a child who'd just been given the best Christmas present ever. His excitement was palpable. He made me excited for him!

"Nick, it means so much that you would share this moment with me. That's incredibly beautiful! You'll do it, brother. I know you will." I could see in my mind's eye Nick's penetrating smile, his arms outstretched to every person individually, his wings wrapped around the whole world as legions of angels helped him share his message. "I can't wait to hear more. I'll see you later this summer, brother. I love you!" And with those words, I was off to cross the Atlantic Ocean.

Geometric patterns of springtime pinks, yellows, and greens sprawled below me as I flew over the French countryside. Stepping off the plane, a display case bursting with macarons the exact same colors as what I'd just seen while flying into France felt visually poetic and warmly inviting.

Armed guards holding assault rifles at every exit felt a bit unsettling as I searched for my train and a place to trade foreign currency. Reading the public transit system maps in French, asking questions in English, and dealing in *francs* in order to get to my hostel in the middle of Paris was a fiery baptism into solo, international travel. But I made it!

For the next few days, I strolled along the streets of Paris. The springtime blossoms enveloped me, while the Parisian cafés and their warm croissants filled my belly. Walking with nowhere to go was one of the most freeing feelings I'd ever experienced in my life. Pictures from my textbooks came to life as I gazed endlessly at Gothic, French Renaissance, and Flamboyant facades. Spending a whole day drawing Auguste Rodin's sculpture, *The Kiss*,[8] implanted more deeply in me what a loving relationship could be: embodied joy.

Days by myself felt timeless. With no reference points, expectations, or the opinions of others, the labels I'd attached to my entire life slowly slipped away. All that was left was a new awareness of myself, something I'd never truly experienced before. Freedom in my mind gave way to living fully present, melting into each moment. A childlike, innocent love for myself bloomed like the pink blossoms of Paris.

Being in France reminded me of Spencer. He'd spent two years in Europe before we were married. I could recognize now the influence his time in Europe had had on him. One day, I called him from my hostel just to see how he was doing, and because I missed him. Our conversation was short. He was cordial.

At night, in a coed dorm room, travelers from around the world exchanged stories in a myriad of languages: French, English, Spanish, and Arabic. As they talked about Morocco, I became interested because it sounded exotic, unlike anything I'd ever experienced. So, when a flat mate suggested I visit, I left for Taghazout the next day.

Arriving in the middle of the night, an attentive driver picked me up barefoot. Waking in my cozy hostel bed, red, orange, and purple textiles tantalized my eyelids while the smell of spices and freshly squeezed fruit juice gently aroused me.

Volunteers at the hostel as well as fellow travelers quickly became my friends and invited me to join them for excursions. They took me to Paradise Valley, their favorite hiking trail. Dates, olives, and a sea of spices sprawled under canopies filled my senses as merchants invited us to buy their wares. The hammam, a Moroccan bath house where a woman in a steam room cleansed our bodies with argan soap, then massaged us with jasmine-scented argan oil, was purifying for my soul.

After being in the country for a week, I was invited to participate in Ramadan, a Muslim religious tradition involving fasting, rest, and personal reflection.[9] We went without food and water while the sun was up. At night after the sun went down, we broke our fast with a bountiful meal. Listening to their prayers spoken over the loudspeaker five times every day reminded me of the devotion I'd lived for so many years in my own religious faith. I wondered if I'd ever believe in anything other than Jesus's love again.

On my last day in Morocco, I was driven to the airport by three friends. It was the seventh day of Ramadan. Stopping by a café, unbeknownst to me, one of them purchased a few things to eat. Upon arriving at the airport, he told me the exact time he'd be breaking fast with his family, then handed me a small box, inviting me to do the same if I wanted to continue in the tradition one last time. I did.

Standing on the tarmac, excited to meet Huxley in England, I could feel the golden Moroccan sun warming my skin. Carefully, I opened the small box and removed the pastry, a token of benevolence from a new friend. Closing my eyes, I took a bite at exactly 7:37 p.m., then boarded my plane. My heart was full.

Huxley's tall frame, bright smile, and exuberant confidence welcomed me to England. Dressed in a black tuxedo tail suit and a partner in a solid black rhinestone studded gown, from a mother's perspective, they looked flawless and danced perfectly in the infamous Empress Ballroom at Winter Gardens in Blackpool. Afterward, we continued our travels to Split Croatia, Plitvice National Park, and finally to Mostar, Bosnia.

Stories of triumph over trials, peppered with pain, from twenty years before were part of every conversation, in each café we visited. Memories of news footage from the Bosnian War in the early years of my marriage came to mind as I walked over the restored Old Bridge and gazed at the east and west banks of the city, previously destroyed but now beautifully rebuilt.[10]

Indiscriminate shelling of Mostar and bitter fighting had physically destroyed the city. Raping, fighting, and ethnic cleansing had led to the deaths of tens of thousands of people. Scars in the corners of the city could still be seen on piles of rubble and bombed-out buildings overgrown with grass and flowers.

The truth of the past was present in the mortar shell holes on the walls of standing buildings. Driving through the countryside, rain pattering on the windshield, Huxley's music filled our rental car while my child sat in the seat beside me. Memories of past war and destruction were replaced by what I was seeing in the present-day landscape: rebirth.

The truth I was seeing with my own eyes was more powerful than the shelling, killing, and war-torn country I had seen on the news. Beautiful rebuilt homes, miles of planted fields, and bounteous gardens whisked by as we drove through the countryside.

True, unbridled hope filled my heart. My mind processed the healing and reconstruction that had occurred in the country I was now seeing with my own eyes. *If an entire population of people and their country could rebuild their lives in such a glorious way, then as a family couldn't we do the same thing?*

True Principles for Telling the Truth and Being Authentic (TRU) Blueprint:

- If you perpetually feel angry, lonely, sad, tired, or any other negative feelings, I invite you to look at how authentic you are. Where are you betraying your true self? Are you being true to WHO you are?

- Obstacles, personal weakness, addictions, and a host of other ailments impede progress. Pretending they don't exist, burying them, or ignoring deep-seated problems doesn't fix them. In fact, in my experience it only makes things worse.

- Failure is part of our life experience. If you're trying, you're going to make mistakes. Life can be messy. You might even fail at something really important. **Being honest in our deepest, darkest feelings to the people we love cannot only free us; it can save our lives.** It did mine, more than once.

- You are the only one who has the power to **align and harmonize your life to the truth of WHO you are, your Personal Guidance System (PGS), and your biochemistry BIO.** You can do it, and if need be, you can do it alone.

- Because you are never actually alone. There is a love that connects us all and when you open to that love, and keep opening to it, it will carry you. **Love never ends. Love is bigger than your pain.** Bring yourself back to you, back to sanity, and back to the health and joy you were born to experience. Joy is your birthright. Live for it.

While completing activities 29–31, you will discover:

- **Activity 29: Learning the Science of Authenticity**

- **Activity 30: Being Honest in Your Deepest, Darkest Feelings**

- **Activity 31: Aligning Your WHO, PGS, and BIO Blueprints**

ACTIVITY 29: LEARNING THE SCIENCE OF AUTHENTICITY

Authenticity is the fundamental principle of well-being. Carl Jung, the founder of analytical psychology said, "the self is the goal of life . . .it is god in us . . .all our highest and deepest purposes strive toward it"[11] Later, in

2008, in a groundbreaking study, Professor Alex Wood and his team drew upon a three-tiered structure to test whether or not authenticity was related to a person's health and well-being. Their results? Authenticity is integral to wellness.[12]

Their research stated that each person has three fundamental parts. These are:

A) **The true self**-awareness, physiological states, emotions, and beliefs

B) **The actual experiences** of intellectual thinking, reasoning, or remembering

C) **The outward behavior,** including actions and communication

Some of the discoveries I personally found to be extremely valuable were that authenticity involves consistency among the three levels of a person, that 100 percent alignment is never possible (in other words, self-compassion is necessary), and finally that external influence is inevitable.

What does that mean for you? Well, to understand this concept, let's look at two examples:

Example #1

A. *Child desires to communicate need to caregiver-true self.*

B. *Child has learned caregiver is not a safe place to express desires-actual experience.*

C. *Child ignores true self's need-outward, resulting behavior.*

<u>Example #2</u>

A. *Wendy Beth desires joy and happy relationships-true self.*

B. *Wendy Beth believes marriage is good, divorce less desirable-reasoning, remembering.*

C. *Wendy Beth adjusts expectations, chooses divorce to experience joy–behavior.*

Discovery Activity

- **Breathe, before you even get out of bed. Do this for at least five minutes today.**

- **What is your number today?** _____

- **List Gratitudes**

  1. _____

  2. _____

  3. _____

As of today, how would you describe your level of authenticity?

- I am never myself. I sell out all the time!

- Mostly I capitulate to what others want me to do.

- At times, I ignore myself so that others feel comfortable.

- Seriously, the privilege of my life is to be me!

Distinguish the three parts of you. (This might take some deeper thinking, but look at the description and examples above.)

A. In the box below, describe or draw your awareness, your needs, your feelings, things about you since childhood, and what you are drawn to when you have nothing else to do (your **true self**):

B. In the box below, describe or draw your thoughts, reasoning, and remembrances (your **actual experience**):

C. In the box below, describe or draw how your actions and your communications play out in your **outward behaviors.**

As you wrote or drew the above answers, where did you find discrepancy in the alignment of your **true self**, your **actual experience,** and your **outward behaviors**?

_____

_____

_____

_____

What two aspects of your life do you see yourself as *authentic?* Why?

_____

_____

_____

What two aspects of your life do you see yourself as *inauthentic?* Why?

_____

_____

_____

What is a common denominator in your times of authenticity? What is it?

_____

_____

_____

What is a common denominator in your times of inauthenticity? What is it?

_____

_____

_____

Write three things you can do to align your true self, your actual experience, and your outward behaviors.

1. _____

2. _____

3. _____

Are you willing to actively incorporate these three things into becoming authentic?

_YES

_NO

Who is someone who you are able to speak freely, openly, and honestly with, no matter what? What quality makes them a safe person for you to talk with?

_____

_____

What is your experience of peace? What does that look like in your life?

_____

_____

- **Set up a twenty-thirty minute phone or in person meeting with someone who you can be authentic with for Activity 33.**

- **Be in Bermuda at least 1x today.**

ACTIVITY 30: BEING HONEST IN YOUR DEEPEST, DARKEST FEELINGS

Integrity is the state of being complete and unimpaired, honest and upright. But what about in our deepest, darkest feelings? Do we really need to be honest even in those parts of ourselves? In my experience, I would say a resounding yes, especially if you're hiding something you think you cannot talk about. That's the thing you must bring into the light.

Dishonesty with ourselves and others at any level erodes our ability to trust ourselves. When we lie, we create false or misleading impressions, building walls inside ourselves and with each other. Lies are barriers to love.

The greatest fulfillment and satisfaction in my life, and the seasons that have brought me peace and joy, even amid challenging times, are when I am 100 percent honest and transparent in my feelings, thoughts, attitudes, and behaviors with myself and others. Darkness, sadness, heaviness, and a distrust of others comes when I am not authentic in my deepest feelings.

Since none of us are perfect and our modern-day culture puts so much emphasis on perfection, it can feel paralyzing and difficult to embrace the parts of ourselves that we see as not perfect. But it is possible with ourselves and with those who we trust.

Kintsugi, an ancient Japanese art, joins broken pieces of pottery with gold. It's not only an artform but a philosophy that embraces the reality of human flaws.[13] The finished product is stunning. I invite us to adopt this idea into our daily lives. Do you believe that you could look at the flaws in your life or in your character as gold? How would that be possible?

One of the challenges in telling the whole truth and being authentic is that people might not know the real you. They might not like what you have to say. When you start showing up as yourself, family and friends may be surprised and confused. But the truth is, their opinion of your honesty is irrelevant. If you want to know who your real friends are, speak or act your truth, and see who stays in your life. Don't be dismayed when some leave. If they love you, truly love you, they will figure out a way to work through any differences you might have.

Remember, real friends and even family want the real you. How many people do you know who apologize for breathing? For having an opinion, for having true desires? For wanting and needing safety and self-expression? Don't apologize for being true to yourself, ever. Just be you!

Discovery Activity

- **Breathe, before you even get out of bed. Do this for at least five minutes today.**

- **What is your number today?** _____

- **List Gratitudes**

  1. _____

  2. _____

  3. _____

- **Along the lines on the pottery, write failures, wrongdoing, personal weaknesses, and the deepest, darkest secrets you currently are dealing with. Because not every person is safe, writing these things may feel too scary. Use code words or images that make sense only to you. Just be honest and get them out of your brain.**

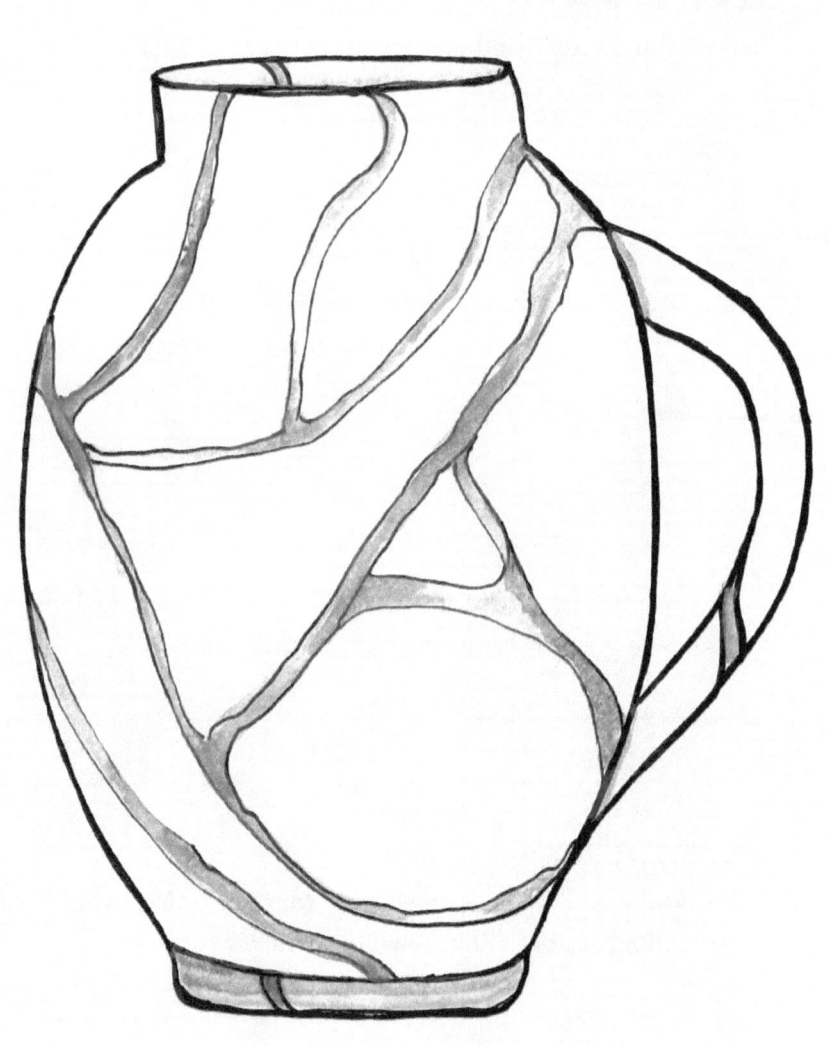

- **Investigate misalignments, trauma, wrongdoing in your life.**

  What did you experience as you wrote your wrongdoings, your weaknesses, your failures, and your deepest, darkest secrets?

  _____

  _____

  _____

  How does your Personal Guidance System (PGS) support you in dealing with all of the things you wrote on the veins of gold?

  _____

  _____

  _____

  Can you imagine thinking about failures, problems, and character weakness as gold? What would that look like for you?

  _____

  _____

  _____

  How do the opinions of others affect your decision-making capabilities in telling or not telling the whole truth?

  _____

  _____

  What percentage of your day do you feel you are capitulating to the opinion of others? And how can you become 100 percent honest in your daily decisions?

  _____

_____

_____

What "hard conversations" are you not having because you are afraid of the consequences?

_____

_____

_____

Is there anyone you need to say "I'm sorry" to? How and when will you make restitution for the following grievances?

_____

_____

_____

What is your Personal Guidance System's protocol in dealing with wrongdoing? How do you let go of guilt and/or shame?

_____

_____

_____

Who do you want an apology from? Why?

_____

_____

_____

What will you do if you never get the apology you are looking for? How will you move forward?

_____

_____

_____

What will change inside of you when you choose to be honest in every relationship? In every situation?

_____

_____

_____

What is the biggest consequence you are currently dealing with from not being 100 percent honest in your deepest feelings?

_____

_____

_____

What will change in your daily life as you gain the courage to become complete and honest and upright?

_____

_____

_____

Can you think of any other obstacles that will get in the way of you living a life of integrity, honesty, and real, raw authenticity?

_____

_____

_____

How will you overcome these obstacles?

_____

_____

_____

- **Be in Bermuda at least 1x today.**

ACTIVITY 31: ALIGNING YOUR WHO, PGS, AND BIO BLUEPRINTS

Recently I watched my grandson employ hundreds upon hundreds of micro-movements to imitate what he saw in the adults around him. He fell so many times. Still, he kept trying until one day all the parts of his brain and his body aligned and he took his first steps. Yeah!

Harmonizing our WHO, PGS, and BIO Blueprints is like learning to walk. It takes time, effective practice, and commitment. In the last thirty days, you may have felt varying degrees of incongruence, like things just don't fit the same way in your life any more. That's exactly what you want! Seeing where you are out of alignment is awareness, and when we are aware, we can then act in the direction of what we want to create.

As your Living Blueprint develops, like the chrysalis of the caterpillar to the butterfly, it may not look like a lot is going on at first from the outside, but inside something extraordinary is taking place.[14] There may be some inherent struggle or uncomfortableness, but please don't stop. You are just getting started. Akin to the metamorphosis and the bursting out of the cocoon that makes the strong wings to fly, putting all the aspects of your Living Blueprint together is the magic that will change your life.

Remember the concept of *marginal gains*?[15] Small, incremental improvements amount to significant improvement when all added together. Your life and your dreams are the most important processes of your existence. Your life will go in the direction you desire when you know and then live honestly in harmony with your Blueprint.

Discovery Activity

- **Breathe, before you even get out of bed. Do this for at least five minutes today.**

- **What is your number today?** _____

- **List Gratitudes**

  1. _____

  2. _____

  3. _____

- **Bring all your Blueprints together . . .**

  Write about the difficulties you have come up against in living fully from your WHO, PGS, and BIO Blueprints thus far in your journey.

  _____

  _____

  _____

  _____

  What have you done when these incongruences creep in during the course of your daily living?

  _____

  _____

Greatest Gift (Activity 17)

_____

_____

Three WORDS (Activity 10)

1. _____

2. _____

3. _____

Source of Inspiration (Activity 18)

_____

Five desired programs running your PGS (Activity 13)

1. _____

2. _____

3. _____

4. _____

5. _____

Eight daily actions steps nurturing your BIO (Activities 21-28)

1. _____

2. _____

3. _____

4. _____

5. _____

6. _____

7. _____

8. _____

Circle what is out of alignment with your actions and behaviors as you look at the previous five questions. Be curious and notice any patterns of discrepancy. Where are you living at full potential? What would you like to do better?

_____

_____

_____

_____

What obstacles are you facing in living from your Blueprint?

_____

_____

_____

_____

What will it take for you to overcome these obstacles and live in congruence with your Living Blueprint?

_____

_____

_____

_____

Are you willing to change in order to live in alignment to your WHO, PGS, and BIO?

_YES

_NO

How are you continuing to track your progress? Is it working? Do you want to implement a new strategy?

_____

_____

What, in the daily living of your life, is the #1 thing you want to do so that you can live in harmony with your Living Blueprint?

_____

_____

- **Do one activity from your Circle of Interests that is in alignment with your WHO, PGS, and BIO Blueprint.**

- **Be in Bermuda at least 1x today.**

If telling the whole truth and living authentically seems too hard to swallow, I promise with daily practice, living authentically and confidently will become second nature. In time, your truth for you trumps any other person's truth for you! This is coming from a past people pleaser, who capitulated to the expectations and opinions of others for many years. Choosing honesty in your deepest, darkest feelings takes you to your edge, allows you to jump, and is the net that catches you.

Still, sharing your true feelings, showing on the outside how you truly feel on the inside, and taking a stand for yourself is an act of courage and can feel scary. It's true. Please don't expect people who are accustomed to you capitulating to their wants to cheer you on. Sometimes, they won't. Many people will, and those are the ones you want a part of your inner circle. They get to be part of your success team, your chosen family.

Of course, there are times when you may not speak your mind. Possibly the timing isn't right, or maybe it's not your place to say something at the moment. It all comes down to knowing WHO you are and your *truest and highest* intentions, following your Personal Guidance System (PGS) and learning to listen and interpret what your biochemistry BIO is telling you so that you can live honestly and peacefully with yourself.

CHAPTER 9 TELLING THE WHOLE TRUTH AND BEING AUTHENTIC

hold onto your dreams
let go of expectations
freedom awaits you

A truly honest and authentic life is not afforded to just anyone. It is earned with an intention to live with integrity, in every thought, feeling, attitude, and behavior, no matter what. Looking for options not yet considered and adjusting timelines and expectations in order to live honestly in love from your Blueprint is a choice only you get to make. And you don't have to give up your dreams.

Still, you may want to get curious and learn new ways of achieving them. Considering unconventional perspectives is always a choice as long as you stay true to WHO you are and your PGS. Commitment to core principles, beliefs, and values, and flexibility in your personal process allows you to ride life's waves more joyously. Trust that the solutions you are seeking will come when you tell the truth, because they will.

Give yourself permission to take a leap of faith. Dig deeper. I promise you, there are answers available that you may not have considered that will not only keep you living more fully but will allow you to experience peace in truth telling.

Often we are presented with situations where we have more than one good option, when it feels like both options are possibilities. You get to choose what is best for your desired outcomes. You can discover what is right for you, if you go deep enough into your true self and remember WHO and where you want to go. Uncover hidden obstacles and speak, even the deepest, darkest truths you think you cannot share. Unburden yourself.

Upon returning to Utah from Europe at the end of May, door after door slammed in my face as I tried to reestablish myself in America as a woman divorcee. Being a homemaker without my own income and then choosing to leave my marriage after twenty-five years of being a stay-at-home mom had not prepared me to be financially solvent on the American economy—not to mention the business bankruptcy of $2 million at our farm. My credit was destroyed; no one would sign an apartment lease with me. Even with my alimony and money earned from art commissions, I could not find a place to live. I was homeless.

Still, I needed to become self-reliant in a career that aligned with my true self. For me, that meant continuing my college degree and creating a career while I was still receiving alimony from my children's father. An innate desire to help others love themselves and move forward toward their highest potential had grown inside me as I had traveled Europe. Raising my own children had been pure joy. Helping others take steps toward actualizing their dreams, just like I'd helped my own children until they took their own powerful steps forward, felt like an extension to motherhood.

I contacted my academic counselor in order to withdraw from the Art Illustration program and pursue a bachelor's in Family Science.[1] This degree just happened to be offered 100 percent online, allowing me flexibility to be mobile and remote in my coursework. Focusing on healthy interpersonal relationships in diverse families throughout a person's lifespan felt aligned with who I was, what I needed, and what I wanted to help others achieve. Once again, everything just worked out.

Excitement for the birth of my second grandchild filled my heart while the turmoil of how to create a safe place to live and create a career swirled around my mind. Our second grandson was born and my heart was once again filled with overflowing adoration for the gift of being his grandma. He was perfect! Not wanting to burden Rhodes, now a father of two, and with my three younger children still traveling themselves, returning to affordable Morocco, if only temporarily, felt like the best thing I could do, especially since my coursework was all online.

Billie, my best friend and the most forgiving, loving mother I had ever known, had already offered me to live with her for the summer, so I had a place to stay. While at her place, Nick called.

"Hi, sister. Do you have a minute to talk?"

I was excited to hear his voice, especially after our last phone call about his psychic reading.

"I'm working with a new coach and he says that I'm ready to take my message to the world. I'm not sure exactly what I want to teach, but I know that I need to make this phone call today. I know I want to do something with *you*." He paused. "What do you think?"

Not being honest with the details of my housing dilemma, I said, "Nick, you have no idea what your phone call means to me. I'd love to create something with you, brother! I'm going back to Europe for a bit, but let's talk about your idea at the retreat this weekend."

The next week, twenty assistants, including Nick and I, met at a self-development workshop deep in the Wasatch Mountains. During one of many conversations with Nick I shared, "While I'm traveling, I'll study, write content, and scope out venues. Everything I'm seeing in my curriculum will support us in helping individuals be honest in uncovering and healing their emotional wounds, connect to their authentic selves, and create meaningful lives. As soon as I get back from Europe, we'll put it all together."

With enthusiasm, he replied, "Sounds great, sista! Looking forward to it!"

I was thrilled and looking forward to it as well.

Before leaving for North Africa, Emma, one of the assistants from the retreat, and I spent time together. My feelings for her were more than friendship. She was a hippie goddess, bright eyed, beautiful, and hyper sensual. A part of me I'd not allowed myself to explore or even feel with a woman since breaking up with Sage was incited. We promised to stay in touch while I was traveling and when I came home. We kept that promise.

When the sun went down, the medina in Marrakech, Morocco came alive. Spices flooded my senses while the sound of snake charmers and the thousands of candles lit by merchants selling their wares illuminated the plaza. I felt like Princess Jasmine venturing into the city of Agrabah as I walked on cobblestone in my linen clothing, sandals, and coral colored scarf.

My hostel was a colorful multi-level dwelling with palace-like architecture, including an interior garden with a turquoise pool to wash its travelers' feet. In the mornings, I'd sit on one of the many balconies, sipping on mint tea, listening to the Salaah, the ritual Islamic prayers I'd learned to love, being spoken over the loudspeaker.

The peace I felt in being back in Morocco and the level at which I was honoring my own real, raw experience with life opened my mind, heart, and body to self-pleasure. Masturbation had always felt taboo, evil, and dirty . . . until it wasn't.

In all my years of healing my sexuality, I'd never truly celebrated, honored, or owned the responsibility of my sexual response system. I'd wanted Spencer to be happy. I'd wanted to have great sex so I could have a happy marriage. I'd wanted to be a good wife. But never once had I wanted to feel sexual pleasure just for me, for my own joyful life. One day, in that perfectly gorgeous setting, self-pleasure allowed me to feel a new level of self-awareness and self-love.

Continuing my travels, I made new friends at my favorite hostel in Tamraght, Morocco.[2] We visited the souk, a colorful, chaotic, exotic marketplace with a sea of aromatic spices and the smell of baking bread. Glancing up, I noticed one of my new friends smiling at me and pointing at the merchant standing next to him, weighing out spices from a brilliant colored bin. When we returned to the hostel, he asked if I wanted to help him make some tea. Since I love tea, I agreed.

Once the steeping time was complete, we gathered cups, then made our way to the rooftop terrace so that we could enjoy the warm drink with fellow flat mates and the brilliant sunset just painting itself over the Atlantic Ocean. As the sky darkened, we moved to a lower terrace around a fire where a young man was singing in Moroccan Arabic what sounded like spiritual songs and playing the gimbri, a three-string, rectangular guitar-like instrument.

Looking into the fire while listening to the rhythms of music, waves of pleasure began rolling through and over me. Within minutes, a building tension in my body was followed by a release of energy, resulting in intense feelings of pleasure in my brain, my heart, my stomach, and my genitals. My face, neck, and chest felt flushed.

Not wanting the feeling to stop but confused at what was happening, I peeked my eyes open so as not to bring attention to myself. *This must be the tea.* I looked around at my fellow travelers, wondering if anyone else was having the same amazing experience. They all seemed to be chipping away at their conversations, totally oblivious to what was happening with me. Relieved, I laid my head back, melting into what felt like the longest and best orgasm I'd ever experienced.

After what seemed like thirty minutes of exquisite bliss, a violent need to purge my stomach forced me to lurch for the door, making my way downstairs to the bathroom. For the next twenty minutes, I vomited, puking the bread, vegetables, and couscous I'd eaten earlier that day at the souk. When I finished, I carefully walked upstairs and sat back down at the fire.

Again, the sounds of the music lulled me into silent waves of rhapsody through and over my entire body. The same building tension was followed by the same rush of energy, resulting once more in intense feelings of orgasmic exhilaration. After what seemed like about twenty minutes, the need to heave and hurl overtook me again. Not wanting to bring attention to myself, I again carefully made my way downstairs, knowing exactly what was in store for me. The waves of pleasure were now mixed with intense retching and profuse sweating in that mosaic tiled restroom.

The rest of the night was evenly split between dry heaves in the bathroom and orgasmic bliss next to a fading fire. As the oceanic air cooled and the tea's effects slowly made its way out of my system, I went back to my hostel bed. Surrendering to the stillness that finally came, I closed my eyes and fell asleep until noon.

We hiked Toubkal, the highest point in the Atlas mountain range.[3] Every time I felt like I couldn't take another step, I would tell myself, *You've had four children naturally. You lived through a divorce. You can do this!* One of my fellow travelers was Israeli with long, flowing hair to the middle of his back. He had the energy of a wild mustang, and the heart of a servant. As we walked to the top of the mountain, he often carried my bag. He was one of the most handsome men I'd ever known and half my age. Something about him also reminded me of Spencer. An untamed Spencer.

A few weeks after our hike ended, and once we'd gone our separate ways, he called me. "Hey, Wendy. Come to Peniche, Portugal. My parents are here and we want to look into opening a hostel together with you."

I was ecstatic. *Is this my answer? Is this how I will create a home for my children? Is this a venue where Nick and I can share our message?* I hadn't been able to create a home for my children in America, but maybe I could do it in Portugal, in a hostel. With a gorgeous Israeli.

"Shallow" by Lady Gaga and Bradly Cooper had just been released.[4] With that song in my ear, while reading a book about bridging cultural differences in the workplace, I flew from Morocco to Portugal. My friend, with his father, met me at the airport.

From the moment I was in their presence together, everything felt different. He was bridled, a completely different version of the man I'd known, trusted, and relied upon in the mountains of Morocco. I knew that feeling, of not being able to be your full self in the presence of certain other people. I missed my friend, the one I'd learned to love–his true self.

For the next six weeks, we studied and planned. His parents were willing to buy the property outright, if needed. In ten years, the hostel would be paid off while at the same time taking care of my friend's and my personal needs. Working with lawyers and accountants, we became residents of Portugal and set up joint bank accounts in preparation to buy the hostel. We brainstormed how to create what we'd both experienced in Morocco at the hostel where we'd first met.

Family style breakfasts and dinners would take place every day. Live music would be played in the garden, around a campfire, under a star-filled sky with new friends pouring in from around the globe. It had been a dream we both cherished, and one that we wanted to give to our guests. In our planning, I shared, "my soul brother Nick and I want to create retreats and workshops where individuals, couples, and families can learn healing treatments, communication tools, and relationship skills." My friend and his parents loved the idea. In everything I imagined, I pictured my children as part of it all, even living with me, if they wanted.

My friend and I decided that the little house on the back of the property we were looking to purchase would be where I would live and a perfect place for my children whenever they would visit. As we continued our planning, an undercurrent of anger in my friend's persona, one I'd not experienced before, began to quietly surface. I believed it was coming from the tension between him and his parents, but it was still unsettling.

In the end, I stepped away from buying the hostel. A ten-year commitment with me staying in Portugal while my children lived in America didn't feel aligned to who I was. Their accessibility to me was my priority. Being a mother was guiding my decisions even though they were adults and not physically with me.

Early one morning, with a heavy heart, while walking on Gamboa beach, I had an idea! *What if I create my own company? I could bring hosts, like Nick, for retreats and workshops to Portugal, filling the beds in my friend's hostel.*

My own sister company would give me flexibility to travel back and forth with my children and it wouldn't tie me to my friend financially. My own company could be the bridge between an international experience and a healing retreat that Nick and I could create together.

Giddy excitement coursed through my whole body as I ran back to our apartment and shared this idea with my friend immediately. He was cautious about my proposal and we decided to think about it over the next couple of months while I went back to America to enjoy Christmas with my children.

Once again, I felt invigorated. I had a plan.

André and I met in Peniche during the hostel negotiations on a cobblestone street under the light of a lamppost. Amidst the sea air, his Portuguese accent and his musky smell were intoxicating. His earth sign was fire, mine was wind, and from the moment we met, our passion was a blazing bonfire.

Kissing him was an electric inducement, sending waves of sexual desire through my whole body. His arms warmed me in the cold night air. But I didn't give myself to him . . . not yet. I'd had too much going on with my children, business meetings, and preparing to return to the United States. I told him I'd be back at the end of January to pursue a business venture.

Six weeks later, I returned to Portugal. André offered to find me a place to live by the beach in Foz do Arelho. Every day I did homework, practiced yoga, and wrote content for mine and Nick's retreats. At night, we ate dinner by candlelight in my apartment.

After dinner, André would smoke his cigarettes. Sometimes we danced. Later we would walk on the beach and drink red wine. Looking into his eyes fanned our growing connection and I felt the sexual and emotional bonding I'd dreamed about in my marriage for so many years. He attempted to teach me Portuguese, then belly laughed when he saw my tongue try to do what he did so naturally. Being with him I could be myself. He loved me.

André introduced me to his son and talked of wanting to create a home together. He took me to a piece of property he'd purchased with remnants of a house and garden waiting to be restored. He plucked bright yellow lemons from the tree tucked away in the corner of his garden and shared them with me. Every few days, we went to the market where he painstakingly chose the perfect cheeses, meats, and bread. His eyes followed me wherever I went.

On the weekends, we'd go into the woods and forage figs, herbs, and watercress. Sometimes we found mushrooms. On occasion, we'd visit his parents in another town. His mother cooked every meal in a brick oven heated with coal. She treated me like a beloved daughter. I wanted her in my life even though we could not understand each other in words. Our hearts were one.

Making love with André was a conscious decision. He was playful and fearless, opening my mind and my heart with every look and every touch whether in my apartment, in the market, or at the beach. In bed, he explored every curve. Our wet bodies became one, in any position, disappearing into his sexual power and my rippling, shaking response. Afterward, we slept wrapped in each other's arms, every night basking in a universe of passion, pleasure, and love I'd never before experienced.

Being with André showed me I was no longer held captive to my sexual trauma with men. I'd broken free from the shackles that had kept me a prisoner for over forty years. I could feel love, both his to me and mine to him. I could feel his sexual response system and my sexual response system working in tandem to create shared experiences. Loving him and being loved by him felt exquisite.

Still, I could not ignore the little patch of eczema that was breaking out in my hands. I knew something in my body was out of alignment. Making love night after night with André outside of marriage, though it felt perfect physically, was out of alignment with a deeper part of myself. Something within my soul, underneath the pleasure I was experiencing and the love I felt for and from André felt empty, hollow, and dissonant. When I looked in the mirror, I could see I was losing something I needed, to be truly happy. Peace.

Still, I continued on. Several months into mine and André's relationship, I felt inspired to attend my own church in Portugal. I could always feel Jesus's love for me, and at the same time, I felt a distinct longing for the connection I'd cultivated with Heavenly Father through my child-rearing years.

My anger at Him for not protecting my children and not making our family a happily-ever-after story had dissipated. And the angst in my soul from ignoring Him caused a tiredness that was ever present, even as I pursued my dreams and experienced romantic love with André. *Should I get married? Then I would not be having sex outside of marriage. Would that solve the problem?* I didn't know what to do, so I lived with my questions, knowing answers would come just like they always had in the past.

Looking up The Church of Jesus Christ of Latter day Saints in Santarem, Portugal was a leap of faith. I'd followed the doctrine as closely as I knew how and I had not been able to create a happy family according to what I had been taught a happy family was. *Why do you think anything will be different, Wendy?*

"Please do not speak to me in English," I said to the missionaries who I met with one afternoon. "I don't want to understand any of the words you speak. I am looking for a very specific feeling. Your words will not convince me."

As the pair of young men in white shirts, ties, and black name tags spoke to me in Portuguese, warm, peaceful feelings like the ones I'd experienced since the blessing in Salt Lake City and before my emotional adulterous conversions began, flooded the hollow parts of my soul. A buoyancy in the form of light infused my heart. My chest felt warm.

André attended with me and in time chose to be baptized. *What if I could feel everything I feel in my relationship and what I feel in my heart at the same time?* I often wondered. *What if he came back to America with me?* A long conversation with a friend helped me check in with myself and discover that I wasn't ready to make the commitment of marriage. Giving up making love and drinking wine was hard, but I was at peace with my choice. I was living my truth. A feeling of rest, tranquility, and lightness seeped into the parts of me living in the unknown.

Deep diving into my spiritual life was strengthened as I created the company to fill my friend's hostel and create the venue where Nick and I could share our message. André was intrigued. He offered his services for the needed construction and renovations of the hostel. Then, together he and I explored The Castle Almourol[5] in the middle of the Tagus River, the Alcobaça Monastery, and many other venues as possible locations for day excursions from the hostel.[6]

Reaching out to Nick and sharing my ideas with him made my international venture more real.

"LOVE THIS!" he texted back. "I'm working with a group of men and it's growing like crazy. The group is all about bringing men back to being real, raw, and authentic. Women have lots of retreats and groups, but this is the first place for men to do the same. I've become friends with the man who started it all, I'll run it by him."

Nick's texts infused more excitement into my already growing enthusiasm!

Months into retreat preparations, my friend chose to sell his hostel. It was just too much of a burden for him to create the space we had dreamed of together, alone, even with his parents as his partners. Deeply saddened for my friend, and for myself, I knew someday in the perfect place, Nick and I would share our message with the world. And somewhere, somehow, I would create a place my children could feel at home, with me, their mother.

Just two months later, my children organized an extraordinary surprise gift for my fifty-first birthday. Each of them, their partners, and my grandsons had written personal letters of praise and gratitude for me. Deeply hidden and previously unknown broken pieces of my heart, mind, and soul fused together as I looked at my grandson's handprints and read the loving words from each member of my family.

Kintsugi, the Japanese art of putting broken pottery pieces back together with gold, filled my mind as their love, from across the ocean, infused into my soul. Loving and raising my children had been the greatest experience I'd ever known.[7] They were my greatest joy. Their words told me that, even though I'd broken their trust in divorcing their father and temporarily abandoned the religion I'd so succinctly raised them with, my efforts as their mother had not gone unnoticed. I mattered to them.

Briggs flew over from Alaska and he and I spent two weeks together. The knee-deep tide that was the temperature of bathwater cradled us every day as he and I, mother and son, played in the soft waves of the warm ocean. Our conversations were short but always heartfelt.

"Are you happy, Briggs?"

"I'm good, Mom."

"Do you ever think about being a dad? Maybe having a relationship?"

"Nah, I don't think so. It looks like you're happy, though."

"I miss being close to you and our family. I'm too far away." Looking over the sea, I thought about my other children across the ocean.

"I miss you too, Mom."

The day he returned to America, my heart ached to be closer to my child. I knew it was time for me to go home. My children had their own lives. Still, I was their mother. They needed me.

A few weeks later, after gathering a pound of baby clams for dinner on the beach, I looked at André coming up out of the water. His rawness, his primal, perfect body walked toward me. His muscles glistened with drops of sea water. He looked at me with an intensity that went deep into my heart even as the sun was setting on the horizon behind him.

Goosebumps formed on my skin as I reveled in the peace, joy, and love I'd found in myself and with him. I was absolutely free to experience all of my feelings and emotions. Committing to marriage with André was not true for me. As much as we loved each other, looking past him, to the ocean waters, I knew it was time for me to go back home. Telling André that I was leaving hurt both of our hearts, but it was my truth, and he fully supported my decision to do what was best for me.

Loving others had always felt natural. I'd raised my children with the idea that there was enough love in the universe for everyone. Now, I knew it to be true in the deepest part of my soul. Jesus's love had carried me and had been my constant companion. An ocean of desire to help others love themselves and find their own truth so that they could actualize their own purpose-driven life was ever present in my thoughts and in my heart.

For most of my life, I'd lived in contempt for myself, but now I knew what freedom felt like. This was the freedom to love fully both myself and another person in a state of peace and happiness. I knew what it felt like to be honest and true to myself and to act from my own conscience. Labels, expectations, and the opinions of others no longer controlled me. Validation came from deep within my own soul and from my source of inspiration. I wanted to help others experience the same freedom.

Upon returning to Utah, I found a small studio apartment complete with walking trails close by and a garage for my car. With large sliding glass doors, the sun coming up over the Wasatch mountain Range was the alarm clock I woke up to every day. The studio apartment was not big enough for any of my children to live with me, but that was okay. I knew that my being present in their lives was so much more important than what I could provide financially or materially.

Asking my sons and several friends for help to move my belongings from storage into my new apartment felt a bit too vulnerable. Spencer had always taken care of that part of life in the past. But now I was on my own. It was up to me to get myself moved into my new place. My boys all agreed to help, but Nick's reply, when I asked for help, "Pretty busy, don't think I can make it," felt oddly detached and hurt my feelings. And he wasn't there to help the day I moved in. In the hustle of getting my life reordered in America, I forgot about my hurt feelings and moved on.

Exploring my new neighborhood, I found a local LDS church on my morning walk. It was a beautiful stone and rock building surrounded by deciduous trees next to the Utah State Capitol. Trepidatious about returning to religious activity in America where I knew I'd understand the language caused me to participate only occasionally. This I shared with my ecclesiastical leader who supported my decision completely. As none of my children attended church, spending time with them was my priority.

Spencer arranged for family pictures to be taken at our first family gathering. I was surprised and elated. Never in our entire marriage had he ever even wanted a family picture. Divorced, he and I took photos with our grandsons. Oddly, I felt that somehow we'd accomplished the impossible. Our marriage was over, but we would always have our children bringing us back together for family activities in an atmosphere of love.

The truth was, in my curriculum I learned our earlier relationship never had a chance. Bonds that we needed–that every couple needs in order to create a happy, healthy relationship–had never formed.[8] Both of us were too wounded to create a healthy marriage. We didn't know how to learn and heal together. Ending the marriage had allowed us both to progress.

As the New Year approached, Spencer and I decided to take the children on a snowboarding/ski trip after the holidays. Accepting a ride home from Spencer, he and I began talking about my transformation over the past couple of years since our divorce. "There are three versions of you. Wendy 1.0, the one before we were married. Wendy 2.0, the version of you while we were married. And Wendy 3.0, the Wendy you are today.

"I like Wendy 2.0. I don't really like Wendy 3.0. It was a lot easier to deal with you when you were in Europe," he said thoughtlessly.

His words were hard to swallow because Wendy 3.0 was actually who I was. Sitting there in the car, I thought, *Wendy 2.0 was the passive wife. A perfectionist, trying to be good enough, begging to be loved, living for everyone else without a voice. Sexually shut down, driving herself into the ground, killing her thyroid, surviving suicide. Wendy 2.0 lived from fear. She was not my authentic self.*

When he dropped me off at home, I called a friend able to talked through emotions. I didn't need validation, but I did want to voice what Spencer had said to me. As I shared my thoughts, I knew the truth, and the truth had set me free. Wendy 3.0, the sensual, free, authentic woman who had emerged since divorcing, combined with the spiritual, organized, thoughtful woman I'd painstakingly created while being married to Spencer was all of me, fully embodied. Through my own experience, I had learned how to experience joy. I knew in whom I could trust and I knew unequivocally what I wanted.

A tectonic shift in my soul rolled through me as I realized I was alive and experiencing joy because I'd trusted in Jesus and been totally honest in my deepest, darkest feelings. The perfectionism, expectations, and the labels I had allowed to stick to me that had almost crushed me to death were gone. In order to live, I'd admitted my failure, been willing to accept accountability for my mistakes, and moved forward in the infinite love I knew available for not just me but every human being alive. In trusting Jesus, I'd been able to make a choice, adjust my expectations, and do anything to experience the joy I knew I was born to feel.

Knowing Spencer didn't want this version of me, that he didn't like the real me, allowed me to finally let go of him, in a way I didn't even realize until that moment I was still hanging onto. For the first time since our divorce, something inside of me was completely released from him. I began dating again.

On December 15, 2019, Billie invited me to join her at a morning Christmas concert. Afterward, we went to a café in downtown Salt Lake City. Meandering, a large pair of ceramic angel wings hung on a bookend caught my eye. Immediately, Nick's psychic reading came to mind. I snapped two pictures and leaned against the wall to edit the image and create a text message. Then I stopped. *It doesn't matter if you send him this picture.* I dropped my phone back in my pocket without hitting send.

Upon returning to my apartment later in the afternoon, our family pictures were in my inbox. For the remainder of the day and into the night, I basked in the love I felt for my children, their partners, my grandchildren, and even my children's father.

The truth is each family member had their own unique journey, creating lives of meaning based on their own beliefs, values, life experiences, and desires. For me, even in the wake of divorce, never had I been so at peace with myself, my choices, and my life. With some of our family photos, I created a social media post in order to share my joy:

I didn't grow up having dreams. I grew up not knowing what was real or what was my imagination. But if I would have had a dream, it would have been to feel the way I feel right now in my own skin. Alive, Authentic, & Loving.

Today, my family doesn't look like I thought it would thirty years ago. It's better. It's real.[9]

Playing Andre Bocelli's, "Because We Believe," I turned up my music as loud as I thought my neighbors would allow without eliciting complaints and I sang to my heart's content.[10] My chest felt warm and I basked in the love I was living in for myself, for my Jesus, and for every human being. I noticed that the eczema on my figure was gone and that my skin was clear and soft. Walking past my bathroom mirror, I liked the woman I was, and she wasn't who I thought I *should* be. I was the real me and I wasn't perfect. I was just me.

True Principles For Your TRU Living Blueprint:

- Living from WHO you are, following your Personal Guidance System (PGS), and nurturing your Biochemistry (BIO) will create an environment within you where **pretending you're okay just doesn't work anymore.**

- Spend time with yourself and discover what incongruences may be disrupting your heart, your mind, or your body. Stop acting like you have the answers when you don't. It's okay. I invite you to get vulnerable. **Real, raw, authentic vulnerability is a doorway to joy.**

- You have access to all the love available to anyone in the universe. **There is an infinite, immeasurable, inexhaustible love waiting for you in this very second.** Each of us must choose and be open to love; it will not force itself upon any of us.

- **Your body can be a message board that can help guide you if you listen to it, if you are curious and aware.** Sharpen your ability to discern when you are in alignment to your true self, your values, your beliefs, and your actions.

- Meditation, slowing down, and not multitasking will help you become more perceptive in tuning into your own heart, body, and mind.

- **If you are not at peace, something, in you, is out of alignment.** If you are battling within, taking the time to be 100 percent honest and uncovering the dissonances can open you to a whole new world of peace and tranquility.

- **Being honest and true first happens with ourselves and then others.** You'll make mistakes, but that's okay. Living is trying, succeeding, failing, and trying again. Over and over again.

- **You can do this!**

WHILE COMPLETING ACTIVITIES 32–34, YOU WILL DISCOVER:

- **Activity 32: Listening to Body Cues to Support Authenticity**

- **Activity 33: Honoring and Being True to Yourself First**

- **Activity 34: Initiating an Honest Conversation with Success Partner**

ACTIVITY 32: LISTENING TO BODY CUES TO SUPPORT AUTHENTICITY

"Awareness heals," says Dr. Michael J. Lincoln, author of *Messages from the Body*. "The key factor in bodily health is the immune system ... what is going on in our consciousness is continuously affecting our body and vice versa. In many ways, the body and the mind imitate and imprint on each other."[11]

A few years ago, two dear friends were hospitalized with life-threatening illnesses. While visiting them both, I witnessed a phenomenon that changed my life and continues to inform my morning practice of waking up and connecting with myself.

One friend, a health practitioner, lay in his hospital bed waiting for someone to give him answers. This friend had little to no desire to learn or change harmful practices deeply embedded in his daily life, potentially killing him. My other friend, to my surprise and delight, when I walked into her hospital room, was actively researching, looking for new information, and speaking to health care workers on the phone in order to find answers, working to *live*.

I have no way of pathologically showing you that their actions had any influence on their prognosis. But I can tell you that the outcome in both of my friends' lives had a huge impact on me and my choices. The friend actively looking for answers and willing to change is alive today. My other friend is not. Please know this activity is *not about negative or critical judgment, only awareness.*

Being aware of our decisions and actively and honestly taking part in our learning and healing journey affects our destiny.

Discovery Activity

- **Breathe, before you even get out of bed. Do this for at least five minutes today.**

- **What is your number today?** _____

- **Schedule a sixty-minute visit, ideally in person, with a success partner for Activity 34.**

- **List Gratitudes**

  1. _____

  2. _____

  3. _____

- **Explore any physical ailments that may be causing you distress.**

What physical ailments or disease are you currently dealing with?

_____

_____

How many hours a day does your ailment or disease affect your life? How does it affect your daily living?

_____

_____

How has implementing your eight biochemistry (BIO) elements affected your current health conditions?

_____

_____

What if your immune system was controlled by your thoughts? What thoughts would you want to change in order to power up your body's capacity to heal?

_____

_____

_____

_____

What is the number one issue you want healed in your mind?

_____

_____

What is the number one issue you want healed in your heart?

_____

What behaviors and actions of yours may have contributed or may still contribute adversely to your health?

_____

_____

What actions done by others may have or are still adversely affecting your health?

_____

_____

What will you do today to stop the above actions from continuing? What will you do today to stop the above actions from continuing to adversely affect your health?

_____

_____

How does following your Personal Guidance System support your overall health?

_____

_____

How do you foresee being authentic affecting your health and wellness?

_____

_____

What do you foresee happening as you listen to your body and look for ways to support naturally healing your mind, heart, and body?

_____

_____

Are you willing to commit to listening to your body and supporting the natural healing capacity in your body?

_YES

_NO

How will you keep track of your progress?

_____

_____

Do you want a visual or auditory reminder to help keep you on track? If so, what will it be?

_____

_____

- **Do one thing from your healing toolkit that brings more awareness to your ability to support your natural healing ability.**

- **Be in Bermuda for twenty minutes at least 1x today.**

ACTIVITY 33: HONORING AND BEING TRUE TO YOURSELF FIRST

You know you better than anyone else does. In fact, you are the only one who knows the whole story about your feelings, your thoughts, and your experiences. You know better than anyone what is keeping you from moving forward and getting your dreams. Truthfully, you are the only one who really knows.

During Activity 17, we did a mirror meditation, connecting with the best parts of ourselves. Today, we'll add a new layer to that activity and go deeper.

Are you ready? Again, a caution here to **stay out of any negative programs or viruses**. Be loving to yourself as you allow your curiosity to wander and your ruthless, compassionate honesty guide you.

For me, the same character flaw I had as a child has been at the root of every problem I've faced as an adolescent and a grown woman. Whether my problem is addiction, dishonesty, depression, anxiety, suicidal ideation, or not speaking my truth, everything boiled down to one thing.

Self-hatred—not feeling not good enough, unlovable, and allowing my mind to run amok with automatic negative thoughts, reminding myself how bad I really am. Learning to overcome this weakness and deleting this virus has been the hardest thing I've ever done and the thing that has changed my life, forever, for the better.

When we really connect to the truth of who we are and attune all parts of our life to our true self, we not only feel peace, we do not feel dissonance. We experience progress toward our goals. Failure to accept all of ourselves, both our light and our dark, can lead to an unbalanced perception of WHO we truly are. Being honest with ourselves comes first, then we can truly show up with others authentically.

By now, every morning you are taking time to just breathe and connect with yourself, either meditating and/or Going to Bermuda every day. These practices are helping you slow down and experience stillness, peace, and the truth of WHO you are in each and every present moment. Today, as you look in the mirror, I invite you to look at your greatest obstacle: a personal character weakness that you're facing.

Discovery Activity

- **Breathe, before you even get out of bed. Do this for at least five minutes today.**

- **What is your number today?** _____

- **List Gratitudes**

  1. _____

  2. _____

  3. _____

- **Sit in front of a mirror looking into your eyes for two-five minutes.**

  What do you see?

  _____

  _____

  _____

  What do you *think* about what you see?

  _____

  _____

  _____

  What do you feel in your heart?

  _____

  _____

  _____

  How are you ready to take full accountability for your life?

  _____

  _____

  What is the next level of real, raw, authentic living you see for yourself?

  _____

What does telling the truth in every part of you look like in the daily living of your life? Write a description. What changes will occur?

_____

_____

_____

How honest are you with the people around you? Do they know who you are and what your values are?

_____

_____

What do you think would change in your relationships if people knew the real, raw, authentic you?

_____

_____

Go back through your BIO blueprint and review all the obstacles you have written. Copy them here. Circle your most incessant obstacle or virus. This may or may not be what you wrote in activity 13.

1. _____

2. _____

3. _____

4. _____

5. _____

6. _____

7. _____

8. _____

How is your biggest obstacle connected to a secret, something you incessantly ignore or are not talking about?

_____

_____

_____

How is this causing havoc in your life?

_____

_____

How is this thing you ignore stopping you from moving forward and keeping you from accomplishing your goals?

_____

_____

_____

_____

_____

Write out a plan of how you see yourself overcoming your biggest virus stuck in your life.

_____

_____

_____

_____

Who is a person in your life who you can be the most real, raw, and authentic with? What attributes do they possess that make them so?

_____

_____

_____

_____

How often do you enjoy authentic conversations with this person and would you like to have them more often? What would that look like for you?

_____

_____

- **Do one thing from your "Circle of Interests" that is the OPPOSITE of your biggest obstacle and that connects you to the most authentic part of yourself.** For example, if self-hate is your biggest obstacle, choose something that inspires self-love. If dishonesty keeps getting in your way, choose something that supports telling the truth.

  What did you notice?

  _____

  _____

  _____

- **Be in Bermuda for twenty minutes at least 1x today.**

ACTIVITY 34: INITIATING AN HONEST CONVERSATION WITH SUCCESS PARTNER

Your Living Blueprint is your compass, in the darkest night and on the brightest days, no matter what circumstances are taking place. If you are in touch with your true self, connected to love, the dawn will come. The sun is always shining, even when it's raining.

Honestly living from your true self, you get to decide who you share your real, raw, authentic life with. Not everyone needs or gets to be in your inner circle. In fact, be careful who you choose to share your deepest feelings with. Not everyone will honor you and your feelings like you were born to be cherished. The more authentically you live from your Blueprint, the more you will celebrate yourself. Then, two things will happen:

- You won't seek outside validation because you no longer need it.

- People will exit your life, leaving individuals whom you can truly be yourself with, who honor WHO you are, and what you want. A real sense of belonging will ensue.

Honesty opens the door to full responsibility and accountability for your life, your decisions, and the outcomes of your choices. Once you take a stand for yourself, living life any other way is incomprehensible.

Discovery Activity

- **Breathe, before you even get out of bed. Do this for at least five minutes today.**

- **What is your number today?** _____

- **List Gratitudes**

  1. _____

  2. _____

3. _____

- **Spend time with your success partner.** Maybe take notes in your conversation. Here are some topics you can discuss:

  - Share with them some of your interests from Activity 6, your source of inspiration, and your eight BIO Blueprints.

  - Discuss your biggest obstacles discovered on Activity 33. Ask them what obstacles or blind spots they may see that you may not be seeing in yourself.

  - Discuss strategies for overcoming the obstacles discussed.

- **Once you have finished meeting with your success partner, write a definitive plan for overcoming your biggest obstacles.** This is your plan. Being honest and vulnerable with a trusted success partner is part of the process, but it's up to each of us to figure out how to overcome our personal obstacles.

  1. _____

     _____

  2. _____

     _____

  3. _____

     _____

- **Make eye contact, then share with your success partner the attributes that allow you to be authentic with them.** Offer gratitude to them for being a person you can be 100 percent honest with. Ask them to share with you a few positive thoughts they feel regarding you as a person whom they choose to spend time with.

- Write your thoughts and feelings from your shared experience.

_____

_____

_____

_____

_____

- **Write your #1 game plan to overcome your biggest obstacle or virus.**

_____

- Will you commit to telling the truth and being authentic by working to overcome your biggest obstacle from this day forward?

    _YES

    _NO

- **Transfer the #1 plan of how to overcome your biggest obstacle to TRU on My Living Blueprint.**

    How will you track your progress?

_____

_____

- **Be in Bermuda at least 1x today.**

Exhaustion comes from the mental gymnastics of pleasing people, as well as acting any other way than what is truthful and authentic and living from the core essence of WHO we are. Being honest with ourselves first and then others is a journey toward freedom and peace of mind and it takes enormous amounts of courage.

Honesty plays a role in creating your best life because, if you're not living authentically, peace will escape you–no matter what you do. As hard as we try, we cannot eat, drink, use drugs, have sex, gamble, or do anything else enough to destroy the truth of WHO we are and what we uniquely need to thrive, experience peace, and move forward toward our dream.

You can hide. You can make yourself sick. You may even mask the truth buried deep inside yourself for a lifetime. But the truth of WHO you are and your innate ability to experience joy at your core center will always be there. Your true self is infinite and innate. And I believe–I *know*–it has absolute value!

STEP 5 - LUV BLUEPRINT

CHAPTER 10 DESIRING LOVING KINDNESS AS A WAY OF BEING

loving kindness is
a choice to make in every
desire and action

You and I have lived in the darkness of hatred. At one time or another, we've been the pawn in someone else's hateful game. Or, we've created and acted out our own destructive battles and self-loathing, blaming, and sabotage. These actions have driven us into a gulf of misery. Evil, or what I refer to as *the absence of love,* is rampant in our world.

Compassion, empathy, understanding, unity, and helping others are antidotes to evil and can be succinctly epitomized into the phrase Loving Kindness LUV, our fifth and last element in creating a Living Blueprint. Nido R. Qubein said, "Hatred is the most destructive force on earth. It does the most damage to those who harbor it."[1] When it is pointed at ourselves, it is especially destructive. But Loving Kindness dispels enmity and infuses light in every moment.

The science of love is explained as a "complex neurobiological phenomenon, relying on trust, belief, pleasure, and reward activities within the brain. Love is a joyful and useful activity that encompasses wellness and feelings of well-being."[2] Loving Kindness is love in action, a superpower, if you will, that when desired and then employed not only changes our state of being for the better, it changes those around us.

In 1975, psychologist J. Philippe Rushton conducted a classic experiment in which 140 elementary and middle school aged children were given tokens for winning a game that they could either keep all of or give some away to a child in need. The children first observed a teacher play the game before being told to practice taking, giving, or neither.

Children gave fewer tokens after watching an adult act selfishly, whether or not the adult verbally taught the concept of sharing. When the adult acted generously, students gave the same amount whether generosity was taught or not—donating 85 percent more than the norm in both cases. When the adult preached selfishness, even after the adult acted generously, the students still gave 49 percent more than the norm.[3] Selfishness was dispelled in the waves of Loving Kindness.

Regardless of our differing cultures, beliefs, or discipline, compassion is at the heart of our human family. In fact, love is so important that it's found amongst cultures and belief systems the world over. In Hinduism, *ahimsa* is more than a religious principle of practicing nonviolence; it's also love, compassion, and patience.[4] *Metta* in Buddhism means benevolence, amenity, and active goodwill for others.[5]

In the Hebrew Bible, *chesed* means love or kindness between people.[6] Similarly, compassion and mercy are central themes in the Quran.[7] The first two commandments in Christianity are to love God, and love thy neighbor as thyself.[8]

The first four parts of Living Blueprint: WHO, PGS, BIO, and TRU are about letting go of the battle in you, clearing barriers and obstacles and living harmoniously in love with yourself. Section Five: LUV is about desiring the attribute of pure love for others and taking action in sharing yourself, your time, your talents, and your resources.

Yes, it's true that a person can *show* loving kindness to others without actually loving. We can even act in loving kindness with barriers for loving ourselves, as I did it for years. But desiring Loving Kindness, the love that moves through us, connecting us to each other, healing us, and changing our hearts has the power to lift us to a higher realm of joyful living.

Fear was trying to stop me. Words I felt deep in my soul stuck in my throat as my heart hammered in my chest. I wanted to share my message of love, hope, and freedom with anyone who might stumble onto my Facebook page. *Creating personal safety from love . . .* that was a thought that had been nudging me for a few days. *I think that's what I want to talk about in today's video.* But I was so afraid. Putting myself out on social media in a teaching video was paralyzing me.

Looking over downtown Salt Lake City, I breathed in deeply. *You can do this. Then you can go for a walk up the canyon later.* With only a couple of weeks home from the southern tip of Spain, I was still basking in the beauty of the snow-capped Wasatch Mountains. Their beauty and magnitude still took my breath away. Remembering Orlo at my door thirty years prior, looking at the same mountain range over her head felt like my life had come full circle.

My heart warmed as I thought of Huxley supporting me in making my dream to help others a reality. Not only had we purchased my new filming equipment together, but we'd spent time reviewing a few videography skills to help me feel more confident in sharing my message. After filming three takes, I sat back, took a deep breath, and prepared to watch the videos. A new message appeared on my screen.

"Nick is dead. He killed himself."

"NO, Nick!" erupted from my throat while at the same time a hole blew through my chest, opening a part of my soul I'd never before experienced. My dream, his confession, our conversation, and his promise all poured from the reservoir of memories at once into my consciousness.

Tears splattered on the message of my phone as I sobbed. "You promised you'd never do this! You said you'd reach out if you ever felt like that again."

Guilt pierced me like an arrow to its mark as the events from the previous day flooded my mind. I remembered the ceramic wings in the bookstore that had reminded me of Nick's wings and his one million angels, the ones I'd snapped a photo of and thought to send to Nick but did not. I'd missed my cue.

Grief engulfed me as I thought about his wife, his children, his parents, his siblings, and his friends like me. *Nick, what happened? Why would you do this? How could you do this to them?* Regret choked the life out of the excitement I'd been basking in just minutes before. Confusion and even anger at his choice to end his life invaded memories of him cheering *me* on–to live and be happy no matter what.

How could you . . . after everything you told me? To me, his choice was the ultimate betrayal to his parents, his partner, and his children. I'd wanted and wished for a relationship like theirs. Needing answers, I called several mutual friends. Everyone was in shock; no one seemed to really know *why* he'd made this choice.

For the remainder of the day I rested, cried, and focused love energy on Nick's children. I thought about how hard I'd worked to stay alive for my own children. How I'd begged God to let me live when I was sick and how the angel had healed me. The idea of Nick's children not having their father for the rest of their mortal lives caused spasms of pain to roll through my entire body. *You must have been in so much pain, Nick. You loved them so much. I'm so sorry I was gone for so long. I'm sorry I didn't send you the angel wings. I'm so sorry.*

The next morning I woke up to the sun, hardly able to allow its warmth to penetrate my sadness. Lying in bed, the finality of Nick's choice weighed heavy on my heart. I was electrified in the truth of choosing life. A time-line from the first moment I saw Nick to the second I learned of his passing formed in my mind. Communication I didn't fully comprehend outside of Nick and I had intertwined our relationship from its inception. The deep sadness I'd seen in him, my dream of his ghastly wound, our conversations, a confession about his gun, the psychic reading, the angel wings. All of it was perfectly clear in my mind. A cellular understanding of the gift I'd been given in my friendship to Nick crystalized in my aching soul.

That afternoon I shared my thoughts and feelings with a mutual friend also deeply saddened by Nick's passing. We walked up City Creek Canyon in the cold winter air talking about anything and everything, but mostly Nick. Our conversation was cathartic. I was grateful for my friend. He left at dusk.

Lying still on my right side, on top of my comforter with my clothes still on, my head rested on my pillow. The reality of Nick's pain, and the pain ensuing from his life now gone felt incomprehensible. Looking out the sliding glass doors, the blackness of the night was overtaking the light. With no lamps on in my room, the gradient glow of the setting sun was hyper visible over the mountain tops. Turning my attention back to my own room, I glanced above the oversized painting of Jesus on the wall opposite my bed.

Nick was there, in the exact same space my brother Johnny had visited me the summer before, after his passing. He was there in an opening, a window, a portal of sorts to another realm. Unlike Johnny, who'd compassionately and simply sat on the portal's edge, comforting me with his presence, Nick, in haste, came toward me. He was frantic. At first, I felt scared. But as he and I began communicating telepathically, peace ensued.

Mine and Nick's essence occupied the same space, but we were two distinct beings. His thoughts and words were felt and heard in my mind. Loving Kindness for him and from him were felt in my entire being. At the same time, his sadness and his grief were heavy. The connection to him in that moment was stronger than talking to someone on the phone, stronger than anything I'd ever felt when Nick occupied the physical world.

"That project is still on the table: show up in your shit no matter what because you are fucking amazing." Those were his first words, and they were so undeniably him, encompassing his energy, his passion, and his power. His anxiousness and his grief filled me. Confused, I didn't understand what he meant.

He continued, *"Sister, I wasn't able to do it; I was too afraid. I didn't know how to tell the truth. Honestly, I was afraid to look like a failure. I was afraid to let people down. Everyone saw me as a "star." I didn't know how to be anything other than what everyone else thought. Worse, I didn't know how to keep going with what was ahead. I didn't have answers. I'm sorry now that I hurt so many people."*

His tone was hurried and anxious. There was no peace in him. He repeated himself more than once. I let myself sit with his words for a moment, as uncomfortable as it made me. I felt somehow that it was my fault—that I should have done something more to prevent this tragedy.

"Nick, if this was your answer, what do you wish would have been different?" My soul was transfixed in our conversation even as the anguish of reality stayed close. I listened to him, hyperaware that I could feel his pain.

"There are people who would have helped me. I did not know it at the time. I couldn't see anything other than pain. But now where I am, there are so many more answers, so many things I realize now I could have done. Life would have changed. Sure, I would have let a lot of people down. But it would have been okay. At the time, however, I couldn't see anything other than what I did."

"But Nick, you are the brightest of stars; to know you is to love you!" I paused. "Did you think about suicide often?"

"No, sister, but it was an option. I didn't know how to ask for help. I promised you I would ask. I promised my wife. But it was an option. It was my out."

He was so adamant, again repeating himself so that I would really get it. It was almost perturbing to me. And I could feel in the deepest part of my soul that at that moment, he hadn't had access to other options or intelligence. "Nick, then why not have this be everyone's option out? If this was your answer, why not everyone else?"

"There was a part of me that told me that I had to be strong. I had to be perfect or I was worthless. There was that part of me that told me I wasn't enough if I didn't take care of everything. So many people tried to tell me different, positive, and uplifting things, but I didn't know how to believe them. If I could have believed them, if I could have opened my heart to the fact that I didn't have to be perfect, that I didn't have to have all the answers. I didn't have to know everything. I only knew how to give. I didn't know how to ask, or receive in return."

As sad as I was at his choice, I was also feeling more and more troubled at the path he'd not only chosen for himself, but for everyone else. The anguish he'd caused his family, his friends, and himself was irreversible.

"So, this was your answer? Is it still your answer, Nick?" I asked incredulously. In my mind, it just couldn't be, but I was willing to be open to what he had to say.

"No, but I was too deep into my own thoughts. I wasn't honest with people about what was going on. I was saying one thing and I was thinking about another. I had a whole dialogue going on that no one could see. But you're right. I did not want to be invisible. If I didn't have the answer, if I wasn't the shining star, if I couldn't give my family and the world what I wanted and what I thought I should give them, there was only one alternative."

Lying on my bed, in the same position *on earth*, having a conversation with Nick, who was fully alive somewhere else, almost felt as if I was having an out-of-body experience myself. Deep empathy toward my human family to perform, provide, and have all the answers in order to be good enough rushed over me. *This world can be a tough place to live.* "Nick, you have a different perspective now. What do you see from where you are?"

"Sister, I see so much love and I see so much pain and I'm sorry. I'm sorry I didn't know how to be honest. I am sorry I didn't talk about my deepest fears. I'm sorry I didn't know how to ask for help. I'm sorry I didn't know how to fail and be okay with it. I'm sorry I'm not there for my children. I'm sorry I've hurt my wife."

Visual images from the first night we met, hearing him talk about his wife, entered my mind. He loved her so much. He adored his children. I'd wanted a marriage like theirs, to be loved like he loved her. Somehow, she and their children would move on.

"What would have helped you, Nick? Knowing what you know now?"

"This I know now. There is nothing to be afraid of. I was so afraid to not be enough. That's why I had to have all the answers. Because even to myself I had to know all the answers. Because in that place of knowing was the only place I felt safe and comfortable, where I felt like I had control. I had power. Mostly I felt out of control and I felt powerless. Now I realize I didn't have to have the answers."

Taking a deep breath while trying to understand Nick, his pain flooded me. I knew those exact feelings of having to have all the answers. But I also remembered the day I stopped thinking I had to know everything and stepped into the unknown. When having all the answers didn't matter anymore. All that mattered was being an example to my children of how to be happy, so that they could be happy too. I went to ask a question, but he pressed on.

"Now I realize I was trying to create perfection. Even then, it wasn't actually perfect. The answer is to ask. There are so many, many solutions. And I wasn't letting anyone past a certain point, and so I wasn't getting any other answers except the one I was coming up with myself."

"Nick, you said 'Show Up in Your Shit.' How does someone do that if they're afraid to let others see that they don't have all the answers? I know from my personal experiences that fear can paralyze a person."

I shifted on my bed, so full of passion about what he was saying because I felt like we were on the cusp of something so big here–a possible solution.

"Actually, Nick, I'm going to take this even broader because in our work we planned to do together, I want to include *anyone* who is contemplating suicide. For example, someone who has dealt with depression their whole life or a person who just lost all their money and possessions or the person who lost the one person in life they could trust. In each of these situations, it seems that no matter what they do, they can't find happiness. Nick, how does someone be completely honest with how they're feeling from your perspective and where you are now? I think the deeper question is, how could you have let some light in?"

"Sister, every situation is different. Some people make the choice I made in the spur of the moment. Some think about it for a long time. I thought about it many times. And I was happy most of the time. I had so much good in my life. It seems simple and obvious now and yet just yesterday I could not do it. It could have been one simple conversation. That's it! Now, I can see how simply just saying the words would have been freedom. That one conversation would have led to another conversation and those conversations would have allowed the love to pour in and the darkness would have dissipated."

"So, Nick, what I hear you saying is that showing up in your shit would have been a conversation–a truthful conversation–letting someone know the deepest, darkest conversation going on in your head."

"Yes. It would have been a conversation, letting someone in and surrendering in my case to the fact that I didn't have all the answers. Yeah, it would have been two things: having an honest conversation and surrendering to the shit that was real in my life."

"Nick, from where you are now, was there a different choice to be made?" Talking was getting laborious. My physical body felt spent and the mechanisms by which Nick and I were able to converse were taking more energy than a typical conversation. But we continued.

"Sister, there were so many other choices. And when I say, 'show up in your shit no matter what,' I mean it does not matter what is going on in your life. No matter how bad you have fucked up, no matter how long you've been a mess, no matter how bad your life is. You have options, you can have a conversation. There is always someone to help you."

Suddenly, Nick's tone and pitch changed. I could tell he was becoming more passionate.

"From where I am now, Wendy, I wish you could see all the options! There are an infinite amount of options to every problem. In the physical world, we think there's only one answer, especially in the pit of despair. Truthfully, there is an infinite amount of pain and obstacles. We are not born or created to figure it all out alone. We are connected. Oh, if you could just see how connected we all are! Just as there are infinite obstacles, I'm telling you there is an infinite amount of love!"

The love he spoke of reminded me of the love I'd felt so many times from Jesus. "Nick, I want to talk about the last part, 'because you are fucking amazing.'"

"Every single soul is amazing, Wendy! It doesn't matter who you are or what you are going through, what you've gained or whatever you've lost, *or what you have or haven't done. You are fucking amazing.*"

"Nick, did you know that about yourself?"

"Well sure, at times I knew it at my very core: I tasted it, I felt it, and I experienced it in my cells. And then there were times everything about myself was based on my results. At those times, my result was the label I determined

about myself. But I could not handle a life in which others didn't think I was amazing–where my mistakes created less than perfect results."

As the truth of his words settled, disbelief grew wild in me, entering my whole body. "Let me get that straight, brother. You knew you were amazing. But you couldn't see a life where others didn't think you were amazing? Is that what you're saying?"

"That's exactly what I am saying, sista! I couldn't handle it if someone else didn't think I was amazing. That's the bottom line. I couldn't see myself existing anything other than successfully. It was either a red light or a green light."

"Oh my gosh, let's talk about that. From the vantage point you have now, what is your perspective about yourself?"

"I would say I'm fucking amazing no matter what anyone thinks! I'm fucking amazing no matter what anyone says! I'm fucking amazing no matter how anyone treated me! I am fucking amazing because I am me."

Hearing and feeling the power of his words as he spoke, I felt myself imploring him to make me understand the answer I was asking for. "How do we share that, Nick? How do we teach that? How do we teach that perspective so profoundly? You have such a higher perspective now. You can see things we cannot see. How do we do that?"

"Wendy, you did it. You allowed your life to crumble and to completely fall apart. You allowed people to judge you. I watched you when you divorced Spencer and when you went to Europe. I cheered you on. You had a taste of your fucking amazingness, and no matter what, you were going to live and be happy. You decided to be okay with looking like a failure. You were okay with having people turn away from you and saying terrible things about you. I wish I could have seen it in myself, but I can see it now. I told you not to give a shit as to what anyone else thought about you. Live your life, figure out your truth, and say it. And that's exactly what you did."

"Nick, I couldn't have done it without you and the rest of my soul family. The day I saw the wings, your angel wings, I was living in love. And I saw those wings and I took a picture to send you and I didn't. I'm so sorry. I know it would have made a difference. Maybe if I would have sent those wings, you would still be here."

"This was always my choice and never your fault that I didn't see another option. But you and I had a plan. I asked you to create something with me when you got back from Europe. I want you to teach people how to live. I want you to teach people how to ask for help. I want you to teach people how to be honest. I want you to teach them to speak their truth no matter what."

As he told me exactly what he wanted me to do, I noticed that the darkness in my room had merged with the outside night sky through my sliding glass doors. Yet inside of me did not feel dark. I felt illuminated and weighed down from the weight of grief I was carrying.

"Sister, there are no walls between us. I'm right here. I want you to teach people how to open up to the love that is available, that never ends, that connects all of us no matter what. I want you to teach people how to live. I want you to teach people how to show up in their shit no matter what because they are fucking amazing."

Nick stayed with me for two weeks. He didn't want to leave. He was excruciatingly sad. Suicide hadn't stopped his pain. And his sadness was heavy, too heavy for me to continue carrying. I felt selfish for wanting my autonomy, for not being able to hold his grief and mine. But I knew how hard I'd fought to be free, to love me, to feel peace and joy, and to live in love. His grief and mine combined was crushing me. One night I told him how I felt.

The next morning when I woke up, he was gone.

In the days following mine and Nick's powerful, life-changing conversation, I shared our experience with both of our families and our mutual friends. Several friends felt called to help me create something that would support individuals in never forgetting and experiencing their value as human beings.[9] We wanted to help others make a different choice than Nick.

Everything I did in my school work connected back to what Nick asked me to do. Teaching people how to live, ask for help, be honest in their deepest, darkest secrets, and how to open up to the love that never ends, that connects us all, became the quintessence of my life. As a mother, I'd first believed, then learned for myself that there was enough love for everyone to be happy. Now with Nick's perspective and directive, I believed even more that happiness and joy was possible for anyone.

Compiling a book of stories of people who had overcome their own dark nights in order to live honestly in love became my goal. Within weeks of Nick's passing, I was having daily one-on-one conversations with people who had dealt with grief, loss, addiction, anxiety, depression, suicidal ideation, and a host of other human ailments. Listening to every story exponentially increased my appreciation for the resilience of the human soul. Every conversation was elevated, purposeful, and conscious, often leading to my own profound spiritual experiences.

In sharing the experiences I'd had with Nick, people's reactions were both positive and negative. "You're crazy if you think anyone will believe Nick came back to you." I also heard, "Tell your story. You've got to tell your story!" Regardless of who said what, I knew what I'd experienced to be true. At the same time, resistance came up and just the thought of telling my *whole* story to someone–anyone–caused my stomach to flip-flop.

While interviewing and trying to write other people's stories, my recognition, admiration, and respect for the significance of each person's story expanded exponentially. Their choices in overcoming insurmountable odds were powerful and life-changing. I could feel their struggle and their triumph. Yet, I simply did not have the writing skills to share their stories to the level that matched their magnificence or to the message I felt commissioned to share. I was frustrated as a writer.

Switching gears, I began studying and researching suicide for a paper I was writing. I came across an article, "Seeds of Despair," from the *USA Today Network*. I read how "more than 450 US farmers across the nine mid-western states had killed themselves from the years 2014 to 2018."[10] Instantly, my mind went to Spencer and the loss of the two million dollars in our pepper crop that resulted in losing our farm. That was his dream. *I wonder if Spencer ever contemplated suicide.* The thought made me cringe. He'd been so graceful through it all. *How had he lived through such a loss?*

Our next family get-together was at Spencer's apartment. He'd heard about Nick's death from the children and offered his condolences. Standing alone in the kitchen with him, I shared the data from the article.

"Did you ever have feelings of wanting to end your life when we lost the farm?"

"No, that's not something I've ever contemplated. That's not how my brain works." Hearing his answer prompted a question in my own mind. *I wonder what makes some people susceptible to suicide, and others not?*

"That makes me happy for you, Spencer." Continuing in the conversation I said, "Nick came back to me, the day after he died."

"That's fucking bullshit," shot out of his mouth as he walked passed me into the living room and sat down. His brusqueness shocked me. He knew I'd seen Jesus and been healed by an angel. *Why would you say that?* Confused, I turned around, noticing he'd joined our children and was now watching a movie. Baffled, I looked deeply at the person I'd been married to for twenty-five years. And, not one whit of me was affected by his words. I knew what I had experienced and his opinion was irrelevant. I had work to do.

Nick's celebration of life was planned for three weeks after his passing. I began a portrait of him for his family. Creating a gift for the people he loved the most had a healing effect on my soul, similar to what I'd experienced in rendering my baby brother Johnny's portrait two years before for my parents. Nick's portrait was displayed on a grand piano among pictures and mementos special to his family. Copies were shared with his loved ones.

As I have worked on this book, Nick's portrait reminds me of the gift of life and my expressed purpose and promise to him to share a message of how to live no matter what, how to ask for help, how to be honest in our deepest, darkest feelings, and how to live connected to love that connects us all.

True Principles For Your Loving Kindness - LUV Blueprint:

- Of all the tools I've employed in my healing and learning journey, the thing that has had the greatest impact on my life and that I believe can have the most impact on yours is desiring and acting in Loving Kindness. This includes **helping others from Loving Kindness, Loving Kindness for one's self, and Loving Kindness from the source of love that connects us all.**

- Loving Kindness is patience, benevolence, empathy, compassion, and gentleness in not only our actions, but in our thoughts both to ourselves and to others.

- **Loving Kindness for others can catalyze our dreams.** As a parent, a child, a sibling, or a friend, acting in Loving Kindness for another person can move the needle in our life more than just acting for ourselves.

- **Honesty in every action is Loving Kindness.** Being honest, especially when you are afraid others will be upset for any reason, takes courage. Secrets of any kind are heavy to carry and telling the truth is one of the most loving things you can do for yourself and others.

- **Telling the truth sets us free.** Being honest in our deepest, darkest feelings opens a doorway to both love and light.

- We each have an appropriate amount of time to take care of ourselves and help those in our stewardship and the people in our circle of influence. **Defining boundaries while helping others** is essential to creating equanimity in our lives.

- There is enough time for what we need and want to do with a mindful time management practice. **Use time and resources in helping acts for others to create a life connected to love.** We can live in Loving Kindness if we choose to do so.

While completing activities 35–37, you will discover:

- **Activity 35: Opening Your Heart, Letting Loving Kindness Be the Catalyst**

- **Activity 36: Defining Boundaries While Helping Others**

- **Activity 37: Accomplishing a Helping Act in Loving Kindness**

Note: Day 37 is set aside for you to accomplish a helping act of Loving Kindness for someone else. As you begin this section, I invite you to think about someone in your life, or a charity that would benefit from your open heart, your time, and your resources.

ACTIVITY 35: OPENING YOUR HEART, LETTING LOVING KINDNESS BE A CATALYST

"Nick" specifically asked me to teach how to be honest in our deepest, darkest feelings. Maybe he understood that for me this level of vulnerability has been learned over a lifetime. Growing up, I lied a lot! When I was eighteen, I became aware that my dishonesty had deeply hurt people I loved dearly. Knowing that I had betrayed their trust changed me. Today, my husband would tell you that I can't tell a lie to save my life. I am proud that he knows me and sees me in this light.

Awareness of and then action toward being real, raw, and authentic, to speak our truth, especially if we are hiding something, is an act of immense courage. A willingness to slow down in order to take the needed time to really understand what our truth is so that we can act with integrity as we move through life is a conscious act of self-love.

Be kind to yourself. Expectations can outweigh our abilities when trying to live honestly in love. Giving ourselves a break when we fall short and looking through the lens of compassion changes our perspective when we are learning to be honest and living from a mindset of Loving Kindness.

Rumi said, "When we practice loving kindness and compassion, we are the first ones to profit."[11] We learn, we grow, we experience grace for others as well as ourselves in our quest to be fully and completely honest.

When we open our hearts to love, and when we choose to be honest in Loving Kindness toward ourselves and others, love works as a catalyst, increasing our motivation and moving us in the direction of what we want. Let me explain.

When I first stopped abusing alcohol and drugs, I didn't do it for me. Love for the child in my belly helped me stay sober. Healing my sexuality wasn't for me either, at first. Years of self-help books, therapy sessions, and practicing sexual techniques with my husband, even when I felt like screaming and running away in order to work through my sexual trauma, sprang from a deep love for my husband and my desire to create the family I wanted.

Most recently, the commitment I made with Nick was the catalyst helping me through personal fear, barriers, and obstacles, allowing me to share my story. Without my promise to Nick, you would not be holding this book in your hands. Helping others from Loving Kindness, Loving Kindness for one's self, and Loving Kindness from the source of love that connects us all can accomplish the impossible.

C.S. Lewis said, "Do not waste time bothering whether you 'love' your neighbor; act as if you did."[12] Compassion for others, feeling into our hearts, and serving others in Loving Kindness, especially when it is so incredibly difficult, changes us, heals us, and can infuse a deep will to succeed no matter what.

Discovery Activities

- **Breathe, before you even get out of bed. Do this for at least five minutes today.**

- **What is your number today?** _____

- **List Gratitudes**

  1. _____

  2. _____

  3. _____

- **Be honest as you answer the following questions about yourself.**

  Without asking others' opinions, ask yourself, how would *others* describe interacting with you?

  - Cold hearted and selfish.

  - Appropriately nice when called upon to be such.

  - Mostly kind, unless I'm having a bad day.

  - The personification of Loving Kindness.

  Honestly, from your heart, think about each person below. How is Loving Kindness communicated from you to others on a daily basis? *From the perspective of . . .*

Your partner?

_____

Your children?

_____

Your parents? In-laws?

_____

Your work associates?

_____

Your friends?

_____

To whom in your world is it *easiest* for you to bestow Loving Kindness upon? Why?

_____

_____

To whom is it *most difficult* for you to bestow Loving Kindness upon? Why?

_____

_____

- Sit quietly for a few minutes and focus your mind's eye on the area around your heart. Place your right hand on your heart and your left hand on top of your right hand. Breathe and feel your beating heart for at least two minutes. What do you feel? Warmth? Pain?

_____

_____

_____

_____

- **Fill in the following columns**

What I *currently* do that helps others.	What I *want* to do to help others.

Write three things you do for others that are difficult but that you know matter.

1. _____

2. _____

3. _____

Write about what you hope your Loving Kindness in the above three actions conveys to another person.

_____

_____

As a child, how were you taught to help others? List a few examples.

_____

_____

_____

Write about any negative experiences you have regarding helping others and showing Loving Kindness.

_____

_____

_____

How might you overcome any negative feelings about serving someone else?

_____

_____

_____

Who is your greatest inspiration for Loving Kindness? Why?

_____

From your perspective, was Loving Kindness a sacrifice for this particular person?

_____

_____

What are the attributes that you see in this person, your inspiration for Loving Kindness?

_____

_____

How has this person's Loving Kindness changed your life for the better?

_____

_____

_____

_____

How would your life be different if this person would not have chosen Loving Kindness?

_____

_____

- **Write a handwritten letter or an email to the inspirational person above. Share your gratitude with them regarding their Loving Kindness.** If this person is no longer alive, you can still write the letter. Maybe even have a personal burning ceremony, allowing the flames to engulf your gratitude as the smoke rises upward.

Which attributes or qualities would you want to cultivate into your life in order to become more loving and kind in every moment? Here are a few examples to get you thinking:

1. Speaking softly and gently in every conversation.

2. Using safe touch as a way to convey love.

3. Smiling at every person you interact with.

4. Really listening to understand before responding.

5. Slowing down and spending meaningful time with others.

Write your own unique list of ways to cultivate and nurture Loving Kindness into your life.

_____

_____

Circle the number one attribute that when nurtured will change your life and the life of your loved ones for the better.

Write the attribute and a detailed explanation of how you plan to live and fully embody this quality. Possibly draw a picture here.

Are you willing to implement this characteristic into your daily life?

_YES

_NO

What will change or shift in your life as your behaviors more fully express this characteristic?

What obstacles do you foresee coming up when you begin implementing this characteristic into your life?

_____

_____

How will you track your progress?

_____

_____

Honestly, what, if any, unresolved issues, in any of your relationships, are you dealing with that may be blocking your ability to show Loving Kindness? Including yourself?

_____

_____

_____

Is there someone you need to have a hard conversion with that you are not? What do you need to say that you are not saying?

_____

_____

_____

Are there things happening in your daily life that are dishonest, blocking you from receiving or giving Loving Kindness to those you want to share with?

_____

_____

_____

How do you react in the moment you experience an inclination toward Loving Kindness? Do you act, ignore, or shut down? Do you open, get curious, explore, and celebrate?

_____

_____

If you have a thought to act in Loving Kindness and you don't, how do you justify your actions?

_____

_____

- **Find one person and give them a hug!**

- **From both today's introspective writing and your last activity, define in one sentence the #1 attribute or quality that you desire to nurture in order to cultivate your ability to desire and choose Loving Kindness in every moment.**

_____

_____

- **Transfer the above attribute or quality to LUV "My Living Blueprint Template."**

  Are you willing to put into action this quality or attribute in all your relationships?

  _YES

  _NO

- **Be in Bermuda at least 1x today.**

ACTIVITY 36: DEFINING BOUNDARIES WHILE HELPING OTHERS

Time—we all get twenty-four hours in a day regardless of our circumstances. How we use this most precious resource is a choice we each get to make. Defining boundaries regarding the amount of time you take for yourself and how much time you help others is another one of those decisions only you can make. Every moment you take time for one thing, you give up something else. There is a cost, a loss, and a gain to every decision.

Without healthy boundaries regarding our time, energy, and resources, helping others can end up being either just another good idea or too over-whelming even to begin. Brené Brown has said, "When we fail to set boundaries and hold people accountable, we feel used and mistreated."[13] I know this to be true.

For me, most of my life I lived without boundaries. I didn't know how to set them. I thought that to be a good daughter, a good mom, and a good wife, I had to take care of everyone else's emotions and needs, giving everything away. It took years to understand that honestly living in love meant taking care of my needs so that I had enough to actually share with others. Without boundaries, eventually we break. But we can change.

You can learn to create healthy boundaries. Living in Loving Kindness from WHO you are, following your Personal Guidance System (PGS), nurturing your BIOchemistry, and telling the truth to be authentic (TRU), creates a solid foundation in your life that can empower you to communicate more effectively. You have a clearer understanding of what you need every day in order to create resilience and success in yourself. You can better gauge what you have to give.

When your cup is full and overflowing, you are better able to share with others. Ezra Taft Benson said, "If you really want to receive joy and happiness, then serve others with all your heart. Lift their burden, and your own burden will be lighter." [14] In my life, as I have learned to create healthy boundaries, this is a truism I have experienced time and time again. A willingness to help others, from Loving Kindness, always helps me first.

Discovery Activities

- **Breathe, before you even get out of bed. Do this for at least five minutes today.**

- **What is your number today?** _____

- **List Gratitudes**

  1. _____

  2. _____

  3. _____

- **Engage in one practice from your Healing Toolkit, then answer the following questions:**

  Do you feel you have healthy boundaries? Write about the boundaries you currently have in place in your life.

  _____

  _____

  _____

  _____

  Does your Source of Inspiration have any guidance on how to act in Loving Kindness and what a healthy boundary would be as you help others?

  _____

  _____

What direction does your Personal Guidance System give you, if any, regarding service to others? Time? Resources?

_____

_____

How will you stay in equanimity with yourself and nurture your own BIOchemistry as you help others? How do you recharge your own battery after you have served others?

_____

_____

What are you willing to commit to doing that would have you helping someone else on a regular basis? Be detailed as you write out your plan.

_____

_____

_____

_____

How often would you like to commit to serving in this capacity?

_____

_____

Are there resources that you need that you do not have in order to fulfill what you want to do? If so, what will you do to secure what you need?

_____

_____

What, if any, resistance are you experiencing in making this commitment?

_____

_____

How will you move beyond this resistance in order to act in Loving Kindness and help others on a regular basis?

_____

_____

- **Make any and all prior arrangements for your helping activity to show Loving Kindness today as you will be accomplishing your plan during your next activity.**

- **Be in Bermuda at least 1x today.**

ACTIVITY 36: ACCOMPLISHING A HELPING ACT IN LOVING KINDNESS

Every day we can choose to live in the wake of Loving Kindness that we personally create. The more love we give out, the more love we get back. This has been my experience. Simple things like the tone of voice we use, or the pleasantries and positivity we add in our speech patterns can create an atmosphere of love that abides in every communication. Or the opposite can occur.

Walls that we can't see build up, barricading us from each other and from the love that is available all around us. Yet, when we use our free will and open our hearts and mind to give and receive in Loving Kindness, the walls dissolve. Warmth fills not only our own hearts, but the hearts of those close to us, if we simply choose it.

As a young, married army wife, expecting my second baby and living far away from family, I felt very alone. One of the other women from my church group quietly began to serve my family. Randomly she would drop off a dinner, or bring me baby clothes she'd picked up at local garage sales. Often she offered to take care of my toddler so that I could take a nap. Her Loving Kindness meant the world to me. Gandhi said, "All other pleasures and possessions pale into nothingness before service which is rendered in a spirit of joy."

Nick came back to me for one reason–to help others. He wanted others to make a different choice than he had made. He wanted others to live, to ask for help, to be honest in their deepest, darkest secrets and to connect to the love that connects us all.

Helping each other one act, one person at a time, is where we begin to create a humanity that lives in love.

Discovery Activities

- **Breathe, before you even get out of bed. Do this for at least** five minutes today.

- **What is your number today?** _____

- **List Gratitudes**

  1. _____

  2. _____

  3. _____

- Check your tone of voice and the words you are using as you communicate with others. How often does your tone convey graciousness, kindness, patience, and love?

  - Never. I'm a jerk and I like it.

  - Mostly I say what I want, unaware of how my communication is received.

- Depends on whom I'm with and how they treat me.

- Trying to be kind, but often falling prey to circumstance and emotion.

- Graciousness, kindness, patience, and love in my speech comes naturally to me.

Can you explain your answer? Why do you think you are like this?

_____

_____

_____

_____

- Spend time today in the act of helping others and showing Loving Kindness. Make sure you leave time for reflection and personal recharge, either before or after.

Write about your experience in helping another in Loving Kindness. How did you feel?

_____

_____

_____

_____

What compensation, in any form, for your time, energy, and resources did you receive?

_____

_____

Why did you choose this particular person or charity? How much time did you spend in the service act?

_____

_____

What would you do differently next time?

_____

_____

What is your #1 takeaway from the act of helping and showing Loving Kindness that you chose?

_____

_____

Do you feel that your action in any way had a negative effect on your BIOchemistry? How did you recharge?

_____

_____

After this activity, how often would you like to commit to serving in a helping role?

_____

_____

Are you willing to give up some of your time to help others on a regular basis? Maybe even every day?

_YES

_NO

Write out a plan going forward that will allow you to help others in Loving Kindness.

_____

_____

_____

- **Be in Bermuda at least 1x today.**

Loving Kindness can act as a barometer, showing us how open and clear we are to experiencing the love available to us. For me, when it's difficult to help others, it's also harder for me to feel deep, abiding love for myself. Helping others can ignite the flame of Loving Kindness.

In the right balance, helping others can take the focus off of our own problems momentarily, help give us a new perspective, and add positive energy into the world around us. Helping others can also bring feelings of satisfaction and fulfillment!

Acting from Loving Kindness has had karmic effects in my life, and I believe the same thing will happen to you, in that what you send out in love will return to you again. Every good thing that has come into my life has come through the merit of Loving Kindness from Jesus, from loved ones, from strangers, and from my every day, ordinary self.

Loving Kindness is like a flywheel building momentum in every action while at the same time smoothing out the rough edges of daily living. Love in a person's life stores positive energy, provides strength, and acts as a reservoir of support and resilience. Just as a flywheel powers a machine, love powers our emotional well-being.[15] The duet "Return to Love" sung by Andrea Bocelli and Ellie Goulding inspires us to look beyond ourselves and _risk it all for love_.[16]

Together, one person at a time, we can slow down, take a risk, open our hearts, then listen to understand and truly serve each other. Love is not visible to the human eye; it must be felt and it presents itself in a variety of ways. It's significant. It's not to be denied, this life-giving energy of Loving Kindness.

CHAPTER 11 LIVING IN LOVING KINDNESS

desiring pure love
surrendering enmity
love is who we are

Life's a journey we mostly walk independently. Even in the most beautiful relationships, it's just you and I alone in our moment-to-moment decisions. Desiring and choosing Loving Kindness in our actions connects us to the love that connects us all. But how do we do that?

The thoughts we choose to entertain, the tone of our voice while communicating, and the words we use detract us from or invite us into the feeling and expression of love. Treating others the way we want to be treated is one of the best ways to connect instantly to love. Feeling sorry and expressing remorse when we fail to act in Loving Kindness also connects us to love.

Loving Kindness is a decision we can make regardless of any other person's actions toward us. Living in love is a decision independent of any relationship status. Living in love, we need never feel alone.

In 1964, during his acceptance speech for the Nobel Peace Prize, Martin Luther King said, "I believe that unarmed truth and unconditional love will have the final word in reality. This is why right temporarily defeated is stronger than evil triumphant."[1] Living in Loving Kindness builds immunity to other people's judgments and opinions of your decisions. Expectations are more easily dispelled.

Your courage, perseverance, and diligence are triumphant, as you move forward in understanding yourself, live from your Blueprint. Utilizing the wisdom you've gained in creating a life based on WHO you are, following your Personal Guidance System (PGS), nurturing your Biochemistry (BIO), and telling the truth (TRU) has positioned you to now choose to live in Loving Kindness (LUV) always.

You have the knowledge and the means to keep your cup full, to respond instead of react, and to show compassion as you live from your Blueprint each and every day. Loving Kindness can flow through you, which means there is never a shortage of love for yourself or for others.

A warm, sunshiny Mother's Day followed the year after my return from Europe. I met all my children at a park for a picnic. We took our first impromptu family picture without Spencer. The moment felt a bit empty. Still, the sun was out, I was home, and I was loving being with my children. Briggs was playing in a spouting fountain in the middle of the park with my two beautiful grandsons. All three of them were sopping wet.

Later in the day, Spencer joined the picnic with an invitation. "If anyone has time, I'm making dinner tonight. Huxley and Briggs, I'm making your favorite chicken." Cocking my head to one side I thought, *Interesting. I've never seen you cook.* Intrigued, I accepted his invitation.

Walking into his apartment, Spencer's ordered and minimalist decorating motif made me smile. He was moving freely around the kitchen, fully conversant on using cooking utensils and preparing food. I was mesmerized. Shocked, actually. All by himself he was measuring liquids, chopping cucumbers, and dredging chicken, something I'd never seen him do in our twenty-five years of marriage. Realizing our children were excited to eat his food because their dad cooking for them had become a habit while I was in Europe filled my heart with gratitude.

After dinner, Spencer showed me his tattoo. On his chest over his heart was a four-inch bull with horns. A little child held the face of the bull and stared into its eyes. The image reminded me of our four little children wanting his attention for their entire lifetimes. My eyes welled up with tears as a beautiful realization sunk in. Through the divorce and while I was in Europe, our children were finally getting the father they'd always needed and desperately wanted.

Later that week, on a beautiful sunny day, we had a family birthday party. Our children outdid themselves planning the festivities. BBQ hamburgers and hotdogs, salads, and various appetizers filled our hungry bellies. Water games, including a child-size swimming pool and a dinosaur that sprayed water from its mouth, were set up for the grandboys. A cornhole tournament ensued for the adults. Rhodes won!

Spencer and I visited in the sunshine. "You've really done a great job connecting with the children, Spencer. It's wonderful to see your relationships with them."

His reply was soft. "Thank you. You set a high bar in the parenting department, Wendy."

Six months after telling me he didn't like the "new Wendy," his kindness felt a bit like the sunshine we were basking in. He left early.

That night when I returned home, I noticed he'd sent me an email. It was late and I was ready for bed, but my curiosity got the best of me.

Wendy,

I'm not really sure why I'm writing this to you, other than a selfish desire to talk to my former best friend. I think I enjoyed Sunday afternoon so much, I'm feeling nostalgic.

I lied to our children and told them I needed to go home because I was tired. The truth is I couldn't hide my sadness any longer tonight. I wish it could be possible for us to be together again. Really. There is nothing I would like more. I meant what I said tonight–I truly don't believe I will ever meet anyone as amazing as you–or that I will love as much as I

325

loved you–and the really scary thing for me is that I don't know if I will ever be able to give someone else my heart. When I promised my heart to you, twenty-eight years ago, it was a forever promise. I seriously doubt I will ever be able to change that fact.

If you ever decided you wanted to commit to each other again-to truly commit–which for me would mean giving up any other relationships with other people–I think I would want us again. I mean it when I tell you I want you to be happy. I really do. I hope with all my broken heart that your path brings you happiness. You deserve it more than anyone I know.

I love you, and I will keep wishing you nothing but a great life.

Your friend. Spencer

My former husband's email caught me off guard. I knew he thought I was a good mom, he'd always said that, but this surprised me more than watching him mirthfully cook for our children. After what he'd said about Wendy 3.0 and what he'd said about "the bullshit" of Nick coming back to me, it didn't make sense. Something had changed in him. On a phone call the next week, he was even more vulnerable.

Spencer had just reread his favorite book, *Illusions* by Richard Bach.[2] The story had helped him understand my experience with Nick and my desire to share what I'd learned. In the book, one of the main characters dies, then returns, imparting wisdom to his friend. Spencer was totally open to discussing my experience with Nick. We did so at length.

Again, I brought up the article about the high suicide rate among farmers during the same years when we'd lost our pepper crop.[3] This time his answer shed light on our experience as a couple, and me as his wife. "Suicide did not cross my mind. That's not something I've ever even thought about, but I was absolutely sinking from despair. I didn't know what to do and your loving response when I told you we'd lost $2 million dollars felt like a life preserver."

He said more, but at that moment, after everything I knew about suicide, for the first time ever in our relationship, I realized that *I had been of value* to Spencer. A part of my heart healed that night.

A few weeks later, Spencer invited Briggs, Huxley, and me to the park for a picnic. I took my guitar and joined them in the sunshine. The next day, we all headed to Park City on motorcycles. A clear blue sky laced with puffy clouds drifted above us. The inkling of being part of a happy family began to sprout in my thoughts. I let it hover on the stage of my mind like the clouds above.

The following week, Spencer invited just me on a motorcycle ride. He picked me up in a pink gingham button-up shirt. He looked sexy as hell. Putting on the helmet he'd bought for me, I jumped on the back of his bike, hyperaware of how close to him I was. Holding on to his waist, with my head in proximity to his, I noticed he was wearing a different cologne than when we were married. Touching him, however, felt familiar and exciting.

Riding along the base of the Wasatch mountain range, the sprawling valley to the right was lit up with the afternoon sun. We went to his house and he played the song "Scars" by James Bay[4] for me. As I listened to the lyrics, I realized Spencer had always loved me. The line in the song, "You try to make a pay phone call to me," sent my mind back to traveling alone. Our eyes locked, and I knew he remembered too. The phone call from Paris.

At that moment I understood why he'd not dated in the three years since our divorce. And why he'd told me, more than once, that life had been easier when I was living in Europe. When I was traveling abroad, he didn't have to see me all the time at family activities. It was then that I understood that his brusqueness was a defense put up to protect his heart. His unkindness was a deflection from his pain.

The evening sun was setting over the Oquirrh mountain range as we walked outside his apartment and up the street to a small grove of trees. With my new understanding of Spencer at the forefront of my thoughts, together we put up a double-person hammock between two trees. Sitting on the hill in front of me, in the evening breeze, I looked deeply into the person I'd spent most of my adult life with. He was not the same man I'd been married to. He was different. He was open to me. Yes, he was still churlish at times, but he was also vulnerable. We talked about his life since moving back to Utah from Iowa.

"What's happened in the last two years, Spencer?"

"I almost lost my job last year. I was already down from our divorce. That was a blow. Having two of my best friends tell me that I had thirty days to make a profit or I was getting fired was another blow. I had to admit to my team that I was failing. All of it together forced me to ask for help, to be vulnerable, to let people know I couldn't do it alone. It was hard, but I did it."

I just listened to the man that I knew so well and was meeting for the very first time. As he talked, I saw tears dripping out his eyes. In twenty-five years, I'd never seen him cry.

Slowly, over the next few weeks, the same thing that had happened when we first met in college began again. We spent *all* our free time together. We ate together almost every day. Conversations and time spent together fell into perfect alignment, just like they had twenty-five years ago. Other relationships and activities slowly dropped out of both of our lives.

I could see that Spencer was very happy! He golfed every day before work. He was taking care of his body by working out with a fitness and nutrition coach. He was aware of our children's needs; no longer were they objects to him. He wanted to spend time with them. He wanted to talk to me about anything. He would cry happy tears in almost every conversation. He took accountability for mistakes in our previous relationship and in our family.

He said he was sorry. He was vulnerable. Seeing him in this light felt like a mirror. He was living his best life.

The battles in my mind that I had lived with for so many years had gone by the wayside. Self-hatred and sexual trauma, issues I had brought to our relationship that had eroded the fabric of our marriage, were healed. Expectations for myself and him to be perfect and that our family live a certain religious standard had been replaced with gratitude and meeting each person exactly where they were at. For every *reason* I'd chosen divorce, we'd both changed!

During one conversation Spencer shared, "I don't go to church anymore. I don't believe in religion, Wendy. Honestly, the world would be a better place without it. If you want me to sit with you when you attend church, I'll do that but just for you. I have no desire to be there for myself."

"I have so many questions, too, Spencer," I admitted, "but I'm okay with not knowing all the answers. Jesus knows everything about us, and in His love I'm absolutely sure." Then, looking away, I remembered the infinite love I'd felt in His presence. It never left me then or now. Turning my head back to Spencer, I noticed he was intently listening to me.

"When I take the sacrament at church, I feel a peace deep in my soul that I don't experience anywhere else. And I've looked. So, I go for that feeling. It's like a light turns on inside of me and I feel lifted, especially if I'm feeling sad. It always works. I want to go back to the temple someday. If you want to go to church with me, it would be nice to sit by each other."

"I'd like that," he said, his clear blue eyes riveted on me.

Spencer's groundedness, his organization, and his absolute calm in the eye of the storm were still the same. He'd been loyal to me. Even in his pain, he'd kept our agreements and fulfilled his financial obligations to me and our children. His work ethic was still second to none and everything in his space was painstakingly neat and tidy.

Our daily conversations continued and the next week he asked, "Would you like to take a drive in the mountains on Saturday and just read together, maybe bring your guitar?"

"I would love that!"

He picked me up early in the day. Warm summer air blew in the window as we listened to music and drove through the Wasatch Mountains for several hours. Being in the seat next to him, doing nothing at all, had the same peaceful effect it always had on my soul. I was still connected to him after everything we'd been through.

Driving for miles while not passing a single car, we finally found a small, isolated meadow next to a stream in the heart of the mountains. Pine trees and quaking aspens surrounded us. His new tent was built in and attached to the back of his truck bed. Lavender colored thistles waist high in full bloom surrounded us. Together we learned how and where all the poles needed to go. Laughing and working side by side, the tent went up easily for our first time.

Crawling in, I took my guitar out of its case and started playing, "Knockin' on Heaven's Door" by Bob Dylan. Spencer was next to me with his book in hand. For the next hour, he dove into his fictional characters and I strummed my guitar. After a while, he moved closer and kissed me. "I want to create a life with you," I heard as he kissed my ear, then my neck.

"Oh, really?" I exhaled. A twinge of self-consciousness crept in as Spencer kissed my mouth, but looking into his eyes, all I could feel was his love. Taking down the tent, we laughed, then kissed some more.

Driving home, I said, "I've loved other people since I was with you, Spencer. I started over not because I wanted to be alone, but because I wanted to create a happy relationship. I've loved both men and a woman. I learned how to set boundaries. I like Wendy 3.0."

"I like Wendy 3.0 too. I think I said what I said because I didn't think I could be with you. But I want to know everything about you, Wendy. Everything. If you're willing to commit to me, and only me, I never want to spend another night away from you." He glanced sideways at me and added, "I trust you. I never thought I could after the divorce, but I do. I trust you, Wendy Beth."

Laying my head back, I rested on his words. No part of me was running away or shutting down like during our marriage. Nor was I missing the past or anyone else. I was fully and unapologetically sharing with him who I was, thankful for the peace I felt in the deepest part of my soul.

That night I slept in Spencer's bed. We made love. It was glorious for him as well as me. The next morning I slept in, then stayed in his bed, swaddled in his sheets till mid-morning while he went to work. An exultant feeling of calm was present as I looked out the window to see the Oquirrh Mountain in the distance, a pinkish-orange morning sky hovering above. His smell lingering, his kiss still fresh on my lips, I thought, *I'm going to marry you.* Spencer was my soulmate.

Eight weeks after my Mother's Day picnic, we were engaged. Living together wasn't an option for me. I already knew sex outside of marriage, even if it was perfect, would make some part of my soul feel empty. Still, I couldn't marry Spencer again without having a clear picture of what sexual intimacy would be like together. I'd already done that once before. Twenty-five years of experience with each other and the changes we'd both made told me everything else I needed to know. My destiny was Spencer and reuniting our family.

Focusing on our love and filled with giddy excitement, we made a reservation for the patio at The Charleston in Draper, Utah, a place Spencer had taken me several times since we'd begun dating. The beautiful, two-story, pre-Victorian brick house turned fine dining restaurant was the perfect place to announce the good news to our children. As it turned out, dinner was just the core six members of our family. Our children's partners nor our grandsons were able to join us.

For the first time in years, Spencer, myself, and our beautiful children were alone, together, just like we'd been growing up as a family. My heart soared. I could hardly contain my excitement! Life felt absolutely perfect.

We realized the next day, however, that all our children weren't ecstatic about our reunion. In fact, some were adamantly against our marriage. More than once we heard, "Don't get married. Take some time. Live together for a year and see if this is really what you both want." Hurt and shocked, the thought had never crossed my mind that our children would not want us to reconcile. I thought they'd be excited to have their parents back together.

The truth was, our divorce was not a single event. It was years of nonworking behaviors, pain, and sadness that had not only hurt Spencer and me. Our children had also been traumatized. As a family, we had done no work together during or after the divorce to help them heal their pain. As I processed, I realized that what was happening was *the thing* I'd struggled with my whole life. The battle was still in me. *Could I live my truth, no matter what?*

So many times I'd allowed people to dictate how I felt about myself, including what I could and couldn't do, or how I should and shouldn't be. My greatest obstacle had been fear of rejection, then capitulating my needs to what others wanted, hoping they would be nice and love me. From my earliest childhood memories, this had been my thinking patterns. It's how I survived. In turn, my boundaries had been trampled on, ignored, and crossed. Creating a life with Spencer was my truth. I knew it in the deepest part of my soul. We moved forward with our wedding plans.

Our family was like a mirror that had shattered during the divorce. Each of us had taken the pieces we needed to survive and recreated our lives. Many conversations ensued, some productive and many not so much. Often, I failed at effective communication. Too many times I spoke from pain. But love always fueled my choice as we moved forward. It was the only way.

Our youngest child, an expert in creating magical events around the world, helped me plan our nuptials. Huxley listened, then walked me through every detail of our wedding day to create our perfect experience. Spencer's only wish was, "Whatever your mom wants, let's make it happen."

Filled with wonder and awe at the miracle I was living, I basked in the moments with my youngest child as we planned an unforgettable experience for our little family. I hoped everyone would choose to be with us.

On August 23, 2020, we woke up above Park City, Utah in the beautiful Wasatch Mountains. The air was crisp as we hiked along a mountain trail with our children and grandsons. Spencer picked me a bouquet of pink, yellow, and lavender wildflowers from the woodland trail we hiked on. Returning to our cabin suite, I took a bubble bath with rose petal water.

"Mom, will you trim our hair before we get dressed?" Huxley asked later in the day. I used my razor to clean up their hair on the backs of their necks for the ceremony. Later, I played my guitar alone in my bedroom. "Walk With Me" by Bella Thorne played in the background as we danced and got ready for our wedding the rest of the afternoon.

Atop the mountain range was a 360 degree of stunning alpine views lit up with the late afternoon sun. A light breeze swept away the heat, leaving just a touch of warmth on our skin. Each member of our family wore natural, earth-toned clothing according to their own style and taste. My white, midi, cotton sundress with eyelet edges and lace-up boots was the perfect juxtapose of rustic elegance. Spencer was absolutely dashing in his ecru shirt, ivory jeans, and tiger eye beads. I carried a mixed bouquet of dried wildflowers and grasses, matching the landscape flawlessly.

Walking down the aisle of The Church of Dirt, I held both my grandson's tiny hands on each side of me as we approached our family already in place amid the rustic pews.

Seeing all of my children in attendance and smiling, Spencer waiting for me under the blue sky and a crude wooden altar, with the sun shining its light on my family, brought tears to my eyes. A dear friend officiated our ceremony, offering words of healing for our whole family. Spencer took a few minutes and apologized to our children for being absent in their lives for so many years. Then he turned to me.

"My darling, Wendy Beth, for fifty-one years I have been searching for the purpose of my life. A few months ago, sitting in our double hammock on the hill, I realized that the purpose of my life is to love you. If I do nothing else in this life but love you well, it will have been a perfect life.

"I want you to know how sorry I am that I haven't loved you better and I am so grateful that you have forgiven me and are giving me this new chance. Thank you so much. I will love you forever.

"In my book of scripture, *Illusions*, he says 'don't be dismayed at the good-byes, a farewell is necessary before you can meet again. And meeting again after moments of lifetimes, is certain for those who are friends.' You are my best friend. I will love you and cry with you every day you desire. I am so grateful to be restarting forever with you today. I love you."

Deeply touched by his words, I picked up my guitar and sang my vows to him,

> *Today on top of this mountain,*
> *I'm going to marry you because I want to.*
> *I was born to be loved by you, to live in peace with you.*
> *I'll be me and I'll love you and together we'll ride our lifetime through,*
> *Baby, it's been a journey to find you.*
> *Our magical mornings are a gift because tomorrow's not a given,*
> *we'll spend the rest of our lives really living.*
> *You be you and I'll be me and together we'll create our infinity,*
> *Baby, it's been a journey to find you.*
> *Richard Bach says, 'If you love something, set it free,*

if it comes back to you it was meant to be.'
Living in love is what we're living,
embracing illusions and loving these children.
Baby, it's been a journey to find you.

I cried the whole time I was singing. To my new heart's joy, so did Spencer.

Our children and our grandchildren tossed rice into the air and we toasted with champagne in the glow of the setting sun. Spencer and I rode down the mountain on his motorcycle. Afterwards, under a cabana at a restaurant, we ate dinner as a family. Looking around my circle of the people I loved most in the world, my heart was filled with awe! *This is my family.*

The truth was choosing to heal my own sexual wounds throughout our marriage and then learning to love me and both of us working to learn and heal during the divorce eventually allowed us to connect as a couple. We had the space and the ability to love each other vulnerably and wholeheartedly. Each other's love freely given was wanted, accepted, and honored.

Reconciliation between Spencer and me happened because compassion and forgiveness, for ourselves and for each other, filled our hearts. Loving Kindness replaced pride, anger, and resentment. Peace in our individual hearts and then in our relationship was the by-product. The past was gone.

For the next three years, Spencer and I focused time, energy, and money on healing our family wounds. Helping each member overcome the trauma of the first marriage and the divorce became mine and Spencer's top priority. It was not easy. We invited all of our children to vacation in Mexico with us. Some joined us; others did not.

We invited all of our children to be with us often, even inviting them to live with us when needed. We started family therapy. Some of our children chose to join us; some did not. Experiencing healing in relationships I thought beyond repair in this lifetime helped me cope when other relationships felt more strained than ever. Learning to let go and allow my children their own process was not easy, but I did it.

Watching Spencer take time to get to know and enjoy his two younger children the way he'd enjoyed parenting when we were first married was healing to my mother's heart. Being part of a healthy, functioning marriage and working to create our family together as partners began to heal my own deep, generational family wounds. Finally, after thirty years, Spencer and I were coparenting.

Life was made even sweeter by welcoming and getting to know our third grandson. His inquisitive, happy spirit brought new life and energy to our family. Oriana, his mother, became like a daughter to Spencer and me, adding to my chosen family. Being a hands-on grandparent with Spencer again was pure joy and a dream come true!

The baby of our family socially transitioned and asked to be recognized as nonbinary while creating a peaceful life with Woodson, a loving and gracious ceramicist. Seeing our youngest child in a safe, loving relationship brought peace to my mother's heart.

The truth was miracles had been a part of my story for as long as I could remember. Spencer and I being deliciously happy together felt like one of the grandest of them all. Not a day went by that I wasn't thankful to be married to him, creating family memories and living our dream together, something I worked tirelessly for over half my life.

Traveling domestically and internationally together was a shared interest we enjoyed often. Walking, hiking, cooking, eating out, talking, and playing games, especially Scrabble, were things we pretty much did every day together. Grandchildren time was cherished and we spent as many moments as we could with our children and their partners.

Almost to the day, three years after our wedding on Guardsman Pass, Spencer and I bought a beautiful off-grid cabin with majestic views deep in the Wasatch mountain range of Utah. I had seen the place in a vision in 2018, so when I saw it in real life, I knew it was ours, no matter what-- quite serendipitous to me since so many remarkable moments in my life had taken place in their foothills. Together he and I began creating our alpine sanctuary.

In the quiet of the evenings, seated on the deck, we nestled under warm blankets together and marveled as the sun gracefully set. The ambient sounds of dusk surrounded us while the night sky gradually unveiled one by one its stars until the entire expanse twinkled with celestial light.

Enjoying these precious moments together was enriched, knowing that we were creating a refuge not only for ourselves but also a place to be enjoyed by our children and grandchildren beyond our own lifetimes. The truth was that the differences that had defined each of us no longer divided us. We both lived from what we believed to be true according to our own experiences, consciousness, beliefs, and values. Me, a disciple of Jesus Christ , and an active member of The Church of Jesus Christ of Latter-day Saints. Spencer, a secular humanist, always willing to sit with me in church any time I ask.[5] Together our belief systems covered an infinite spectrum of possibility.

We both agreed that the biggest difference in our relationship today from the beginning years was that individually we took 100 percent accountability for our personal happiness. We had no expectations that the other person was responsible for filling our cup. Living our personal Blueprints was up to each of us. Never did we try to change the other.

Knowing who I am, honoring my gifts, and living my truth brought peace and joy to my soul. My experiences with my Personal Guidance System have often been a leap of faith-building trust in my Source of Inspiration over the past thirty-four years. As I have learned, changed, and understood better how to be true to myself and not betray my truth, I saw that commitments continue to create structure and support toward my happiness as I keep them with integrity.

My Biochemistry began a state of change through menopause and I adjusted to new horizons of how to care for my aging body. Some days I felt my years more than others. Taking the time to care for myself, if it ever was a luxury, became an absolute requirement in feeling mentally awake, physically strong, and spiritually attuned as I began the second half of my life.

Asking for help, telling the truth no matter what, and being authentic with Spencer were key ingredients in creating my ultimate relationship. I created a life where my well-being and living in love was the atmosphere in which I enjoyed both my interests and time with my loved ones–a space in this world where my feelings, thoughts, and ideas were seen, heard, validated, and respected.

Loving Kindness and compassion for myself prevailed even and especially when I fell short or failed. The grace I was given by Jesus and freely gave my children, and others, was something I learned to give myself. Every day was a new opportunity to live truly, choose wisely, and act kindly from the wisdom of my own unique Blueprint.

Recently while volunteering at a LGBTQ Pride Center to distribute food for the homeless dealing with food insecurity, I sat and watched as people from all faiths and walks of life participated in a community helping act. I contemplated the many times I, in my own church, had been a participant of the exact same type of service opportunity.

In a world of inequality and cultural divisiveness, on that beautiful spring morning, I felt absolutely united with humans helping other humans in complete compassion and Loving Kindness. Once again I was reminded that for each of us, every dawn is a new day to use our free will to live fully and dance between our decisions and our destiny.

True principles for your LUV Blueprint

- **Making and keeping commitments can calm the mind, bring peace to our everyday lives, and create structure by which to build our life upon.** When we trust ourselves to keep our commitments, our discerning capabilities are sharpened, allowing us to make wiser choices.

- **You are 100 percent in charge of your happiness.** No one else can fill your cup. No one else knows what you need. Of course, others can support you, but ultimately it's up to each of us to create a happy life.

- If your Personal Guidance System is not taking you to pure Loving Kindness for yourself and others, I invite you to examine it and make adjustments. You were born to be happy. It is available to us all.

- **Other people's opinions of you are irrelevant.** Let go of needing other people's approval. Knowing WHO you are, following your Personal Guidance System (PGS), nurturing your biochemistry (BIO), telling the truth and being authentic (TRU), and desiring, then choosing Loving Kindness (LUV) will change the trajectory of your life and give you the absolute confidence you need to stand up for what is true for you.

- Live your life, and let the opinions of others float away like smoke from a fire.

- The dance between your destiny and your decisions is a perfectly unique creation that you were born to, not only become the master of, but learn to exquisitely enjoy.

While completing activities 38–40, you will discover:

- **Activity 38: Making and Keeping Commitments**

- **Activity 39: Accepting 100 Percent Accountability for Your Happiness**

- **Activity 40: Living in Love, Scheduling Check-Ins**

ACTIVITY 38: MAKING AND KEEPING COMMITMENTS

Personal integrity can be subjugated to the business of life, to the moments when all hell's breaking loose . . . or that's when it can be fortified. We get to decide. And trusting ourselves is integral to our personal happiness and to living in love. Zig Zigler, one of the most influential thinkers said, "It was character that got us out of bed, commitment that moved us into action, and discipline that enabled us to follow through."[6] Living from your Blueprint is a commitment to your happiness, to your evolution, and to your forward movement in spite of adverse experience.

Commitment, as a binding agreement, acts like a structure holding aspects of our life together. How strong that structure or commitment is, we choose. When life gets chaotic, when it feels out of control to any degree, look at how you keep your word. It can so easily be taken for granted. Are you keeping your promises to yourself and others? Do you trust yourself to keep your commitments?

Commitments can keep us centered and focused on our goals. When we get lax in our commitments, life can start to feel wobbly and our internal foundation isn't as resilient. Living committed to your WHO, PGS, BIO, TRU, and LUV Blueprints will support you in maintaining a strong, daily internal infrastructure for your life. You can feel safe and move forward even when circumstances outside of you are unstable

Discovery Activity:

- **Breathe, before you even get out of bed. Do this for at least five minutes today.**

- **What is your number today? _____**

- **List Gratitudes**

  1. _____

  2. _____

  3. _____

- **Set up a thirty-minute conversation with one of your success part-ners for activity 40.**

- **In each shape, list your commitments to**

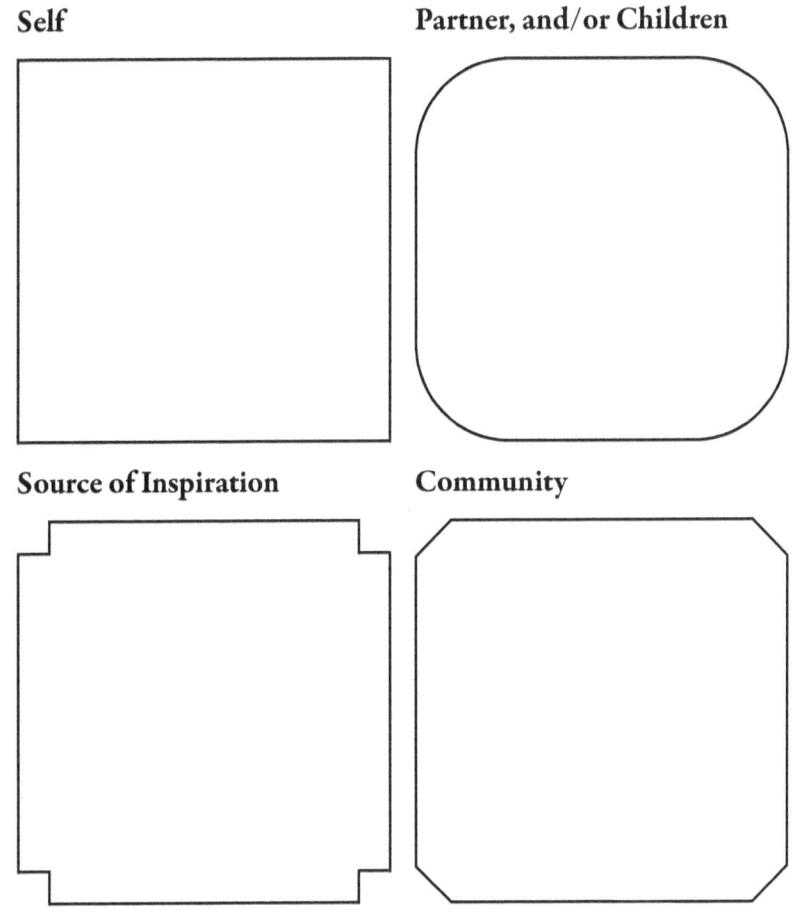

Self

Partner, and/or Children

Source of Inspiration

Community

Are your commitments balanced? Do you want them to be?

_____

_____

_____

Where are you lacking in commitment? Where are you overcommitted?

_____

_____

_____

Write down the #1 reason you over or under commit.

_____

_____

_____

What is the number one thing you would like to do differently in your commitments?

_____

_____

_____

How well have you kept your commitments thus far in your Living Blueprint? If anything, what is breaking down for you in keeping your commitments?

_____

_____

_____

Does your Source of Inspiration help you keep your commitments? Does your Personal Guidance System help you keep promises to yourself? How?

_____

_____

_____

Center and ask yourself, what is the most important thing you can do to keep your commitments to yourself and others?

_____

_____

_____

o **Commit to at least one hour every week planning your WHO, PGS, BIO, TRU, and LUV Blueprints into your DWM daily/ weekly/monthly routine.**

Take planning notes for yourself for the upcoming week and month here.

WHO BLUEPRINT

_____

_____

_____

PGS BLUEPRINT

_____

_____

BIO BLUEPRINT

TRU BLUEPRINT

LUV BLUEPRINT

Looking at the notes you have prepared from your weekly planning session and your own "My Living Blueprint Template," add the items you want to commit to, track, and be accountable for in your DWM Tracker.

You can print them out from the resource tab at wendybeth.org or track your progress in your own electronic spreadsheet.

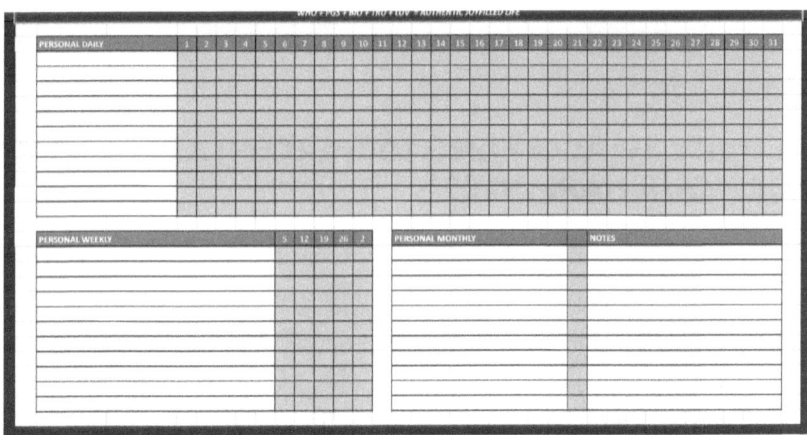

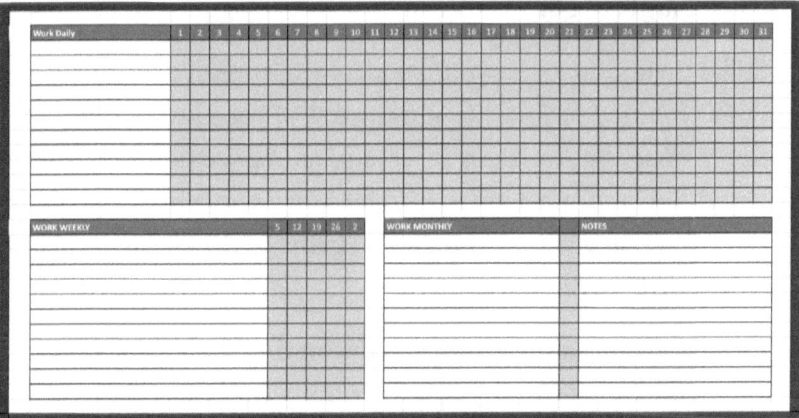

What day and time will you spend planning the daily and weekly application of your Living Blueprint?

_____

_____

- **Add this date and time to your personal calendar and to My Living Blueprint.**

- **Be in Bermuda at least 1x today.**

ACTIVITY 39: ACCEPTING 100 PERCENT ACCOUNTABILITY FOR YOUR HAPPINESS

Personal happiness and connecting to love is up to each of us. Two things I've found that exponentially increase our ability to connect to love and be happy are first, NOT multitasking, and second, NOT comparing ourselves, our efforts, or our actual results, to anyone else. I know it's hard, especially when there's so much to do and when it looks like everyone else is having so much fun and doing better or worse than we are. Each of us is perfectly unique.

Still, I invite you to put your blinders on and fixate on the five programs you want running in your life and the rest of your Living Blueprint. Focus creates results. The American Psychological Association website notes that the mind and brain are not designed for heavy-duty multitasking.[7] Focusing on the task at hand allows us to fully experience the gifts that each moment our beautiful life brings.

Comparing ourselves to others and worrying about what others think of us robs us of our happiness. Literally, it steals our peace of mind. Dr. Daniel Ahem, in his book *Change Your Brain, Change Your Life,* said, "Stop worrying about what others think of you. Base your thoughts, your decisions, and your goals on what you want and what is important in your life"[8]

This quote from Charles Mackay, a Scottish writer, helps me focus on my life's purpose and helps me let go of other people's opinions of my life and my decisions. "You have no enemies, you say? Alas, my friend, the boast is poor. He who has mingled in the fray of duty that the brave endure must have made foes. If you have none, small is the work that you have done. You've hit no traitor on the hip. You've dashed no cup from perjured lip. You've never turned the wrong to right. You've been a coward in the fight."[9]

Life experiences, aspirations, families, and what brings us joy are perfectly uniquely our own, and can be contaminated by outside expectations and opinions. Even our own children and our parents, the people we know the best and who know us, are completely different from us. If you think about it, what others think of your life and what makes you feel fulfilled and satisfied are really no one else's business. And vice versa.

Discovery Activity

- **Breathe, before you even get out of bed. Do this for at least five minutes today.**

- **What is your number today?** _____

- **List Gratitudes**

    1. _____

    2. _____

    3. _____

- **Focusing on NOT multitasking and NOT comparing yourself to anyone else creates something that represents all five elements of your Living Blueprint.**

    WHO, PGS, BIO, TRU, LUV-Refer to My Living Blueprint page.

    - A piece of clothing decorated with Living Blueprint acronyms.

    - A vision board showing your intentions.

    - A comic strip depicting all parts of your Blueprint.

    - Drawing or writing your Blueprint on your water bottle.

    - Design a spreadsheet to track your progress.

    - An exercise routine embodying all five aspects.

- A poem that you may or may not share with others.

- Paint, draw, or sculpt a piece of art.

- A mobile to hang from the ceiling.

- Choreograph a dance routine.

- Produce a video.

What to do with your creation:

- Display it in a prominent place, reminding you to choose from your Living Blueprint.

- Share it with a family member or friend. Encourage them to discover and design their own Living Blueprint.

- Share it on social media and tag #myliving blueprint.

  As you worked singularly on your project, what did you notice in your brain, heart, and body? Did you feel your heart? What about your thoughts? Where were they leading you?

  _____

  _____

  _____

  _____

  What would be the value to you in your life in letting go of multitasking?

  _____

  _____

  _____

Do you tend to compare yourself to others? How does that make you feel?

_____

_____

- **If comparison is a virus you are trying to delete, try this. On a separate sheet of paper, write down all the things about you and your life that you think are better than someone else. Then, write down all the things about your life that seem worse than someone else. Now, burn the list.**

What would change in your everyday life if you let go of all comparisons plaguing your thought process?

_____

_____

_____

What does a life free of comparison and focused on your own perfect Blueprint look like?

_____

_____

_____

- **Be in Bermuda at least 1x today.**

ACTIVITY 40: LIVING IN LOVE AND SCHEDULING CHECK-INS

One of life's little secrets is that joy is experienced in the journey as much, if not more, than it is in the destination. Amelia Earhart, one of the most inspirational American figures in aviation, said, "The most difficult thing is the decision to act. The rest is merely tenacity. The fears are paper tigers. You can do anything you decide to do. You can act to change and control your life; and the procedure, the process, is its own reward."[10] Living in Loving Kindness is its own reward.

Sam Harris, in his book, *Letter to a Christian Nation,* shares a tenet of the Jains ideology that can inspire all of us to live closer to love regardless of our religion, gender, age, culture, or nationality. It states, "Do not injure, abuse, oppress, enslave, insult, torment, torture, or kill any creature or living being."[11] To the degree that we live this principle is up to each of us. But in a world full of hatred, violence, trauma, and pain, we would do well to abide by its precepts a little closer.

You have a clearer understanding of WHO you are and are living from WHO you are. Your source of inspiration and the Personal Guidance System (PGS) you have chosen is taking your life in the direction you want to go. Nurturing your Biochemistry is becoming second nature and no longer are you subjugated to popular opinion because you are learning to unapologetically tell the truth and live authentically (TRU). Loving Kindness (LUV) is becoming an integral part of your daily routine, allowing you to live in love.

I'm so excited for you because I know what it feels like to have a conscious plan by which to move toward your dream. Feelings of hope and excitement are no doubt part of your everyday experience now.

As you continue to live the principles and practices you've uncovered and created in your WHO, PGS, BIO, TRU, and LUV Blueprints, I invite you to revisit this process twice per calendar year. Doing so will allow you to update your commitments as you change, develop, and evolve. As you continue to nurture your true self and others, asking for help when needed, and being honest in your deepest, darkest feelings, I believe that you will continue to experience your own joyful, peace-filled life, and your personal happily ever after!

Discovery Activity

- **Breathe, before you even get out of bed. Do this for at least five minutes today.**

- **What is your number today?** _____

- **List Gratitudes**

    1. _____

    2. _____

    3. _____

- **What does Living in Love feel like for you?**

    _____

    _____

    _____

    _____

- **How can you move forward in the world more consciously, living in love in every thought and action?**

    _____

———————————————————————————————

———————————————————————————————

———————————————————————————————

- **Spend time celebrating with a success partner today. Share with them your creation from Activity 39. Explain the five parts of Your Living Blueprint.**

- **Schedule with yourself (add to your calendar), the date five months from now when you will revisit your Living Blueprint.**

- **Be in Bermuda at least 1x today.**

You and I were born to manifest our highest and most glorious selves. Reading, writing, learning, healing, and continuing to move toward our dreams has brought a new awareness to our own personal existence and our ability to progress toward what we want.

Living from WHO you truly are, as well as learning and following your PGS are lifelong processes. Give yourself the time you need to trust yourself and your source of inspiration. Kahlil Gibran in the Prophet taught, "Be patient toward all that is unresolved in your heart and try to love the questions themselves . . . like blocked rooms and books that are now written in a foreign tongue. You do not now see the answers, which cannot be given you because you would not be able to live them . . . the point is, to live everything now. Live the questions . . . you will gradually, without noticing it, live along some distant day into the answer."[12]

You have discovered and designed your own unique Living Blueprint, moving you out of destructive patterns and suffering into awakening and innovating your own magnificent soul. The fundamental principles of Living Blueprint, *when lived consistently,* will continue to create equanimity in your life.

Commitment to telling your truth and you being authentic is making the world a better place is no small thing. Dedication to not only your own growth and evolution but to our whole human family is changing the world one choice at time as courage continues to outweigh your fears!

Ultimately, my friend, despite our diverse cultures, values, and areas of expertise, one universal truth remains unwavering, compassion from Loving Kindness is the common thread that connects us as a human family.

Its significance is not confined to any particular religion, belief system, or discipline. Across various corners of the world, love manifests itself in myriad forms. As we navigate through earth life together, let us build a world where Loving Kindness in every moment is the truth guiding us all.

EPILOGUE

Six years after walking away from my baby brother's funeral, Spencer received a text. "Wendy's mother is very sick. She may or may not make it through the night. She has a blood clot that has moved to her lung, her heart rate is too high, and the cancer is causing problems. I thought you would want to know."

Instinctively, I decided to go see my mother in Montana. Spencer made arrangements and joined me. By the time we arrived, my mother was out of the hospital and back at home, but she was thin, pale, and gaunt. She was so weak, she looked like she was dying.

For some reason, looking at her reminded me of being in her bed alone as a small child. She was gone, delivering a casserole to someone in need. However, the essence of her and the smell of her hair was all around me as I snuggled deep into her sheets.

That day, increasing pain forced her back to the hospital, and within forty-eight hours, she was flown by life flight to The Huntsman Cancer Institute in Salt Lake City. Shortly thereafter, I flew to Utah to see if I could be of support to her and my father.

Witnessing my heartbroken father help his wife, my mother, out of the hospital bed to her walker so that she could move her legs to help her circulation showed me a side of my parents I'd never experienced: my mother's vulnerability and my father's tender Loving Kindness in their relationship.

My sister and I spent the better part of one morning showering our mother. She lovingly lathered her long, beautiful hair as I kept warm water running over her naked body. As the water ran over my mother's frail shoulders and through her silver hair, I sensed and could almost see the immense burdens she'd carried in her mortal journey. I'd hoped they would run down the drain with all the bubbles. Her strength humbled me.

Though never raised in the same household, one liners learned from our mother kept coming to mine and my sister's thoughts, then dropping into the hallowed conversation.

"It's all about your choices."

"Live and learn."

"We don't get to choose our consequences."

"Life's a journey."

All three of us laughed. Our mother's wisdom was the voice inside both her daughters' heads.

At the request of my mother, I braided her hair so that it would not get tangled in all the IVs, cords, lines, and tubes running in, out, and around her body. She looked like an Indian princess, reminding me of the many moments we spent camping together as a family when I was a little girl.

As I braided her hair, the same essence I'd experienced as a small child surrounded me. My mother, the smell of her hair, and her wisdom inside my head.

For the next two months, my mother and I continued our conversations telephonically, she at her home in Montana and me at mine in California. More than once she apologized and explained why she'd been a "terrible mother" to me. I told her I believed she had done her best, and that with thirty-three years of motherhood experiences myself, I had a lot more mercy for her than I had had for her as a young mother.

Together we shed many tears. She asked me to help her compile all her receipts and get her finances in order. We made a plan for me to return to Montana and spend time together in the Helena Montana Temple, something she'd been wanting to do since its dedication on June 18, 2023.

Two months later, before we had a chance to do her finances and before we went to the temple, my mother peacefully passed away, surrounded by her family, including me. Two weeks after she died, she returned in a dream and gave me specific directives as to how to share this book and the truth of what had happened in our family. I deeply appreciated her directive.

My mother's and my journey throughout this life was not easy. In fact, it was very, very painful and hard. But I would do it all again if it meant experiencing the joy I have today, feeling loved by her before she died, and loving her with my whole heart and soul.

Making decisions from my Living Blueprint and choosing Loving Kindness, no matter what, allowed me to forgive both my mother and myself. Fully embracing sacred moments with her before she died was another miracle in my undeniable, authentic, joy-filled life.

As you live your own magnificent journey, I hope you embrace every moment authentically, expecting joy, even when life is hard. Because, even when it's raining, remember the sun is always shining.

If you or someone you know is looking for encouragement, direction, help, or additional assistance on what to do next, I invite you to reach out to me at any of following: I am happy to work together in person, over the phone or through video.

wendybeth.org.

https://linktr.ee/wendybeth.

instagram.com/wendybeth.

https://www.facebook.com/wendy.cozzens.

Much love to you, my new friend.

APPENDIX
MY LIVING BLUEPRINT TEMPLATE

My Greatest Gift (Activity 17)

Own your gift.

My Success Partners (Activity 4)

1.

Turn here for a connection.

2.

WHO: "Three Words" (Activity 10)

1.

2.

Live from these attributes.

3.

PGS:

My Source of Inspiration
(Activity 18)

Consult and follow in every decision.

My Top Five Interests (Activity 6)

1.

2.

3.

Enjoy one-two of these EVERY day.

4.

5.

My Healing Toolkit (Activity 14)

1.

2.

3.   *Do this when "How Am I" scale drops to 7 or below.*

4.

5.

My Desired Running Programs (Activity 13)

1.

2.

3.   *FOCUS time, thoughts, and energy on these.*

4.

5.

BIO:

- Nurturing My Biochemistry Every Day (Activities 21-28)

1.

2.

3.

4.

5.   *Do these every day to nurture your body.*

6.

7.

8.

TRU: **Tell the Truth and Be Authentic (Activity 34):**

Overcome your biggest obstacle with this.

LUV: **Choose Loving Kindness (Activity 35):**

Desire and nurture this to Live in Love.

Weekly Planning Day/Time (Day 38): Add reminder alarm to phone calendar

Calendar your Blueprint 1x every week.

Two Dates to Update Living Blueprint (Day 38): Add reminder alarm to phone calendar

Update your Blueprint 2x every year.

Living Blueprint DWM Tracker

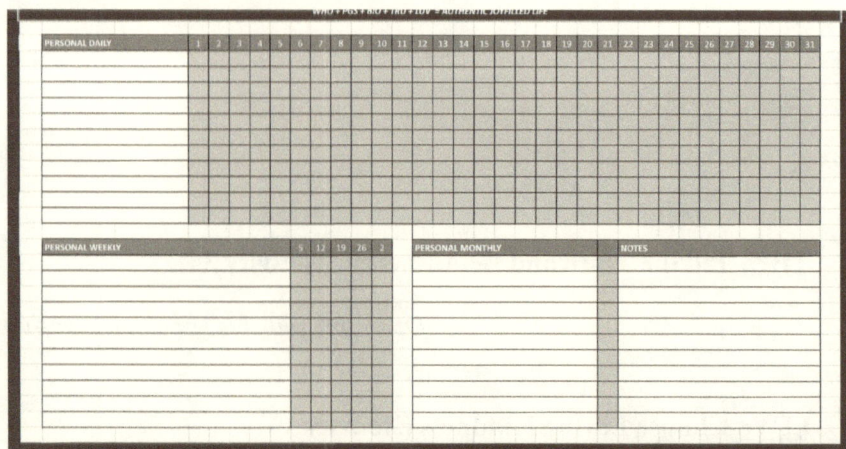

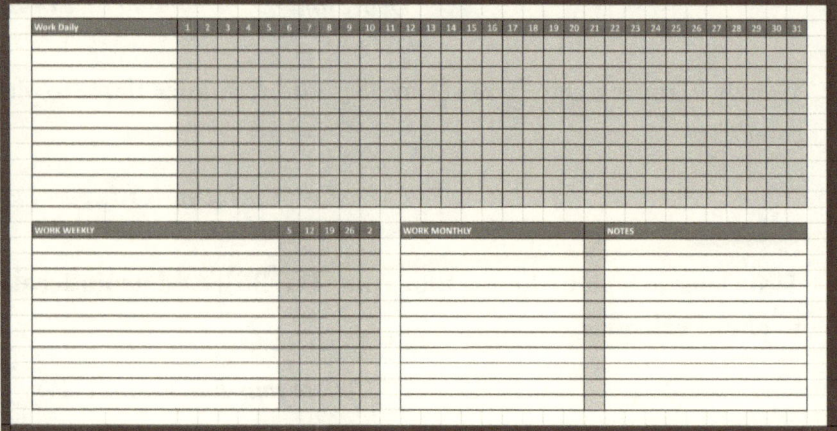

<u>Please visit wendybeth.org resources for:</u>

- **<u>Electronic Living Blueprint Trackers for Google Docs.</u>**

- **<u>PDF printables for My Living Blueprint and DWM Tracker.</u>**

- **<u>Examples of aligned weekly planning sessions, My Living Blueprint Template, and DWM tracker.</u>**

NOTES

Letter to My Reader

1. Western, S. *Coaching and Mentoring: A Critical Text*, (SAGE, 2012).

Introduction

1. "Global Inequalities," IMF, March 1, 2022, https://www.imf.org/en/Publications/fandd/issues/2022/03/Global-inequalities-Stanley.

2. World Health Organization: WHO. "Suicide, » August 28, 2023, https://www.who.int/news-room/fact-sheets/detail/suicide.

3. "Suicide Statistics," (n.d.), Centers for Disease Control, accessed November 13, 2023, https://www.cdc.gov/suicide/index.html.

4. Clear, J., "Marginal Gains: This Coach Improved Every Tiny Thing by 1 Percent," February, 4, 2020, https://jamesclear.com/marginal-gains.

Chapter 1

1. Bible Gateway, John 8:3, (n.d.) https://www.biblegateway.com/verse/en/John%208:31.

2. Cronkleton, E., "10 Breathing Techniques for Stress Relief and More," *Healthline*, March 24, 2023, https://www.healthline.com/health/breathing-exercise.

3. Armenti, P., "For There Is Always Light: Amanda Gorman's Inaugural Poem, 'The Hill We Climb' Delivers Message of Unity," *The Catbird Seat*, The Library of Congress, January 22, 2021.

4. MSEd, K. C., "Abraham Maslow Quotes about Psychology," ThoughtCo., February 24, 2019, https://www.thoughtco.com/abraham-maslow-quotes-2795686.

5. Keller, Helen, "Alone We Can Do So Little. Together We Can Do So Much," (n.d.), The American Foundation for the Blind, https://www.afb.org/blog/entry/happy-birthday-helen.

6. "Legs Up the Wall Pose," *Yoga Journal*, December 9, 2022, , https://www.yogajournal.com/poses/legs-up-the-wall-pose-2/.

Chapter 2

1. Monson, P. T. S., "Patriarchal Blessings," November 8, 2021, https://www.churchofjesuschrist.org/study/manual/gospel-topics/patriarchal-blessings?lang=eng#title1.

2. Wood, Therese, "Visualizing the Evolution of Global Advertising Spend (1980-2020)," *Visual Capitalist*, Aug. 31, 2021, www.visualcapitalist.com/evolution-global-advertising-spend-1980-2020.

3. Wikipedia, "Venn Diagram." October 25, 2023, https://en.wikipedia.org/wiki/Venn_diagram

4. Grady, C., "Why Marianne Williamson's Most Famous Passage Is Cited as a Nelson Mandela Quote," *Vox*, July 30, 2019, https://www.vox.com/culture/2019/7/30/20699833/marianne-williamson-our-deepest-fear-nelson-mandela-return-to-love.

5. Rubin, R., *The Creative Act: A Way of Being: The Sunday Times Bestseller* (Canongate Books, 2023.)

Chapter 3

1. Branch, Susan, *30th Anniversary Heart of the Home, Notes from a Vineyard Kitchen*

2. "About GI Bill benefits | Veterans Affairs," Veterans Affairs, July 18, 2023, https://www.va.gov/education/about-gi-bill-benefits/.

3. *Corinthians 13*, (n.d.), https://www.churchofjesuschrist.org/study/scriptures/nt/1-cor/13?lang=eng#p4.

Chapter 4

1. Gong, E. G. W., *Sacrament*, (n.d.), https://www.churchofjesuschrist.org/study/manual/gospel-topics/sacrament?lang=eng#title1.

2. Nelson, P. R. M., *Book of Mormon*, (n.d.), https://www.churchofjesuschrist.org/study/manual/gospel-topics/book-of-mormon?lang=eng#p15.

3. Christofferson, E. D. T., *Bible*, (n.d.), https://www.churchofjesuschrist.org/study/manual/gospel-topics/bible?lang=eng#p30.

4. Talmage, J., *Jesus the Christ*, (Winchester, MA: University Press, 1915).

5. Rand, A., *The Fountainhead* (Signet Book, 1952).

6. Orwell, G., *1984* (HarperCollins,2013).

7. "Camp Humphreys," Wikipedia, October 10, 2023, https://en.wikipedia.org/wiki/Camp_Humphreys.

8. "Demilitarized Zone," Wikipedia, September 8, 2023, https://en.wikipedia.org/wiki/Demilitarized_zone.

9. "Buddhist Temple, Wikipedia, October 31, 2023, https://en.wikipedia.org/wiki/Buddhist_temple.

10. "Post-traumatic Stress Disorder (PTSD)-Symptoms and Causes," Mayo Clinic, December 13, 2022, https://www.mayoclinic.org/diseases-conditions/post-traumatic-stress-disorder/symptoms-causes/syc-20355967.

11. Holland, E. J. R., *God the Father*, (n.d.), https://www.churchofjesuschrist.org/study/manual/gospel-topics/god-the-father?lang=eng#title27.

12. Bass, E., L. Davis, & P. Bateman, "The Courage to Heal," *Violence & Victims*, 9(4), 1994, 381.2-383, https://doi.org/10.1891/0886-6708.9.4.381a.

13. Frankl, V. E., *Man's Search For Meaning: The Classic Tribute to Hope from the Holocaust* (Random House, 2013).

14. "Alternative Treatments," *TIME Magazine*, 2022.

15. "Find A.A. Near You," Alcoholics Anonymous, (n.d.), https://www.aa.org/find-aa.

Chapter 5

1. "President Declares 'Freedom at War with Fear,'" September 20, 2001, https://georgewbush-whitehouse.archives.gov/news/releases/2001/09/20010920-8.html.

2. "Chakra," Wikipedia, October 19, 2023, https://en.wikipedia.org/wiki/Chakra.

3. "Temples," The Church of Jesus Christ of Latter-day Saints, (n.d.), https://www.churchofjesuschrist.org/temples?lang=eng.

4. "My Hero," [video], YouTube, 2014, https://www.youtube.com/watch?v=GT2f-WM86oQ.

5. Owens, D., *Where the Crawdads Sing* (UK: Hachette, 2018).

6. Napier, A. Y., PhD, & C. A. Whitaker, MD, *The Family Crucible* (Harper Collins, 2011).

7. Donovan, D. M., M. H. Ingalsbe, J. Benbow, & D.C. Daley, "12-Step Interventions and Mutual Support Programs for Substance Use Disorders: An Overview," *Social Work in Public Health*, 28(3–4), 2013, 313–332, https://doi.org/10.1080/19371918.2013.774663.

8. Gallwey, W. T., *The Inner Game of Tennis: The Classic Guide to the Mental Side of Peak Performance* (Random House, 2010).

Chapter 6

1. Amen, D. G., *Change Your Brain, Change Your Life: The Breakthrough Programme for Conquering Anger, Anxiety, Obsessiveness and Depression* (UK: Hachette, 2009).

2. "Friedrich Nietzsche," Wikipedia, November 10, 2023, https://en.wikipedia.org/wiki/Friedrich_Nietzsche.

3. Instagram, (n.d.), https://www.instagram.com/adamgrant/.

4. Collings, T., "Viparita Karani: An Ayurvedic Guide to Legs Up the Wall Pose," *Paavani Ayurveda*, January 29, 2021, https://paavaniayurveda.com/blogs/ayurvedic-yoga/viparita-karani-an-ayurvedic-guide-to-legs-up-the-wall-pose?gad_source=1&gclid=C-jwKCAiA0syqBhBxEiwAeNx9N7u_gvoSDXXYoOnM4xK8S6k-JahFlZPopSUIpttpZM4t2JPZNLmsrcBoCCk4QAvD_BwE.

5. Wendt, T., "Parasympathetic Nervous System: What to Know," *WebMD*, November 3, 2022, https://www.webmd.com/brain/para-sympathetic-nervous-system-what-to-know.

6. Chopra, Deepak, *Deepak Chopra -Official website*, (n.d.), https://www.deepakchopra.com/.

7. Iyengar, B. K. S., "Light on Yoga : Yoga Dipika, in *Allen and Unwin eBooks*, pg. 449, 1968, http://ci.nii.ac.jp/ncid/BA58492356.

8. Watso, J. C., & W.B. Farquhar, "Hydration Status and Cardiovascular Function, *Nutrients*, *11*(8), 1866, 2019, https://doi.org/10.3390/nu11081866.

9. Huberman, Dr. Andrew, "How to Feel Energized & Sleep Better with One Morning Activity," Huberman Lap Clips, [video], YouTube August 10, 2022, https://www.youtube.com/watch?v=WDv4AWk0J3U.

10. Carroll, J. L., *Sexuality Now: Embracing Diversity* (Cengage Learning, 2012).

Chapter 7

1. Godbey, J.K., & S.A. Hutchinson, "Healing from Incest: Resurrecting the Buried Self," *Arch Psychiatr Nurs*, Oct:10(5):304-10 1996, doi: 10.1016/s0883-9417(96)80039-2. PMID: 8897713. Victims become Perpetrators.

2. Iyengar, B. K. S., *Yoga: THE PATH TO HOLISTIC HEALTH.* Pg. 234, 2001, https://openlibrary.org/books/OL8156123M/Yoga.

3. Kagan, J., "Skilled Nursing Facility: Definition vs Nursing Home," Investopedia, November 20, 2020, https://www.investopedia.com/terms/s/skilled-nursing-facility.asp

4. "Deschutes River," (n.d.), Rivers.gov. https://www.rivers.gov/rivers/river/deschutes.

5. Ibid.

6. "The Federal Government Takes on Physical Fitness, JFK Library, (n.d.), https://www.jfklibrary.org/learn/about-jfk/jfk-in-history/physical-fitness.

7. APA PsycNet. (n.d.). https://psycnet.apa.org/record/2018-34837-0.

8. Savage, B. M., H.L., Lujan, R.R. Thipparthi, & S. E. DiCarlo, "Humor, Laughter, Learning, and Health! A Brief Review," *Advances in Physiology Education*, *41*(3), 2017, 341–347, https://doi.org/10.1152/advan.00030.2017.

Chapter 8

1. Kolk, V. D., & A. Bessel, *The Body Keeps the Score: Mind, Brain and Body in the Transformation of Trauma*, (Penguin Books, 2014), https://ci.nii.ac.jp/ncid/BB2901461X.

2. "Facts about Suicide," *Suicide*, CDC, (n.d.), https://www.cdc.gov/suicide/facts/index.html.

3. Brown, Brené, "Listening to Shame," TED, [video], YouTube, March 16, 2012, https://www.youtube.com/watch?v=psN1DORYYV0.

4. "Authentic," *Merriam-Webster Dictionary*. 2023, https://www.merriam-webster.com/dictionary/authentic#:~:text=%3A%20worthy%20of%20acceptance%20or%20belief%20as%20conforming%20to%20or%20based%20on%20fact.

5. Neskowin Beach State Recreation Site-Oregon State Parks, (n.d.), https://stateparks.oregon.gov/index.cfm?do=park.profile&parkId=161.

6. "Dealer Takes All: Inside One of Seattle's Biggest Opioid Busts," *Seattle Met.*, November, 7, 2022, https://www.seattlemet.com/news-and-city-life/2019/03/dealer-takes-all-inside-one-of-seattle-s-biggest-opioid-busts.

7. Wood, A. M., P.A. Linley, J. Maltby,M. Baliousis, & S. Joseph, "The Authentic Personality: A Theoretical and Empirical Conceptualization and the Development of the Authenticity Scale,"

Journal of Counseling Psychology, 55(3), 2008, 385–399, <u>https://doi.org/10.1037/0022-0167.55.3.385.</u>

8. Rodin, M. "The Kiss", Musée Rodin, (n.d.), https://www.musee-rodin.fr/en/musee/collections/oeuvres/kiss.

9. "Ramadan," –Wikipedia, September 28, 2023, <u>https://en.wikipedia.org/wiki/Ramadan.</u>

10. "Bosnian War," Wikipedia, November 13, 2023, https://en.wikipedia.org/wiki/Bosnian_War.

11. Owens, L. S., & S. A. Hoeller, *Jung, Carl Gustav, and The Red Book: Liber Novus*, Audible (14:48-15:20), 2014.

12. Wood, A. M., P.A. Linley, J. Maltby, M. Baliousis, & S. Joseph, "The Authentic Personality: A Theoretical and Empirical Conceptualization and the Development of the Authenticity Scale," *Journal of Counseling Psychology*, 55(3), 2008, 385–399, https://doi.org/10.1037/0022-0167.55.3.385.

13. Motoki, "Kintsugi as a Metaphor for Life," - o *Medium*, April 12, 2023, <u>https://medium.com/@motoki/kintsugi-as-a-metaphor-for-life-9f79d3b24ad3.</u>

14. Pliska, Z. *Hello, Little One: A Monarch Butterfly Story* (Page Street Kids, 2020).

15. Clear, J., *Atomic Habits: An Easy & Proven Way to Build Good Habits & Break Bad Ones* (National Geographic Books, 2018).

Chapter 9

1. "Exploring Careers in Family Science," *NCFR*, (n.d.), https://www.ncfr.org/about/what-family-science/

careers?gclid=CjwKCAiA0syqBhBxEiwAeNx9N0Y3ciBSlzZ38vg-
Zun-i0TrO2Q70yZzeJjEivw1jO20lzq08igfxihoC-UMQAvD_BwE.

2. "Morocco," Wikipedia, November 15, 2023, https://en.wikipedia.
org/wiki/Morocco.

3. Toubkal National Park, (Official GANP Park page), (n.d.), https://
national-parks.org/morocco/toubkal.

4. Lady Gaga, "Shallow," –Google, (n.d.), https://www.google.
com/search?q=shallow+lady+gaga+lyrics&oq=shallow+lady+-
gaga&aqs=chrome.2.0i131i355i433i512j46i131i433i512j0i512l3j4
6i340i512j0i512l4.10516j0j4&sourceid=chrome&ie=UTF-8.

5. "Castle of Almourol," https://www.portugaltravel.org/gam-
boa-beach-penicheCastle of Almourol.

6. https://en.wikipedia.org/wiki/Alcoba%C3%A7a_Monastery

7. Kemske, B., *Kintsugi: The Poetic Mend* (Bloomsbury Publishing,
2021).

8. Nichols, M. P., *The Essentials of Family Therapy* (2014).

9. Cozzens, W. B., "Wendy Beth's Facebook Post," Facebook December
15, 2019.

10. Bocelli, Andrea, "Andrea Bocelli: Because We Believe," - Live from
Studio Ferrante Aporti, Italy / 2007 [video], YouTube October 23,
2015, https://www.youtube.com/watch?v=foKSmlMnt-U.

11. Lincoln, M. J., *Messages from the Body: Their Psychological Meaning*,
2006.

Chapter 10

1. "Dr. Qubein Biography," Office of the President, September 6, 2023, https://www.highpoint.edu/president/dr-qubein-biography/.

2. "The Neurobiology of Love," *PubMed.*, June 1, 2005, https://pubmed. ncbi.nlm.nih.gov/15990719/.

3. Rushton, J. P., "Generosity in Children: Immediate and Long-term Effects of Modeling, Preaching, and Moral Judgment," *Journal of Personality and Social Psychology*, 31(3), 1975, 459–466, https://doi. org/10.1037/h0076466.

4. "Ahimsa," https://en.wikipedia.org/wiki/Ahimsa.

5. "Metta: How You Can Help," (n.d.), https://www.mettainstitute. org/mettameditation.html.

6. "Chesed," Wikipedia, September 12, 2023, https://en.wikipedia.org/ wiki/Chesed.

7. Shah, Z. H., "Two Hundred Verses about Compassionate Living in the Quran," *The Muslim Times*, January 21, 2022, https:// themuslimtimes.info/2013/10/29/three-hundred-verses-about -compassionate-living-in-the-quran/.

8. Oaks, B. P. D. H., "Two Great Commandments," October 5, 2019, https://www.churchofjesuschrist.org/study/general-conference /2019/10/35oaks?lang=eng.

9. "Home," *YourAbsoluteValue*, (n.d.), https://www.yourabsolutevalue. org/

10. Sherry, Mike, "Seeds of Despair: Hundreds of Farmers are Dying by Suicide," *Flatland*, March 25, 2020, https://flatlandkc.org/news-issues/ seeds-of-despair-hundreds-of-farmers-are-dying-by-suicide.

11. Rūmī, M. J. A., C. Barks, R.A. Nicholson, A.J. Arberry, & J. A. Moyne, (2004). *The Essential Rumi*, (San Francisco: Harper ebooks, 2004), http://ci.nii.ac.jp/ncid/BA74847838.

12. "C. S. Lewis," Wikipedia, November 6, 2023, https://en.wikipedia.org/wiki/C._S._Lewis.

13. "7 Brene Brown Quotes that Are Pure Life-Changing Gold," *Medium*, December 14, 2021, https://medium.com/live-your-life-on-purpose/7-brene-brown-quotes-that-are-pure-life-changing-gold-1f5faa9d9dd6.

14. "Top 200 Ezra Taft Benson Quotes," –*QuoteFancy*, 2023 (n.d.), https://quotefancy.com/ezra-taft-benson-quotes.

15. "Flywheel_ What Is a Flywheel?"– Google, (n.d.), https://www.google.com/search?q=what+is+a+flywheel&oq=what+is+a+-flywheel&aqs=chrome..69i57j69i59l3.3688j0j4&sourceid=-chrome&ie=UTF-8#fpstate=ive&vld=cid:d7f5c0b5,vid:7K-4W4hA6aV4,st:0.

16. "Return to Love, Andrea," Google, (n.d.), https://www.google.com/search?q=return+to+love+andrea&oq=return+to+love+an-drea+&aqs=chrome..69i57j33i160l5.15267j0j4&sourceid=-chrome&ie=UTF-8.

Chapter 11

1. "The Nobel Peace Prize 1964," NobelPrize.org. (n.d.), https://www.nobelprize.org/prizes/peace/1964/summary/.

2. Bach, R., *Illusions: The Adventures of a Reluctant Messiah* (Delta, 2012).

3. Sherry, Mike, "Seeds of Despair: Hundreds of Farmers are Dying by Suicide," *Flatland*, March 25, 2020, https://flatlandkc.org/news-issues/seeds-of-despair-hundreds-of-farmers-are-dying-by-suicide.

4. "James Bay–Scars," [video], YouTube, August 28, 2015, https://www.youtube.com/watch?v=oVslvM30EWI.

5. "Secular Humanism," Wikipedia, October 21, 2023, https://en.wikipedia.org/wiki/Secular_humanism.

6. "Zig Ziglar Quotes," *BrainyQuote.com*, BrainyMedia Inc, November 14, 2023, https://www.brainyquote.com/quotes/zig_ziglar_132507.

7. "Multitasking: Switching costs," *APA* March 20, 2006, https://www.apa.org. https://www.apa.org/topics/research/multitasking.

8. Amen, D. G., *Change Your Brain, Change Your Life: The Breakthrough Programme for Conquering Anger, Anxiety, Obsessiveness and Depression* (UK: Hachette, 2009)..

9. Mackay, Charles, "No Enemies," read By Margaret Thatcher, Poem Animation. Poetryreincarnations, [video], December 25, 2020, YouTube, https://www.youtube.com/watch?v=ixXH-vtcxeo.

10. Patel, H., "Sow Something Now, Reap Later. Sow Nothing Now, Regret Later," *Medium*, December 25, 2021, https://medium.com/afwp/sow-something-now-reap-later-sow-nothing-now-regret-later-b1a9c55c1b71.

11. Harris, S., *Letter to a Christian Nation: A Challenge to the Faith of America* (Random House, 2011).

12. Gibran, K., *The Prophet* (BoD–Books on Demand, 2019).

BIBLIOGRAPHY

"Adult Development and Aging." *Journal of Gerontology*, 41(2), 296, 1986, https://doi.org/10.1093/geronj/41.2.296a.

Amen, D. G. *The End of Mental Illness*. Tyndale House Publishers, Inc., 2020.

Ariza-Montes, A., G. Giorgi, A.L. Leal-Rodríguez, & J. Ramírez-Sobrino. "Authenticity and Subjective Well-being within the Context of a Religious Organization," *Frontiers in Psychology*, 8, (n.d.), https://doi.org/10.3389/fpsyg.2017.01228

Baily, E., S. Matz, W. YouYou, & S. Iyengar. "Authentic Self-Expression on Social Media Is Associated with Greater Subjective Well-Being," *Nature Communications*, (n.d.), https://doi.org/10.1038/s41467-020-18539.

Balcetis, E. *Clearer, Closer, Better: How Successful People See the World*. Ballantine Books, 2020.

Barney, B. *Shine the Light Within: 5 Steps to Lighten your Soul Through Forgiveness: Vol. One* (first). All Things Possible, 2018.

Brady, T. *The TB12 method: How to Achieve a Lifetime of Sustained Peak Performance*. Simon and Schuster, 2017.

Boehm, M. *The Wild Woman's Way: Reconnect to Your Body's Wisdom*. Simon and Schuster, 2021.

Bourzat, F., & K. Hunter. *Consciousness Medicine: Indigenous Wisdom, Entheogens, and Expanded States of Consciousness for Healing and Growth*. North Atlantic Books, 2019.

Brown, B., *Braving the Wilderness: The Quest for True belonging and the Courage to Stand Alone.* Random House, 2017.

------. *Dare to Lead: Brave Work. Tough Conversations. Whole Hearts.* Random House, 2018.

.Callister, T. R., & R. L. Millet. *The Infinite Atonement: Illustrated Edition.* 2013.

Cameron, J. *The Artist's Way: 25th Anniversary Edition.* National Geographic Books, 2016.

Collins, J. C., & J. Collins. *Good to Great: Why Some Companies Make the Leap . . . and Others Don't.* Random House, 2001.

Comer, R. J., & J. S. Comer. *Fundamentals of Abnormal Psychology.* Worth Publishers, 2021.

Cronkleton, E. "10 Breathing Techniques for Stress Relief and More." *Healthline.* March 24, 2023, https://www.healthline.com/health/breathing-exercise.

Deisseroth, K. *Projections: A Story of Human Emotions.* Random House, 2021.

Deslandes, A. C., H. Moraes, C. Ferreira, H. Veiga, H. Silveira, R. J. O. Mouta, F. Pompeu, E. S. F. Coutinho, & J. Laks. "Exercise and Mental Health: Many Reasons to Move," *Neuropsychobiology,* 59(4), 2009, 191–198, https://doi.org/10.1159/000223730.

Dispenza, J. *Becoming Supernatural: How Common People Are Doing the Uncommon.* Hay House, Inc., 2017.

Ferrell, J. L. *The Peacegiver: How Christ Offers to Heal Our Hearts and Homes.* Shadow Mountain, 2012.

Fleming, S. M. *Lost Canyon: A Story of Loss, a Journey of Healing.* 2012.

G, A. M. D. *Change Your Brain Every Day: Simple Daily Practices to Strengthen Your Mind, Memory, Moods, Focus, Energy, Habits, and Relationships.* Tyndale House Publishers, 2023.

Gawdat, M. *Solve For Happy: Engineer Your Path to Joy.* Pan Macmillan, 2017.

Giele, J. Z. *Family Policy and the American safety net.* 2013.

Gilbert, E. *Big Magic: How to Live a Creative Life, and Let Go of Your Fear.* Bloomsbury Publishing, 2015.

Hardy, J. W., & D. Easton. *The Ethical Slut, third edition: A Practical Guide to Polyamory, Open Relationships, and Other Freedoms in Sex and Love.* Ten Speed Press, 2017.

Harrison, C. C. *He Did Deliver Me from Bondage.* Windhaven Publishing, 2012.

Hay, L. *Heal Your Body: The Mental Causes for Physical Illness and the Metaphysical Way to Overcome Them.* Hay House, Inc., 1995.

Institute, A. *The Anatomy of Peace: Resolving the Heart of Conflict: Easy Read Comfort Edition.* 2008, Read How You Want.Com.

Jarvis, C. *Creative Calling: Establish a Daily Practice, Infuse Your World with Meaning, and Succeed in Work + Life.* HarperCollins, 2019.

Jesper, A. "What Justifies Judgments of Inauthenticity," *Crossmark*, HEC Forum (2018) 30:361–377.

Johnson, S. M. *Attachment Theory in Practice: Emotionally Focused Therapy (EFT) with Individuals, Couples, and Families.* Guilford Publications, 2019.

Junger, S. *Tribe: On Homecoming and Belonging.* UK: HarperCollins, 2016.

Kahneman, D. *Thinking, Fast and Slow.* UK: Penguin, 2011.

Kosilo, M., M. Costa, H. Nuttall, & H. Ferreira. "The Neural Basis for Authenticity in Laughter and Crying," *Scientific Reports*, 2021, https://doi.org/10.1038/s41598-021-03131-z.

Lamott, A. *Bird by Bird: Instructions on Writing and Life*. Canongate Books, 2020.

Landes, D. S. *Wealth And Poverty of Nations*. UK: Hachette, 2015.

Lee, M. J. *Pachinko*. Grand Central Publishing, 2017.

Levine, L. E., & J. Munsch, J. *Child Development: An Active Learning Approach*. SAGE Publications, 2016.

Liu, J. J., A.N. Dalton, & J. Lee. "The 'Self' Under COVID-19: Social Role Disruptions, Self-Authenticity and Present-Focused Coping." *PLOS ONE*, 16(9), 2021, e0256939. https://doi.org/10.1371/journal.pone.0256939.

Lundberg, G., & J. Lundberg. *I Don't Have to Make Everything All Better: Six Practical Principles that Empower Others to Solve Their Own Problems While Enriching Your Relationships*. Penguin, 2000.

Maltz, W. *The Sexual Healing Journey: A Guide for Survivors of Sexual Abuse (revised edition)*. Harper Collins, 2001.

Maslow, A. H. *Motivation And Personality*. Prabhat Prakashan, 1981.

Markman, H. J., S.M. Stanley, & S. L. Blumberg. *Fighting for Your Marriage: A Deluxe Revised Edition of the Classic Best-seller for Enhancing Marriage and Preventing Divorce*. John Wiley & Sons, 2010.

Maxwell, S., PhD. *The Talk: What Your Kids Need to Hear from You About Sex*. National Geographic Books, 2008.

McConaughey, M. *Greenlights: Raucous Stories and Outlaw Wisdom from the Academy Award-winning actor*. UK: Hachette, 2020.

Newman, G. "The Psychology of Authenticity." *Review of General Psychology*, 23(1), 2019, 8–18. https://doi.org/10.1037/gpr0000158.

Nagoski, E. *Come As You Are: Revised and Updated: The Surprising New Science That Will Transform Your Sex Life*. Simon & Schuster, 2021.

Nichols, M. P. *The Essentials of Family Therapy*. 2014.

O'Leary, J. *On Fire: The 7 Choices to Ignite a Radically Inspired Life*. Simon and Schuster, 2016.

O'Keefe, P. A., C. S. Dweck, & G. M. Walton. "Implicit Theories of Interest: Finding Your Passion or Developing It?" *Psychological Science*, 29(10), 2018, 1653–1664. https://doi.org/10.1177/0956797618780643.

Robinson, S. E. *Believing Christ: The Parable of the Bicycle and Other Good News*. 2002.

Ruiz, D. M., & J. Mills. *The Four Agreements: A Practical Guide to Personal Freedom*. Amber-Allen Publishing, 2010.

Sacks, O. *On the Move: A Life*. Pan Macmillan, 2015.

Satterfield, J. M. *A Cognitive-Behavioral Approach to the Beginning of the End of Life, Minding the Body: Facilitator Guide*. Oxford University Press, 2008.

Sheldon, K. M., R.M. Ryan, L.J. Rawsthorne, & B.C. Ilardi. "Trait Self and True Self: Cross-role Variation in the Big-Five Personality Traits and Its Relations with Psychological Authenticity and Subjective Well-Being." *Journal of Personality and Social Psychology*, 73(6), 1997, 1380–1393, https://doi.org/10.1037/0022-3514.73.6.1380.

Sincero, J. *You Are a Badass: How to Stop Doubting Your Greatness and Start Living an Awesome Life*. UK: Hachette, 2016.

Smith, J. J. "The Lectures on Faith." DigiCat.2022.

Suzuki, S. *Zen Mind, Beginner's Mind: Informal Talks on Zen Meditation and Practice*. Shambhala Publications, 2010.

Tolle, E. *The Power of Now: A Guide to Spiritual Enlightenment*. New World Library, 2010.

Van Epp, J. *How to Avoid Falling in Love with a Jerk*. McGraw Hill Professional, 2008.

Voss, C., & T. Raz. *Never Split the Difference: Negotiating as if Your Life Depended on It*. Random House, 2016.

Wagner, E. *Chief Engineer: The Man Who Built the Brooklyn Bridge*. Bloomsbury Publishing, 2017.

Walsh, F. *Normal Family Processes: Growing Diversity and Complexity*. Guilford Press, 2012.

West, R., & L.H. Turner. *Interpersonal Communication*. SAGE Publications, 2019.

Yip-Williams, J. *The Unwinding of the Miracle: A Memoir of Life, Death and Everything that Comes After*. Random House, 2019.

Zhu, L., L. Li, X. Li, & L. Wang. "Mind–Body Exercises for PTSD Symptoms, Depression, and Anxiety in Patients with PTSD: A Systematic Review and Meta-Analysis." *Frontiers in Psychology*, 12, 2022, https://doi.org/10.3389/fpsyg.2021.738211.

ABOUT THE AUTHOR

Wendy Beth is a fellow traveler, speaker, and Soul Guide. Her purpose and passion is to help others work through confusion, loss, and suicidal ideation–issues she faced and overcame. Utilizing her degree in family science, Wendy Beth not only offers her true story but a powerful, practical 40-day journey to help you gain traction towards your own happily ever after.

Thank you. Because of each of you, this book exists:

Les and Leona, for coming to SLC, saving my life, and giving me a soft place to land in 1990.

Family members – you know who you are! For repeatedly telling the truth, for validating my pain, and for being honest with me. I love you!

All my bishops in the LDS church, for being a loving, revelatory place of peace and safety.

Jeremy, for wanting to share your good news with me, trusting me with "our project," and validating every spiritual gift I have ever been given.

Chandler, for pulling up a chair for Jer in our first meeting, cheering me on from the onset of my "keeping my promise," and then introducing me to Bridget.

Daniel, Pam, Priscilla, Michael, Rick, Masha, Jessica, Maria Jose, Rebecca, Joan, Jared, Gary, Kashturi, Madison, Allysa, Shaelene, Brita, Steve, Steph, Michel, Adam, Brad, Shari, Liz, Spencer, Masha, Hadlee, Jo, Joshua, and Chandler, for reading and reviewing *Living Blueprint* and giving me valuable feedback. This book is amazing because of each of you!

Christina, for your hands-on expert clinical review and advice! And for your affirmation and encouragement of the *Living Blueprint* project!

Shari, for being the best example of "forgiving others" I have ever seen. For being a safe place to lay my head, cheering me on since I began this book, and helping create a beautiful book cover for *Living Blueprint*.

Rebecca, RHG Publishing, Chisom, Misti, Shannon, etc., for EVERYTHING you did to publish this book and get my legs under me so that I could share the message of *Living Blueprint*.

Bridget and Hannah, for being the only writing mentor and editor who could have gotten my story out of my heart, brain, and body. I'm serious! Your compassion, patience, and trust in your processes were the space I needed to tell my story and uncover *Living Blueprint*.

Christina and Jamie, for always building me up as a mother on some of the most challenging days of writing this book and for cheering me on to create a space for myself in this world.

Joshua, for the gift of peace, knowing that my grandsons were safe and enjoying life with an amazing father as I focused on writing this book.

Allysa, for your feedback that pushed me to be even more transparent and share more of my story to help others learn and heal and create joy-filled lives.

Michel, for celebrating me and for helping me with social media, to step out of my shell and let others see me, Wendy Beth, so that I could share this message with the world.

Maddie, **Lexi**, and **Abraham**, for loving and being a safe place for some of the most important people in my life.

Carter, **James**, and **Sol**, for bringing light into my life throughout the process of writing this book. You were often in my thoughts!

Shaelene, for listening, talking, and being with me on some of the heaviest days while I wrote this book.

Jacob, for making me smile and even laugh through my tears as I prepared this book.

Spencer, my love, for being a rock so I can be a kite and fly free. For choosing our family, especially during the divorce, and for saying "I'm sorry." I belong with you, darling.

Jesus, for loving me long before I loved myself, carrying and healing my pain, never leaving me comfortless, and showing me, in person, how to love and treat others—no matter what.

Father in Heaven, for filling me with your spirit and bringing so many people willing to love, support, and help me discover, design, and share *Living Blueprint—A True Story: Five Principles to Creating an Authentic Joy-Filled Life.*

For an ever-expanding thank-you list, visit wendybeth.org and click on "Thank you." I am continually adding to this list as it is one of the ways I find healing and joy in my everyday life.

REVIEWS

"I read the entire book in one sitting. I could not stop- what a life lived. Wendy Beth's story had me more hooked than all the reality TV shows, yet filled with such beautiful insights and special reminders. Loved that she was able to blend taboo topics . . . mention events that most keep quiet in family situations . . . with honesty and pure authenticity . . . but the ending . . . I'm still getting choked up. What a great ending. So beautiful."

~ Michael Scott, Commercial Photographer, USA

"The gut-wrenching life journey of Wendy Beth reminds us of the importance of seeing the soul within each person without placing artificial labels. Her courageous triumph is a testament to human resiliency. The book also surfaces the discussion of gender fluidity versus gender dichotomy, as different societies see it differently. It is my hope that folks will find it in them to engage with an open heart by taking the message in this book to build a more inclusive world for all our children. Nothing is more important than love, understanding, and compassion. Nothing!"

~ Dr. Kashturi Henry PhD, CTP, Six Sigma Black Belt Founder & CEO, Kas Henry Inc. & Ennobled for Success Institute (Belize)

"*Living Blueprint* is the most open, raw, and honest book I have ever read! Wendy Beth has verbalized the effects of living in a fallen and broken world with an honesty and frankness uncommon in our culture today! She has cleared a path, illuminating a way out of the darkness of guilt and shame. Developing a new daily rhythm of healing and growth in conjunction with love and community. She walks you through the maze of unhealthy thinking, finding value and worth in the tools developed. It will take some hard work, digging deep, and letting go. Forever changing the trajectory of your life. Rebuilding your foundation on love and truth will bring the joy you seek. I enthusiastically recommend the journey! Thank you, Wendy Beth; your story resonates with so many!"

~ Pam Howard

"From day one of the forty-day journey . . . pinpointing WHO I am and what makes me WHO I am has been a blessing going through the Living Blueprint process . . . it's almost like God had a hand in you choosing me to be part of this journey."

~ Daniel - Father

"Wendy Beth eloquently describes her journey with such intimacy that you not only feel it as your own but also realize that it is possible for us to learn to coexist with pain. By reaching out in faith, we can accept our human experience, fostering connection, a sense of belonging . . . Her "Blueprint" delves into your deepest feelings, helping you see your story as a whole, creating a "Visual map" to observe and learn from the thoughts and feelings buried deep within our hearts. This book is both refreshing and compelling to read!"

~ Maria Jose, Santiago, (Chile)

"*Living Blueprint* is viable proof that a person can triumph over unfathomable tragedy with a rare fortitude and character that truly is authentic. The raw honesty was at first a frightening and frustrating experience but necessary for me to understand the depth of human frailty and pain that so often leads to overwhelming despair. Wendy Beth and the Living Blueprint can help you emerge from a life of exhaustive pain, anxiety, and fear with no foreseeable future to a life of genuine joy, freedom, and contentment. She is a brave, wise, and gentle warrior with the courage to bare all for the enrichment of others. Cheers to Wendy Beth (and Spencer) for their naked vulnerability."

~ Gary Little, NHA

"My favorite part of the 'Living Blueprint' journey has been discovering new tools I can use for self-care and achieving my absolute BEST. The "Three Words" have been very powerful. It's only been a week since I discovered them, but I am connecting my thoughts, feelings, and decisions to my three words in one week. It's incredible. I have a new weapon to use against my demons."

~ *Beta Reader Number Two*

"Wow, what a powerful gift Wendy has given readers! Her vulnerability and willingness to expose and share some of the deepest, most personal parts of her incredibly sacred journey allows her to be very relatable to those wading through the messier parts of life. Lessons learned are shared from experiences, providing tools and principles readers can apply to their lives, inviting change and a way out of suffering. Thank you, Wendy, for bringing light and hope where despair and darkness has been living for far too long! Thank you for sharing your beautiful story!"

~ *Joan, Wife, Mother, Grandma, RN*

"In our very young years growing up, we can't control what is brought to us; however, once we grow up, that's where our self-control comes into play to do something different and learn from what was put on us. Wendy Beth's story is a beautiful awakening of her authentic spirit. This story will help people gain their own strength and resolve so that they too can live a life that was meant for them, uncovering their own strengths so that they too can do it freely without having their pasts destroy their present or future."

~ *Steven Zeiger*

"I feel as if I went on this journey with the author. I cried, laughed, was heartbroken, and felt peace at the end. I absolutely plan on 'Going to Bermuda' daily! This book is soulfully honest with a raw look into the author's true journey to find who they are. This book is well written and is full of tools to help the reader find where you are at in life, and help you find your true happiness in your own life's journey. The timing for me in my life was perfect."

~ *Priscilla Miller*

"Wendy Beth's courage to share the intimate details of her journey is a beacon of hope, showing that even in the darkest moments, healing is possible. Wendy created a relatable and authentic guide for those navigating their own hardships as she intertwines her personal story with a practical workbook, creating a powerful combination to help those seeking tools for healing. Wendy's story is a gift to those who need it most, and her brave narrative will leave a lasting impact on those who read it."

~ *Brita Bigler Peterson#1 International Bestselling Author www.britapeterson.com*

"I long to have grown up in a loving and nurturing home, being taught all the tools to live my life successfully so I wouldn't have to deal with the painful, energy-robbing effects of generational alcoholism, various abuse, low self-worth, trust issues, and toxic relationships . . .

Unbeknownst to Wendy Beth, she has given me a much-appreciated gift of learning more ways to overcome various ongoing personal challenges by designing my own unique blueprint. She gives forty engaging activities that are meant to help me grow into the person I want to be by being accountable to myself. Some are easy, but some require me to come out of my comfort zone to write down my deepest, never-shared thoughts. I love that this book is a product of Wendy Beth overcoming her very difficult challenges and her willingness to share proven self-help tools with us in an encouraging and loving way."

~ *Rebecca Westfall (Germany)*

"In this day and age, where the market is saturated with numerous self-help books, *The Living Blueprint* is a breath of fresh air, an inspiring, intimate conversation. Not only is it rich with thoughtful, practical tools for improving the reader's quality of life, but it is Wendy Beth's courage, honesty, and pure love from her heart that weave this manuscript and make it a transformative, hope-giving experience for anyone looking to embrace life's perfect imperfections."

~ *Masha Maria, (Russia) artist @itsmashamaria earthisforlovers.com*

"This book is worth the read. It is well written with a clearly laid-out path for the reader to follow to create a better life for themselves. The exercises are well explained, and although the work can be a little daunting, Wendy Beth makes it clear it can be attained if you follow her steps."

~ *Madison Frederick #1 International best-selling author https://www. madisonfrederick.com/*

"I first met Wendy Beth in California in 1993. I commend her for being so open and truthful, and feel certain that others will find strength through reading her story. Wendy Beth has exemplified the virtues she writes about as long as I've known her. She doesn't just recommend Loving Kindness, she lives it. This Blueprint has been vital to Wendy healing herself and her relationships. She practices what she preaches. I remember her teaching me about 'Going to Bermuda' back in 2012. She sincerely wants to help others grow and evolve into their best selves. She genuinely works towards authentic connection, and vulnerability in relationships. You will find that in these pages. I know bringing the practices found in the pages of *Living Blueprint* to others is so important to Wendy Beth because she has a heart filled with love for mankind and a desire to lift and help. After reading this book, I feel confident that you will love and appreciate Wendy Beth the way I do."

~*Jo Skeen*

"Wendy Beth, my soulmate, is the best person I have ever known. She is incapable of purposefully harming anyone–in thirty years, I have never even seen her contemplate doing so. Losing her was the biggest regret of my life, and her forgiveness and our second chance is my biggest blessing. *Living*

Blueprint includes her raw and vulnerable story of how she transformed her life from unbelievable pain to incredible happiness. Her authenticity can be uncomfortable, but ultimately it is a guide to a dream-like life. I can say this with confidence as we are on this journey together."

~ *Spencer Cozzens (President, IA3 Consulting)*

www.ingramcontent.com/pod-product-compliance
Lightning Source LLC
Chambersburg PA
CBHW030351130626
46549CB00004B/1450